186 Continuoor

Cleij

KN 83

LEAVE A LITTLE TO GOD

Essays in Judaism

BOOKS BY ROBERT GORDIS

LEAVE A LITTLE TO GOD

Essays in Judaism

By

ROBERT GORDIS

BLOCH PUBLISHING COMPANY
NEW YORK

PRINTED IN THE UNITED STATES OF AMERICA
BY GANIS & HARRIS, NEW YORK

To the men and women—
and above all, the youth—
of my beloved congregation
Temple Beth-El
of
Rockaway Park

Preface

These introductory lines, I am afraid, must inevitably take on the character of a confession. Since 1931 it has been my privilege to serve as Rabbi of Temple Beth-El of Rockaway Park, New York. During these three and a half decades I have preached many hundreds of sermons. Some of them, in radically revised form, found their way into print as essays or as chapters in some of the books which I have written during these years.

However, I steadfastly refrained from publishing a book of sermons, being conscious that the rhetoric of discourse differs fundamentally from the style appropriate to the printed page. In this connection, as my sons have not hesitated to remind me, I was wont to quote the statement of Rabbi Judah ben Nahmani: *Debharim shebikhethabh 'iy 'attah rasha'iy le'omran 'al peh; debharim shebe'al peh 'iy 'attah rasha'iy le'omran bikhethabh,* "Words set forth in writing you are not permitted to present orally; words delivered orally you are not permitted to set down in writing" (*B. Gittin* 60b; *B. Temurah* 14b).

The chances are that I would have continued to adhere to this standpoint, had it not been for the friendship and generosity of my loyal friends, Paul and Rose Hirsch and Arthur and Miriam Hirsch. Ever since 1961, they have been printing the High Holy Day sermons which I delivered in the pulpit of our Temple. The very attractive publication that they have so generously produced each year has been sent to the members of our congrega-

vii

tion as a Hanukkah gift. It is only fair to add that these discourses have evoked a very appreciative response.

Several friends have accordingly suggested that these sermons, augmented by a few others, ought to be made available to a wider public in more permanent form. For the High Holy Days offer the Jewish teacher a superb opportunity to present the fundamental insights and ideals of Judaism in popular form. It is hoped that through the medium of these discourses, laymen and, in particular, our youth may be led to a fresh appreciation and a deeper commitment to the Jewish heritage. I have sought to interpret the Jewish tradition in terms relevant to the modern age and in a spirit of sympathy for our generation, which is confronted by massive problems and perplexities virtually unparalleled in history.

The three sections of this book correspond, it seems to me, to the three basic areas of concern of living religion. The first section, "The World," seeks to deal with the impact of science and the implications, legitimate or not, which have been drawn from it, affecting the content of religion and the validity of its world view. The revolutionary transformations which modern technology has wrought in the conditions and conduct of modern life are discussed. The effort is made to present a vital and meaningful faith for twentieth-century man that will draw upon the wisdom of the past and be responsive to the call of the present.

The second section, "Israel," deals with the status of Jewish life today in the United States, in the State of Israel, and throughout the world. The problems and ills which beset the Jewish people are set within the framework of the values that are to be found, and are all too often ignored, in the Jewish heritage. Of particular concern are the role of Jewish youth in the Jewish community and the agonizing question of the meaningful survival of Judaism in the open society of the future.

The third section, "Man," analyzes some of the problems of the individual who strives to achieve his personal well-being in a new and chaotic world. The abiding issues of sin and forgiveness, of tragedy and joy, which become particularly poignant with advancing years, are treated here. The attempt is made to shed some light upon the perennial and agonizing question of man's suffering in a world created by a good God. This, the greatest mystery of human existence and the chief stumbling block to faith in God, cannot be ignored.

It should be emphasized that I have sought to speak to the laymen, and particularly to our young people, who are no less concerned with these issues than the scholar or the thinker. While the material is rooted in Jewish tradition and experience, I venture to hope that it will prove of interest, and perhaps of value, to men and women outside of the Jewish community, since we all share the same human condition. Perhaps, too, my colleagues in the rabbinate may also find stimulation and interest in these pages, and younger students may derive some guidance from this effort to transmit the timeless truths of Judaism to our times.

If warrant is needed for departing from the rabbinic injunction against consigning oral material to writing, the Talmud itself supplies it. For the Talmud, which was originally oral in form, was ultimately written down, "because of the danger that the Torah might be forgotten" *(Rashi ad locum)*. In point of fact, the school of Rabbi Ishmael disagreed with Rabbi Judah ben Nahmani at the very outset, and declared that "both oral and written discourses may be put into writing" *(ibidem)*.

I have, accordingly, assembled the discourses delivered during this decade, adding the first sermon, "Leave a Little to God," and the concluding sermon, "The Ultimate Goal," which originally appeared in my book, *A Faith for Moderns*. It need hardly be pointed out that all the material in this volume has been revised for publication in its present form.

The determining factor for the issuance of this volume still remains to be given. In the spring of 1965 my beloved congregation celebrated my thirty-five years of service to Temple Beth-El. I pray that this volume may prove a not unworthy monument to these years during which we have lived and labored together for the cause of Judaism, and created invisible though indestructible bonds of brotherhood with one another.

As has been the happy destiny of nearly all my books, the present volume has had the benefit of the learning and accuracy of my devoted friend, Rabbi Abraham I. Shinedling. With exemplary generosity and meticulous care, he gave the manuscript a critical reading, proofread the volume, and prepared the index of Biblical and Rabbinic passages. As each of these discourses in turn was hammered out on the anvil of thought, it was refined and enriched by the wise insight and critical judgment of my dear wife, Fannie, to whom my rabbinical career owes its inception, as well as whatever measure of success it has attained.

It is my hope that this volume may bring to Jews and non-Jews greater understanding and a deeper appreciation of the relevance and truth of Judaism. May it help advance the age-old and ageless task which has been enjoined upon us by our tradition— to love all God's children and to bring them nearer to the Torah.

ROBERT GORDIS

Rockaway Park, N.Y.
Purim, 5727

Contents

THE WORLD

Leave a Little to God

It is May 24, 1844. A bearded scientist with a group of colleagues is seated at a table tapping out some sounds on a little instrument before him. Moments later, forty miles away in Baltimore, the message is received—"What hath God wrought!" The world stands jubilant and thankful before a modern miracle. The telegraph has been invented, and a new era of human communication has dawned.

It is September 13, 1959. The news is flashed around the world and banner headlines in the newspapers announce—"Russians Land Rocket on the Moon, Time Calculated Within Eighty-four Seconds." Before this extraordinary achievement of man's intellect the free world stands frightened and dismayed. A new era of possible human annihilation has dawned, and some are even tempted to murmur, "What hath Satan wrought!" And each succeeding achievement in outer space leaves us more terror-stricken or more blasé, resigned to an apparently inevitable course that will lead to cosmic disaster. In fact, we have already transferred the minor hazards of earthbound creatures to the heavens. The inevitable has already happened—a collision has occurred in outer space between two unmanned spacecraft!

The brave new world for which men prayed and hoped for centuries has been ushered in, but it has left us prematurely old and frightened by its prospects. If we seek a refuge from the international scene by turning to the domestic front, we find no peace. Corruption, crime, delinquency, and fraud seem universal. Massive problems create crises, and the massive crises threaten us with catastrophe. No wonder hope and confidence are fled and everywhere there crouch anxiety and foreboding, if not terror and despair. On the threshold of the New Year how can we muster both the energy and the will to face the future?

A century and a half ago, the French tyrant Napoleon was master of Europe. In Spain an embattled English army under the Duke of Wellington was trying to resist his advance. One day a young lieutenant came into the British general's tent with a map clutched in his trembling hands: "Look, General, the enemy is almost upon us!" "Young man," the General replied, "get larger maps. The enemy won't seem so close."

If we wish to understand the shape of things to come, we cannot be satisfied with the headlines of today. We need the perspective of history, the full record of man's past struggles, defeats, and achievements. We are accustomed to speak of the path of human history as though men advanced on a straight highway. Actually, man's progress is best compared to a pendulum, for it is characteristic of human nature that we do not go forward in a straight line, but fluctuate from one extreme to the other. To borrow the language of the physicists, men go from one action to an opposite and almost equal reaction.

II

When our primitive ancestors first emerged upon this planet, they were animals—with one difference. They were intelligent enough to be frightened, to feel helpless before a vast and unknown world filled with countless dangers lurking everywhere. Hence man, and man alone, peopled the hills and the valleys, the seas and the skies, the rivers and the trees with invisible beings, with spirits, gods and demons, fairies and witches, who were powerful and could determine man's fate.

As time went on and man began to organize his ideas, the gods were now assigned special spheres of sovereignty, given different functions and arranged in families, with elaborate rituals created to win their favor. But in ancient religion, as in primitive times, man saw himself as helpless and dependent on the whims and caprices of the spirits, their favor or their displeasure. Man was the plaything of the gods. The ancient Babylonians, for example, who were kinsmen of the Hebrews, had a tradition about the Flood similar to ours in the Bible. But while the Torah tells us that it was man's colossal wrongdoing that impelled God to visit that catastrophe upon the human race, the Babylonians ascribed it to the fact that men on earth were making so much noise that the gods could not sleep! One can well sympathize with their outraged feelings! The Greek myths in which we take delight today were not legends to the Greeks. The tales of the gods on Olympus, using human beings as the instruments and the victims of their greed, their jealousy, their lusts, and their quarrels, constituted religious truth in the Greek world.

When the great religions of the Western world arose out of the bosom of Judaism, man's position underwent a change, but not as radically as is sometimes thought. To be sure, he was no longer a plaything of capricious and unpredictable gods. Man was now the creature of a God of Justice and Mercy. But man's position of total dependence did not change. To accept this total surrender became the mark of piety. The mightiest religion of the West, Christianity, taught, "Believe on Me and ye shall be saved." The most militant religion of the East, Mohammedanism, declared that man's destinies were totally predetermined by Allah, and that the only course for man to adopt was Islam, total submission to Him. For most teachers of religion, man, being a creature of God, was nothing, and God was everything.

But whether or not, as the song writers tell us, "love is a many-splendored thing," it is true that man is a many-faceted being. In their churches and cathedrals, men continued to echo the idea that man is nothing, but in their laboratories and plants, their factories and fields, men were acting on the contrary theory that man is everything. The ancient Greeks, who were the architects of our civilization, had a phrase for it: "Man is the measure of

all things." The advancing tide of science kept strengthening
man's confidence in his own powers. Cynics and disbelievers now
whispered that instead of God's creating man, it was man who
had created God. As technology progressed and blessings without
number poured forth from the cornucopia of invention, man
could hardly be blamed for regarding himself as the lord of the
universe, the creator and monarch of all he surveyed.

Few stopped to ask, "Whence came man?", who obviously did
not create himself; or "Whence came the green earth?", which
existed before man; "or the planetary system?", which existed before the earth; "Or the universe?", which antedated our planetary
system. Who could blame the German biologist Ernst Haeckel
for announcing triumphantly that he had solved "The Riddle
of the Universe."

A little over a hundred years ago, in 1859, Charles Darwin published his "Origin of Species." Many men were persuaded by the
evolutionary theory and other scientific achievements that science
had dethroned God as Creator and enthroned man in His stead.
From the generous treasure-house of science came not only ships
and cars, planes, radio and television, and millions of gadgets and
instruments of all kinds. The scientists broke down the barrier
between matter and energy. They pierced the mystery of the
hitherto unbreakable atom. They peered into the very constitution of the world and fashioned new elements at will. Was it not
true that man was the prime creator in the universe? The only
hymn that still made sense was:

> "Hail to thee, great Science,
> From whom all blessings flow."

The pendulum had swung widely from one extreme to another.
First God was everything and man was nothing. Now man was
everything and God was nothing.

III

But the oscillation of the pendulum was not ended. As man's
intellect through technology was bringing him one rich gift after
another, as homage to a king, man's intellect through science was

undermining his position on the throne. Psychology declared that man was a bundle of primitive instincts and his reason merely a false front, an empty façade hiding irrational impulses. Anthropology suggested that there were no moral standards, only varying customs among different peoples, and that these could be discarded at will. The rise of industry in the nineteenth century had led to the mechanization of man and made of man a tool, a hand, a cog in a factory. The twentieth century brought the human race to the brink of a far more horrible fate—the manipulation of man. From being a tool of production, man became a tool of domination. He could be sold anything—a toothpaste, a candidate for public office, or a new fascist or communist order of society, not on the basis of any intrinsic merit or rational evidence, but under the spell of the new technique. There are levels of manipulation. It began, more or less harmlessly, with advertising, went on to "public relations," and reached its highest point—or its lowest—in organized brainwashing, in propaganda and the mass hysteria on which dictators have climbed to power.

Suddenly man discovered that he could do everything, but that he himself was nothing. His powers were limitless, but wherever he turned he was helpless. When, toward the end of the nineteenth century, Alfred Nobel invented dynamite, he joyously reported that fact as proof positive that with so horrible a weapon available to the nations, war could never take place again. Now, two World Wars and fifty smaller wars later, we know that we can wipe out the human race completely through nuclear bombs. We can plan the exact place and moment of total annihilation, yet no one is sure that men will not take the fatal step.

If we avert our gaze from the world stage and look about us, we find everywhere else that man is helpless. There always have been criminals in society and malefactors in public office. Now the tragedy does not lie merely in the quantitative increase of wrongdoing. Today we take it for granted that there will be widespread breaches of trust in government, in the corporations, in labor unions, in public institutions, in the press, and on television. The breakdown of the American family is highlighted by the fact that one out of four marriages in the United States now ends in divorce courts. Illegitimacy, abortions, and adultery are increasing alarmingly, bringing in their wake a staggering burden of human misery and degradation.

Our moral crisis goes far deeper than the spiraling rise of juvenile delinquency, vandalism, and crime. This is by no means limited to underprivileged minority groups, but has infiltrated into the so-called better homes and finest communities. The crisis is qualitative. In the past, society as a whole, and the offenders in particular, recognized the moral standards against which they had sinned. To use the common legal term, they knew right from wrong. Today the criminal derides the judge before whom he stands. He did it for "kicks," or for gain, for "dope," or out of sheer viciousness, and society, deep down in its heart, does not know right from wrong either. That is the essence of the tragedy. In the words of the Psalmist, *Ki hashatot yeharesun, tzaddik mah pa'al.* "For the very foundations are destroyed; what can the righteous man do?" If Oliver Goldsmith were alive today he might be tempted to lament:

> *"Ill fares the land to hastening ills a prey,*
> *Where science accumulates and men decay."*

Does not that mean that the human race is the end of the road? Have we not exhausted all the possibilities? First man was nothing and God was everything. Then God was nothing and man was everything. Now God is nothing and man is nothing. Behind the alternating bluster and blandness of our enemies, the ineptness and ignorance of our own leadership, behind the wealth of science and the spiritual poverty of man, are we not hearing a voice of doom, "Nothing art thou and unto nothing shalt thou return"? This is the agonizing question confronting mankind.

IV

There is, however, a sound more powerful than the blast of atomic explosions and the noise of jet planes roaring over our heads, a still small voice, first heard on Sinai. Judaism, which first revealed the one Living God to a world steeped in paganism, still has a message in this hour of imminent catastrophe for mankind groping in darkest despair. Against the fear which has gripped human hearts that we stand at the end of the human adventure stands the authentic message of Rosh Hashanah.

Judaism has its own view of man's role in the universe. For the Torah, man is not a plaything of divine caprice, nor even a helpless and corrupt creature at the mercy of an omnipotent Power. On the other hand, man is surely not the prime creator of his world, the total master of his fate. In the most profound teaching of the Jewish tradition, man is neither a helpless plaything, nor a worthless creature, nor a self-creator—he is, in the words of the Talmud: *shuttapho shel hakadosh barukh hu bema'aseh bereshit.* "The co-partner of God, the Holy One, in the work of creation." This great cosmic partnership rests upon the profound Biblical concept of man set forth in the opening chapter of *Genesis,* which declares that Man was created *betselem 'elohim,* "in the image of God." What does this vivid Hebrew phrase mean? Obviously, it does not mean a physical resemblance between God and man, because God has no form and man's body has much the same attributes as the animals around him. It means that man possesses part of the nature of God—the gift of reason and thought, the love of beauty manifest everywhere in the world, the unconquerable yearning for righteousness which never dies in the human soul, and above all the capacity to create, to mold and fashion the world, which is the hallmark of God Himself. Man is the only creature who can conceive of a past and of a future. In William Hazlitt's words: "Man is the only creature that can laugh and weep, because he is aware of the gulf between what is and what can be."

What are we doing here in God's world? The hymn of the Daily Prayer Book has the answer: *Barukh 'elohenu shebera'anu likhevodo.* "Blessed is our God who has created us unto His glory."

The Midrash boldly spells out the meaning of this cosmic symbiosis, this partnership of God and man. Basing itself on a great passage in *Isaiah* (43:12)—*attem 'edai, ne'um hashem, va'ani 'el.* "Ye are My Witnesses and I am God"—the Midrash (*Shoher Tob,* ed. Buber 255a) interprets, *Keshe'attem 'edim 'ani 'el, ukeshe'ein 'attem 'edim 'eini 'el.* "When ye are My witnesses, I am God, and when ye are not My witnesses, I am no longer God." As surely as man cannot build the world without God, God cannot build without man. In Robert Browning's poem, Antonio Stradivarius, the famous violin maker, says, "God cannot build a violin without Antonio."

What does it mean to recognize that God and man are partners? What practical consequences flow from this insight into man's relationship to God? I find the answer in an utterance which the great Solomon Schechter, the first president of The Jewish Theological Seminary of America, was accustomed to repeat, "Leave a little to God." Note what he did *not* say. Not, "Leave it all to God," for then man becomes nothing. Nor, "Leave nothing to God," for then man is doomed to failure. "Leave a little to God" —that is the counsel we need. We must do our share and know that God will do His. *Action and faith both must be our watchwords. To work and to wait must be our program—passion and patience, both are needed for life.*

With this insight we can confront the major crises of our age and conquer. With the threat of world-wide annihilation posed by the cold war hanging over us, two clear-cut alternatives exist. We may choose to surrender to Communism or wage an all-out war against it and run the risk of blotting out the human race. There are siren voices urging one or another of these courses upon us. But there is a third possibility, slower, more painful, far less simple, making greater demands upon us—the effort to coexist on this planet even with those whom we cannot wholly trust. To this end, we must use the United Nations and direct diplomatic negotiations, trade relations, and cultural exchanges, all as instruments for preserving the peace. But this course of action requires high intelligence and firm resolution, and, above all, patience without end.

Whence shall this patience come? It can come only from faith, from the assurance that if we do our part, God will do His and the painful process of "peaceful co-existence" will lead to a happier state of affairs. This faith is no mere whistling in the dark. For God has taught us through His prophet, *Lo' tohu bera'ah lashevet yetzarah* (*Isa.* 45:18), "He created the world, not for chaos but for human habitation." It is a fact that our social and economic system has undergone vast changes in the last hundred years. So, too, far-reaching changes are taking place in Soviet Russia, and we can be certain that the tempo of change will increase. What will emerge will be in accordance with God's purposes for the world, not Mr. Johnson's or Mr. Brezhnev's, or yours, or mine, but something different and something better than what either our adversaries or we possess at present. *Lo' tohu bera'ah lashevet yetzarah.* "God created the world not for chaos, but for human habitation." We must work and wait and leave a little to God.

Or let us turn to our homes and our families. How often do we see the children we have loved and nurtured wander off into new and perilous paths, apparently becoming strangers to us and all that we hold sacred? Across how many of our homes might we inscribe the title of Shaw's play, "Heartbreak House." All too often we are tempted to feel that all our efforts in rearing our children, in setting before them standards of reverence and responsibility and in inculcating loyalty to truth and goodness, have been wasted. We know we did not do a perfect job, for perfection is with God alone, but we did the best we could, and behold the consequences! Here again Schechter's words have a message for us, "Leave a little to God." Action and faith, passion and patience, are needed in this cosmic partnership. In the words of Koheleth, *Baboker zera' 'et zarekha uva'erev 'al tannah yadekha,* "In the morning sow your seed and in the evening do not let your hands be idle. For you cannot tell which of them will prosper or whether both of them will be good." From faith in God comes patience. If we wait, we shall discover that the seed we have planted has not fallen on fallow ground. Our plowing and planting of the field have not been wasted, because God's sunshine and rain have also been working from above. What will grow in our children will be new, and it may be different from what we are accustomed to, but we can hold fast to the faith that the best of what we have known and loved will not be utterly lost. The good and the true are immortal.

"Leave a little to God." Do your share and He will do His, for He created the world not for chaos and destruction, but for human habitation and joy.

Hayom harat 'olam. "On this day of Rosh Hashanah the world came into being." The majestic Musaf Service in its threefold structure proclaims the life-giving truth of man's relationship to God as co-partner in creation. The *Malkhuyot* proclaim the sovereignty of God—God rules the world as our Father and our King. Nor do we have to go it alone. For the *Zikhronot* recall that God is mindful of man's struggles and agonies, his weaknesses and frustrations, his capacity for goodness and greatness. And out of the sovereignty of God and the significance of man comes the third section of the Service, the *Shofarot,* paying tribute to the Shofar, which was sounded on Sinai at the giving of the Law and will be heard again proclaiming the Messianic age.

The Shofar is symbolic of the cosmic partnership of God and man. On Mount Sinai it was said: *Mosheh yedabber veha'elohim ya'anenu bekol,* "Moses spoke and God answered him with a loud voice." Let us speak and act for the right and then leave a little to God, knowing that He will not fail us. Together we can go forward to build a world worthy of God's greatness and man's hopes.

II

For Whom the Shofar Blows

I

This is the jet age, when we move through space almost at the speed of sound. If only we possessed a Time Machine and could travel with equal rapidity through time! I would wish to move the gears into reverse and whisk ourselves backward across the centuries to the eighth century B.C.E., to Samaria, the resplendent capital of the Kingdom of Israel.

What would we find? A country at the high point of prosperity. Its government is stable; its borders have been enlarged and are secure. Its trade, both domestic and foreign, is flourishing. Luxury is widespread. Magnificent palaces and country houses dot the landscape, resounding to feasting and celebration. The carousers are stretched on couches decorated with ivory, and eat the richest delicacies, to the tune of viols and harps. With the new leisure comes a blooming of culture—everyone fancies himself an artist. Religion, too, is prospering. The temples are crowded; offerings are plentiful, and the priests are busy at the altars. Patriotism, piety, and prosperity are everywhere.

Suddenly the peace is broken by an interloper. Into the capital comes an uncouth figure, and a foreigner to boot. He is a farmhand and a shepherd from the frontier town of Tekoa in Judah, and his name is Amos. He is not impressed by what he sees or, more accurately, he is so impressed that he peers beneath the surface. Behind the façade of the prosperity of the rich he sees

13

the grinding poverty of the poor. The piety of the Temple grows
fat on the plunder of the weak. In the seats of government he
sees the claws of tyranny; the halls of justice are the abode of
oppression and bribery. The peace and the security of the state
are only the calm before the storm, the fitful sunshine before the
fateful hurricane.

It is late, very late, almost too late, unless men heed the warning. And Amos cries out: *Hayittaka' shofar ba'ir ve'am lo yeheradu?*
"Can the shofar be blown in a city, and the people not tremble?"
Amos called for a transformation, for *teshubhah*, a return to the
old principles taught by Moses and the prophets. God demands
not ritual, but righteousness, not beautiful music in the Temple,
but lives that are beautiful because they are rooted in harmony
and peace.

> Remove from Me the noise of your songs
> And the melody of your viols I refuse to hear,
> But let justice well up as the waters
> And righteousness like a mighty stream.
> *(Amos* 5:23-24)

The people do not hear, or if they hear, they refuse to understand. When Amos completes his tirade, the authorities make
short shrift of him. The government officials, the military leaders,
the Temple officials, the men of affairs, hard-headed and realistic,
laugh at the crackpot who announces doom at the peak of prosperity. Being a foreigner, Amos is given the unanswerable reply—
he is told to go back where he came from! With the subversive
out of the way, Amos is quickly forgotten and life goes back to
normal.

But not for long. Within twenty-five years after Amos' appearance everything is lost. In 722 the kingdom is destroyed; the
country is left a shambles. The Kingdom of Israel disappears forever. The population is uprooted and goes down into history as
the Ten Lost Tribes. All that remains of that era of prosperity
and peace are some ruins in Samaria uncovered by archaeologists
—and the deathless words of Amos.

II

Twenty-seven centuries have elapsed since that day. Instead of tiny Israel, the stage of human events embraces the entire earth. The city of Samaria had a far smaller population than Queens County today. Nearly everything is changed—but not the principles which Amos proclaimed.

The danger of instantaneous and total destruction by atomic bomb may, perhaps, be a little further off now than in the recent past. The "hot-line" wire between Washington and Moscow is a tiny step in the right direction. The limited ban on nuclear testing is far more important, because it will help to clear the atmosphere of nuclear fall-out, which threatens unborn generations. It may help establish a climate in which the world may move, however hesitatingly, toward disarmament and the peaceful resolution of differences. What greater blessing can we ask for on the New Year but that we may progress from imminent danger toward the hope of survival?

But atomic annihilation is not our only peril—there are many roads to destruction. History knows of civilizations that were destroyed by some natural calamity, by a volcanic eruption, like Pompeii in Italy, or the island of Delos in Greece. The *fall* of the Roman Empire may have been caused primarily by the incursion of barbarian tribes—but the *decline* of the Roman Empire had slower, less dramatic, subtler inner causes.

History knows of an even more striking illustration of inner disaster. The most brilliant civilization of the ancient world was that of the Greeks. Here a small people, within a few centuries, produced the Golden Age. Centered in Athens, there arose a brilliant group of creative geniuses who laid the foundations of science, philosophy, art, and literature for the Western world. In a few short years Greek culture was carried to every corner of the earth.

Then, inexplicably, at the time when all the world was doing it homage, the glory that was Greece faded and died. The Greeks suffered what Sir Gilbert Murray has described as "a failure of nerve." Greek culture lost its creative gift, its driving power, its cutting edge. The Greeks found themselves without any confidence in the future, because they lost their sense of purpose in the present. Greek civilization was not destroyed from without— it decayed from within.

As we turn from the ancient past to the living present, it becomes clear that it is inner decay and moral rot that confront our age. Nor is the peril limited to the United States or to the Free World. The spiritual malady is endemic, world-wide, and its symptoms are limitless.

Never have Americans had so many pleasures and so little satisfaction and serenity in life. We have only to begin with the family —the foundation of society, the center of life for the individual, his refuge and comfort, his earliest school, his lifelong shelter. Today the family is often an empty façade. Always there were differences between the generations, but today the gap has become a yawning abyss. The complaint of the prophet Micah is truer today than when first uttered:

> The son reviles the father,
> The daughter rises up against her mother,
> The daughter-in-law against her mother-in-law,
> A man's enemies are the members of his own household.
>
> *(Micah* 7:6)

Peace is best kept between parents and children by holding them apart, at arm's length, as much as possible, so that the old folks will neither be seen nor heard, and will not "interfere" with the lives of the young people. Recently there was a discussion program on T.V. concerned with "The Family and the City." One of the panelists was a charming young woman, by profession a family counsellor. She explained, as the most natural thing in the world, "My husband and I came to New York immediately after our marriage to get far away from his parents and mine."

Yes, ours is an "emancipated" generation that has cast off many of the taboos of family loyalty, and surrendered many of the traditional standards of personal conduct. Let us forget tradition and ask an even more basic question: Is our age happier? There is one irrefragable test—the phenomenon of divorce. Nearly one marriage out of four now ends in the divorce court, leaving a trail of bitterness and heartache and suffering, not only for the adults, but often for children whose lives are warped by this disaster. Judaism quite properly does not regard divorce as a sin, for a hate-ridden relationship is no longer a marriage. But Judaism sees divorce as a tragedy, for every divorce is a tombstone erected on the grave of love and high hopes for happiness once cherished by two young people.

Juvenile delinquency is no longer front-page news—it has lost its sensational quality. It is one of the routine facts of life. It penetrates into every segment of society. Not only the poor but our middle and upper class families produce an ample quota of youthful delinquents and criminals, who are only a reflection of the actions and attitudes of their elders.

Some time ago, the American playwright Arthur Miller wrote a very perceptive piece on the causes of juvenile delinquency. His analysis is clear from his title, "The Bored and the Violent." Alcoholism, drug addiction, vandalism, and even murder for "kicks" are not uncommon, because our youth are bored and the bored become the violent. Both the beatnik and the delinquent are rebels without a cause. Says Miller: "Delinquents are a living expression of our universal ignorance of what life ought to be, even of what it is, and of what it truly means to live. What the country has to decide is what it is going to say if these kids should decide to listen."

III

That is the rub—what shall we say to them and to ourselves? What is our national purpose? America was born and grew great —not merely prosperous, but great—because it had a purpose. Our sense of national purpose undergirded the Declaration of Independence and was embodied in the Preamble to the Constitution:

> We, the people of the United States, in order to form a more perfect Union, establish justice, insure domestic tranquility, pro-

vide for the common defense, promote the general welfare, and secure the blessings of liberty to ourselves and our posterity, do ordain and establish this Constitution for the United States of America.

The national purpose was not limited to our nation—it began at home, but its goal was the world. As Abraham Lincoln reminded us, our nation was conceived in liberty, and dedicated to the proposition that *all men* are created equal. We confidently expected that democracy would be the destiny of all men.

What remains basic today of all the goals in the Constitution? Only providing for the common defense seems to remain, and even this purpose we are prepared to serve by being short on insight and long on expenditures.

What about the other, ultimate purposes which justify the common defense? What about insuring domestic tranquility? The race riots, the rising crime wave, the gang wars, the senseless vandalism, the mounting horror of traffic deaths—what we have done is substitute for domestic tranquility the growing use of tranquilizers.

The most inclusive national purpose is promoting the general welfare. To be sure, men have always been interested in their own personal and group interests, but there always was a perception of the public good, a sense of the common weal, of the needs of the country as a whole. Today our democracy has become a field of battle by pressure groups. Corporations, labor unions, manufacturers' associations, the churches, the universities, the A.M.A.—all are interested in getting the most for themselves out of the public treasury or the national wealth. They do not usually put it as candidly as did Charles E. Wilson when he identified the general welfare with General Motors. But when President John F. Kennedy pleaded, "Do not say, 'What can my country do for me?', but 'What can I do for my country?' ", his remark was widely laughed at as naive, or dismissed as political oratory.

Before the general welfare can be attained, as the Constitution recognizes, comes the establishment of justice. Thank God, there still are untold numbers of elected and appointed officials, legislators, judges, lawyers, and police officers who are dedicated to

advancing and maintaining justice—or we should be on the verge
of national collapse.

Yet how often have we fallen away from the sense of *noblesse
oblige,* from respect for one's office and the sanctity of one's oath,
or even for one's self?

Several years ago, there was a sensational traffic case in New
York City. A young man, the son of a judge, had driven a car at
high speed and had killed five people in the process. There are
some grounds for believing that he was drunk at the time, that
he left the scene of the accident, and possibly was also involved
in a car-stealing ring. Yet I do not find his alleged misconduct
the nub of our moral tragedy. What about the ethical standards
of three judges on the bench, all sworn to administer justice, who
dismissed all the charges against the offender in a hearing which
lasted exactly five minutes—one minute for each life snuffed out!
Hypocrisy, it has been said, is the tribute which vice pays to virtue.
Today even hypocrisy is too high a price, and so the motions of
legality and order are dispensed with.

Recently, we had a Governor sitting in the Executive Office of
a state in the Union. Within easy reach of his desk, I am sure,
there was a copy of the United States Constitution that he had
sworn to uphold and the Bible on which he took his oath. He
had only to open his Bible and read the twenty-first chapter of
Deuteronomy. The Bible ordains that when a murder is discovered in an open field, the elders of the nearest city are to be held
morally responsible for permitting conditions to develop that
made such violence possible. They have to undergo a public act
of expiation and proclaim, "Our hands did not shed this blood"
(*Deuteronomy* 21:7). Governor George C. Wallace did not merely
permit lawlessness in Alabama; he incited it, day after day, week
after week, month after month. After twenty-two bombings of
Negro homes and businesses in Birmingham without a single arrest came a bloody climax in the murder of six children. The
blood of these innocents cannot be washed away by offering a
reward for the capture of the murderers.

We are today the contemporaries of a revolution—the struggle
of the Negro to achieve the justice and equality set forth in the

Constitution and explicitly granted to him a hundred years ago in the Emancipation Proclamation and in the Fourteenth and Fifteenth Amendments. For a long time, the struggle was relatively free from violence and bloodshed, a high tribute to the moral discipline, the patience, and the loyalty of our Negro fellow citizens. How many of us or of our children could match the dignity and the courage of a little Negro girl walking up the path leading to a Southern school on the first day of official desegregation?

Revolutions are never pretty—they are always painful. The violence which they engender destroys much that is good, and so there have been excesses in the struggle. With the hostility or the apathy of the white majority, no wonder that some extremists are gaining in strength who insist that the only way to achieve justice for the Negroes is to perpetrate injustice against the whites. The Black Muslims preach that the day is coming when the whites will be destroyed in retaliation for the crimes committed against the blacks. It is being proposed in some quarters that employment quotas for whites be introduced in various industries, thus correcting the crime of white racism by substituting black racism in its place. Anti-Semitism, the infallible barometer of the moral decay of a society, is on the rise among Negroes. The spokesmen for "black power" insist that they advocate only political and economic power for Negroes. It is undeniable that for thousands of their fellows it is a rallying cry for violence.

But who is responsible? Is it the Negro who, for a hundred years, waited patiently for his white fellow citizen to begin to live up to his professions? Or is it the white man, who read in his Declaration of Independence, "All men are created equal, if they are white, and have been endowed by their Creator with inalienable rights, if they are not colored"?

Democracy is not on the march today. It is on the defensive, and our Communist foes know it full well. Time was when Americans had faith in the world-wide future of American democracy, not because it was American, but because it was democracy. With all their hearts they believed that freedom was the inevitable destiny of all men. Benjamin Franklin, writing in 1789, said: "God grant that not only the Love of Liberty, but a thorough Knowledge of the Rights of Man may pervade all the Nations of the Earth, so that a Philosopher may set his foot anywhere on its surface, and say, 'This is my Country.' "

Many of us will remember that in our own lifetime Americans poured out their blood in a war whose announced purpose was to make the world safe for democracy. It is true that the goal was not achieved, because our ideals were not matched by our realism and wisdom. Because of this moral defeat and even greater disasters that followed, disillusioned idealists became confirmed cynics, *with nothing to live by and nothing to live for, and therefore nothing to live with.*

It is this disease of the spirit that has infected not only our criminals and delinquents, but also the rank and file of the American people, the vast majority of young people and adults, who are decent and law-abiding. Arthur Koestler describes our youth today as the "silent generation." "They seem," he observes, "to have no aspirations except getting on in their professions, marrying early, and going on holidays in the family car. Thus, the super-historical age has produced a generation which seems to live outside history."

In James Reston's words, "The charge against this emerging generation is not that they believe in wrong things, but that they don't believe in anything." I believe that he is mistaken. There was a time when people believed in Heaven and Hell. They still do—only the definitions have changed. Heaven is a country club. Hell is the time that people must spend by themselves, and with their television sets out of order.

IV

What has happened to modern man? We shall not fall into the trap of lamenting the "good old days" and deluding ourselves into believing that earlier generations were paragons of virtue and wisdom. Men always were torn by lust, by fear, by greed, by envy. Hypocrisy and pretense are not modern inventions. Twenty-five centuries before Sigmund Freud, the prophet Jeremiah declared,

'Akobh halebh mikkol ve'anush hu', *mi yeda'enu*, "The heart of man is perverse above all things, and exceedingly weak. Who can understand it?" (*Jeremiah* 17:9).

The one great difference was that in the past men believed that they possessed an answer to the fundamental questions of life, which modern man has lost. Marshal Ferdinand Foch, the hero of World War I, declared, "If you don't believe, you can't fight." The truth goes deeper: "If you don't believe, you can't live." We have lost the solid core of faith, the fundamental sense of a purpose in life.

If we have really lost it for good, we are lost forever. But I fervently believe that we have only mislaid it. In our speed, in our reckless drive to get on, to get ahead, we have lightened our baggage and now have no garment to cover the nakedness of our souls.

But the truth does not have new models each year, like cars or women's hats. The eternal is always contemporary—the truth, always modern. It was Moses, the Prophets, and the Sages of Israel who first enunciated the great truths concerning God by which men can live. These principles, accepted by Christianity from its Jewish source, became the bedrock of Western civilization. They were never fully realized, to be sure, but never totally lost sight of either. They always served as a flying goal toward which men aspired and by which they judged themselves and society. Now these pillars of the world are being washed away. Is it any wonder that the temple of civilization is in danger of destruction?

Against this peril, the Shofar sounds a note of warning, as it did in Amos' day. But the Shofar is also the herald of truth, the Emancipation Proclamation of the human race, for if we hear the truth, it will make us free.

First and foremost, the Shofar announces the *Malkhuyot*, the sovereignty of God. We live in a world which was called into being by a wise and good Creator, and is governed by Him in justice and in truth.

There still are those who believe that science has made this faith impossible—or at least unnecessary. A hundred and fifty years ago, Napoleon Bonaparte met the famous French astronomer, Pierre Laplace. "I understand, M. Laplace, that you have written a five-hundred-page book on the universe without mentioning God even once," said Napoleon. "Yes, Sire," replied the astronomer, "God is a hypothesis I can do without!"

But those who maintain this idea are far behind the vanguard of scientific thought, which is acutely aware of the legitimate functions and limitations of science. More and more scientists are echoing the words of Louis Pasteur: "A little science estranges men from God, but much science leads them back to Him." And, we should add, when men return, they will be more mature, more understanding, because of the journey that they have undertaken, the experiences that they have undergone, the ideas that they have encountered.

Science is no substitute for religion, any more than religion is a substitute for science. Both are indispensable enterprises of the human spirit.

Science has shed welcome light on what laws govern the world in its operation. But it knows next to nothing about the beginning and the end of things. The creation of the universe, the nature and origin of life, the emergence of man, the source of language, of society, of the family, the meaning of death—even these "scientific" questions are still beyond the purview of science. If reality may be compared to an alphabet, science can be said to read the middle letters, from B to Y, but not the first and the last, Alpha and Omega, A and Z.

But the limitations of science go deeper. The scientist seeks to answer important questions, "How," "When," "Where?" But there are even deeper questions, eternal issues which are outside its competence, "Why," "Who," "Whither?" When a scientist speaks out on these issues, he is only a man wrestling with the great mysteries. On these basic questions it is the philosopher, the moralist, the religious teacher, to whom we must turn for light and leading.

Turn our backs upon science? That would be the height of folly, for science is a superb instrument for helping us get to our goals, but it cannot tell us what goal to choose. Without a car we could not reach a distant destination, but we do not ask the car to decide what should be our destination.

Moreover, science, far from displacing God, discloses new evidence of His presence day by day. Each succeeding scientific discovery reveals more and more of the pattern of order and harmony in the world—it demonstrates that this world is not lawless but lawful, not an accident but a plan, and we live not in chaos but in a cosmos. In the words of the poet, "The laws of nature are the ways of God." Today the progress of science has made Francis Bacon's words far more reasonable than when he first uttered them: "I had rather believe all the fables and legends of the world than that this universal frame is mindless."

We sound the Shofar to proclaim: *Hashem 'Elohav 'immo uteru'at melekh bo,* "The Lord, our God, is with us and the trumpet blast of the King is in our midst."

But that is not all. Since God created the world, it bears the stamp of its Creator, who possesses not only power but intelligence, not only intelligence but righteousness. When we sound the Shofar for the second time we proclaim, *'Attah zokher ma'ase 'olam,* "Thou rememberest the events of all ages." As surely as the natural world is governed by physical laws, the human world is governed by moral laws. Scientists did not invent gravitation or the conservation of matter; they discovered them in the world. So the Hebrew prophets did not invent the idea that morality is the basic law of human society. They discovered this truth through the wisdom of their hearts and saw it validated in the cosmic laboratory that we call human history.

The history of man on this planet is the record of the rise and fall of civilizations, for which the scientists, historians, and philosophers offer countless reasonable theories. The Prophets of Israel would not quarrel with these explanations, but they would go deeper. *No civilization has yet survived permanently because none has deserved to survive. No society has thus far avoided destruction because no society has yet been built upon the foundations of true righteousness, or has even been willing to move unflinchingly toward the goal. As Proverbs says, Tsedakah teromem goy vehesed le'umim hattat,* "Righteousness exalts a nation, but sin is the disgrace of peoples." The prophets would add, "Not merely the disgrace, but the disaster of nations."

In our day, we saw the greatest assault ever attempted against the principle of righteousness as the bedrock of civilization. Adolf Hitler confidently announced that he was building the Third Reich which would last a thousand years. He exaggerated by nine hundred and ninety!

In their individual lives, as well as in their group activities, some men believe that they can manage to escape the consequences of the Law of Consequence, which declares that righteousness is the only sure foundation of well-being and that evil must lead to destruction. The results may be postponed—they cannot be avoided. In the days when Americans were known as happy-go-lucky optimists, they used to tell the story of the tourist who fell off the top of the Empire State Building. As the horrified workers rushed to the windows, they saw his body hurtling by. Gaily he waved to them as he passed the 47th floor, "Don't worry about me, I'm just fine—so far!" As Koheleth pointed out long ago, it is because the law of Divine justice operates slowly and is sometimes delayed that men's hearts are filled with the vain hope that they can sin and somehow escape the consequences, as though it were possible to imbibe alcohol without limit and not get drunk.

'Attah zokher kol hanishkahot, "God remembers what we vainly seek to forget." Right and wrong are no figments of men's imagination; they are rooted in God's world. Obey them and live, violate them and perish. In the words of Isaiah, *Vayigbah Hashem Tsebha'ot bamishpat, veha'el hakadosh nikdash bitsedakah,* "The Lord of Hosts is exalted through justice, and God the Holy One is sanctified through righteousness" (*Isa.* 5:16).

Finally, we sound the Shofar for the third time as a clarion call to man's action. Man must act because he is responsible; he is responsible because he is free; he is free because he was created *betzelem 'elohim,* "in the image of God."

Here again science has been both a boon and a stumbling block. Science has shed welcome light upon the conditions under which man must live and work and struggle. But we have repaid our debt to science by debasing the coinage, by converting its insights into alibis. It is true that we are shaped by our biological heredity, that we are limited by our psychological make-up, that our behavior is fashioned by our social and economic environment.

But the great truth upon which religion insists and which is demonstrated by life every day is that we are *conditioned* by these factors, but not *determined* by them. There are limits which we cannot escape, but within these limits we are free to govern our lives. Unlike the lower animals, man is not completely at the mercy of his environment. He can modify it, rise above it, rebuild it altogether. From the slum areas of our great cities have come both gangsters and heroes, enemies of society and benefactors of humanity, money-grubbers and idealists. At the other end of the social scale, rich homes have been the breeding-ground both of sinners and of scholars, of playboys and patriots, of cynical wasters as well as leaders of the people.

No man is a prisoner of conditions, unless he himself has fashioned the bars. Yes, man comes into a world not of his own making, but the area of his freedom is great. In the words of the *Piyyut* on Yom Kippur, "We are like clay in the hands of the potter." We are partners with God in shaping our human clay either into a palace or a prison.

What we do with our individual lives, what our country does with its destiny, what civilization itself achieves, depends upon our faith in God, our allegiance to morality, our sense of responsibility. Given these truths, we shall rediscover a sense of purpose in the world.

Why were we placed in this world? To this most profound of questions our tradition gives a clear answer: *Barukh 'elohenu shebera'anu likhevodo*, "Blessed is our God who has created us unto His glory." Man's duty is to enhance the glory of God. "Where is God's glory?", we ask in the Kedushah; and we answer, *Kevodo male' 'olam*, "His glory pervades the world." It is our sacred duty, our joyous privilege, to enlarge the boundaries of God's kingdom through the cultivation and love of beauty, the

search and the love of truth, the pursuit and the love of righteousness.

The Shofar speaks to us of God and of the world, but most of
all of ourselves. Its piercing and plaintive notes are a warning.
In its antique accents, we can hear the message of the modern
poet:

> If we really want to live,
> We'd better start at once to try.
> If we don't—it doesn't matter,
> But we'd better start to die.

But the Shofar bears also a message of hope:

*Hahayyim vehammavet natatti lephanekha hayom haberakhah
vehakelalah (Deuteronomy 30:19).* "Life and death do I place before you this day, the blessing and the curse. Choose life, so that
you and your children may live."

III

The Revolution in Man

I

According to an old tradition, Adam turned to Eve one day in the Garden of Eden and said, "You know, my dear, we are living in an age of transition!" Ever since, men have always felt that their particular time was a period of change. Nonetheless, some ages are more rapid and violent in their transformations, more unsettling than others. Such an era is the midpoint of the twentieth century in which we live. Our era will undoubtedly be regarded as a period of worldwide revolution, with conflict, chaos, and catastrophe crowding on one another's heels.

The headlines of our newspapers each day chronicle the ebb and flow of the revolution. Think how much has happened within our lifetime. In a half century—two major World Wars and a dozen other conflicts, the bloody rise and the bloodier fall of fascism, the emergence and victories of communism on four continents, and its continued threat to the democratic West, the irruption of strident nationalism in the Far East, Southeast Asia, and throughout Africa, racial strife in South Africa and the United States, with echoes everywhere. The world is girding itself for a struggle between communism and capitalism, between dictatorship and democracy. We can only hope that it will be fought with weapons of peaceful competition rather than through nuclear annihilation.

Far less noticeable in the headlines, yet even more ominous, because it is in full swing on both sides of the Iron Curtain, is an inner revolution taking place within the nature of modern man himself. Because we are heading into dangerous and uncharted waters, there is a vast sense of unease among us in this age of security, a deep-seated, scarcely identifiable hunger in this age of affluence. William Butler Yeats described our age to perfection:

> Things fall apart; the center cannot hold,
> Mere anarchy is loosed upon the world. . . .
> The best lack all conviction, while the worst
> Are full of passionate intensity.
>
> *(The Second Coming)*

In the last Presidential campaign in 1964, the two leading candidates both expressed this vague but profound feeling of dissatisfaction with life. Senator Barry M. Goldwater spoke of "a virtual despair among the many who look beyond material success to the inner meaning of their lives." President Lyndon B. Johnson declared, "We haven't been keeping faith with tomorrow, or with ourselves." To put it epigrammatically, if not grammatically, millions never had it so good or felt so bad.

II

What has happened to modern man? We often hear it said, "You can't change human nature." The proposition is highly debatable, but what is certain is that "you *can* change human behavior." A process which began nearly two hundred years ago with the Industrial Revolution has been gaining momentum, and as the results have been accumulating, man has been transformed. The first and most obvious effect has been the *mechanization of man*. Science and technology have showered a horn of plenty upon men. A host of labor-saving devices has removed the drudgery and the back-breaking toil involved in many necessary activities. The development of machines has increased productivity on the farm, in the factory, and in the office beyond man's wildest imaginings. Only a fool or a hypocrite would lament the advent of these products of man's inventive genius that have eased his burdens and added to his blessings.

The tragedy is that our scientific and technological inventiveness threatens to make men superfluous. Among the labors which they save us is the labor of living itself. Today computers can solve in a few moments awesome mathematical and statistical problems that would require thousands of man-hours. We are also told that the computers can now think for us. One can almost hear a symphonic chorus of modern machines singing to the obsolescent creature that is man:

> Anything you can do,
> I can do better than you!

And I mean "anything"! According to one report, these machines are beginning to reproduce themselves! If so, they will surely make men totally unnecessary!

Because of the automobile, walking has joined the roster of lost arts. Today there are new neighborhoods that are built without sidewalks. Recently, a man sued for damages on a charge of false arrest. He had been stopped one evening by a policeman on the ground of suspicious behavior. The patrolman explained to the judge, "I saw him walking on the street."

Among the other decaying arts is the art of letter writing. Ours is an age when ready-made greeting cards are available for every purpose. Today you can buy a card to explain that you forgot to send a card to apologize for having forgotten to send a card at the birthday of your husband's cousin.

Another dying skill is the art of reading, in a time of comic books, tabloid papers, picture magazines, and non-books. According to surveys that one can scarcely believe, the average American child spends forty hours a week in front of his television screen. Is it any wonder that T.V. succeeds in weaning our children away from the laborious task of translating black symbols on a white page into ideas that need to be understood and analyzed? The "good guys" and the "bad guys" are always easy to identify on T.V. And as for our vaunted "education boom," a responsible study of American college graduates claims that they read an average of one book a year.

Our newspapers devote many pages every day to sports, but this sport is no child's play, but big business. The free, uninhibited activity of amateurs has, fortunately, not disappeared, but it is getting rarer. Spectator sports have undermined the physical fitness of the American people. This, in spite of the more ample food and better housing enjoyed by this generation. Paul Grossinger, the manager of the famous Catskill resort, spoke out of a wealth of experience, "The biggest thing that has changed is the customer himself. He puts a much greater emphasis on creature comforts. He's an observer, not a participant."

Mechanization speeds the process of *depersonalization*. In the past, men laid great stress upon the power and the significance of names. God's name was tantamount to His essence. As for a man, his name embodied his personality. That is why we are flattered when our name is remembered and feel hurt when it is forgotten. Today we are being stripped of our names in favor of numbers that can fit into the slits of our automatic machines. It is ironic, and not a little pathetic, that an effort was made in California to launch a revolt against the replacement of telephone exchanges by numbers. People were struggling to hold on to some vestige of personality, even if it was only the name of a telephone exchange. The revolt collapsed when the State Public Service Commission denied the petition.

This mechanization of man which began in the nineteenth century prepared the ground for the *manipulation of man* in the twentieth. Totalitarianism in all colors—black, brown, red and yellow—has perfected the art of manipulating the souls and controlling the minds of men to a degree impossible and undreamed of in earlier ages. Hitler could never have achieved his sway of terror without the radio, nor could he have exterminated many millions of human beings without the improvements of technology.

"Brain-washing" is not a technique limited to our enemies. It is the stock-in-trade of all the forms of propaganda which are being let loose in our own country in every political campaign. We can see in operation the principle which Hitler laid down in *Mein Kampf,* "When you tell a lie, make it a big one, because of even the most outrageous lie something inevitably

sticks and adheres." The public relations industry and the advertising fraternity would modify this only slightly, "Make the lie as
big as you possibly can and yet get away with it." In his book,
"The Rape of the Mind," J. A. M. Meerloo describes how the
process works:

> "Man's mental laziness, his resistance to the hard labor of think-
> ing, makes it relatively easy for Totalitaria's dictator to bring his
> subjects into acceptance of the Big Lie. At first the citizen may
> say to himself, 'All this is just nonsense—pure double-talk,' but
> in the very act of trying to shrug it off, he has become subject to
> the power of the inherent suggestion. That is the trick of double-
> talk. Once a man neglects to analyze and verify it, he becomes
> lost in it and can no longer see the difference between rationale
> and rationalization."

One of the first goals of the manipulation of men has been their
desensitization, to make them impervious to the promptings of
conscience or to sympathy for the suffering. Here language proves
an invaluable tool. Hitler did not murder six million Jews, he
"liquidated" them. We have no poor, only "the lower income
brackets." Two-thirds of the world's children and millions in the
United States are not perpetually hungry; they are merely suffering from "malnutrition."

"Sensitivity," said the French novelist Jules Romains, "is the
mark of a civilized man." What shall we say of a generation which
is being systematically and cynically desensitized? The irruption
of crime and delinquency in America and throughout the world
is a commonplace. Undoubtedly there are many causes for this
widespread violence. The contrast between the affluent members
of society and millions who are destitute, the easy accessibility of
luxuries on the one hand, and the lack of bare necessities on the
other, the feeling among the underprivileged that they have no
stake in society—all these factors play their part. But the quick
recourse to violence, the ease with which men inflict brutal punishment upon their fellows without any compunction, is the end-
result of a long process of desensitization.

A few years ago the world was shocked by an incident which
was repeated several times. One night a young woman was mur-

dered in three stages. The crime was carried on before the eyes of over thirty of her neighbors, none of whom lifted a telephone from the safety of his apartment to summon aid. A respectable housewife explained why she did not let her husband call the police. "I didn't want him to get involved." When the criminal was finally arrested, the same respectable citizens filled the court-room and shrieked like maniacs, "Hang him!"

In the past, many of our admission tickets to plays and other events used to carry the phrase, "Not good if detached." Today we have made detachment, noninvolvement, isolation, our high-est ideal of conduct. When we cease being persons and are no longer sensitive to one another, we invite *the breakdown of human communication*. We constantly boast of the achievements of modern technology in making all the world a single neighbor-hood, in speeding transportation and improving the means of communication. Marya Mannes has pointed out that this is an illusion:

> "The more people are reached by mass communication, the less they communicate with each other. The proliferation of one-way messages, whether in print or on air, seems to have increased rather than lessened the alienation of the individual. Friendly, gregarious America is full of intensely lonely people for whom radio and television provide the illusory solace of company."

One of the most frightening aspects of the racial violence that has disfigured our country during the past few months is a dis-covery which we should have made long ago: that men and women of different races may live side by side for years and never know one another, that neighbors may be not merely strangers, but enemies.

This is true not only across the national borders or the barriers of race. It is true even on the most personal and intimate of levels. From time immemorial men have complained that parents and children did not understand or respect one another. Tension be-tween the generations is, in large measure, inherent in the human situation. As each generation builds upon its predecessor, but diverges from it, growth and progress take place. But today this gap has become a yawning chasm.

To overcome the difference between the generations, some American fathers delude themselves into believing that they are their sons' "pals" and are acting accordingly. Women, being more realistic, seem to be less prone to this form of self-deception. Be this as it may, by adopting this stance of false equality the fathers surrender in advance whatever moral authority they might have had in molding their children's lives during the formative years. After all, it will not be long before the son will play baseball better than his father, who will then remain only an "ex-pal."

Another method for building friendship with children, very popular in this age of gadgets and of "keeping up with the Joneses," is to shower them with elaborate toys, luxuries, and other super-fluities. Yet these devices do not really succeed. A youngster in the United States said about his father to a counsellor, "I want to talk with him about my inner life, but we always end up talking about things." And the situation is similar on the other side of the Iron Curtain. In one of the most successful plays on the Soviet stage, a son gets drunk and then musters the courage to say to his father, "You have decided that silence is the most convenient way of lying to me."

Between nations, between races, between neighbors, between friends, between parents and children, between husbands and wives, true communication has become rarer as men are de-humanized.

Modern man is now master of all he surveys, but is he free? Peter Berger said, "Man is not so much a slave, as a clown." Now what is a clown? He is a man whom we do not recognize as our brother. His face bears a painted smile and his true features are unknown to us. He does not speak to us in words, and his inner-most emotions are unknown. At his mishaps we laugh because we do not see him as human.

III

The dehumanization of man is far advanced in the present. What of man's future? The distinguished French philosopher and jurist Jacques Ellul writes that Western man in 1970 will, above

all else, want and seek security. He says, "By 1970 nearly everyone in the North Atlantic sphere will be comfortably housed, well
fed, enjoying ample leisure and adequate medical care, traveling
more and in general, richly entertained." But "the man of 1970"
will also be a "complete extrovert," satisfied with his work and
his associations but unhappy if cast on his own resources. If I may
put it into simple terms, man will have mastered everything except
the art of living with himself.

Another observer, the English essayist E. V. Lucas, arrives in-
dependently at the same conclusion: "It is idle guessing the future
of the world. A Third War? A relapse to barbarism? A world of
ant-states, with aristocracies or bureaucracies in control of inarticu-
late masses mechanically tending machines? A world of welfare-
states, inhabited by orderly hordes of Philistines, largely preoc-
cupied with physical enjoyment and sport, 'telly' and belly? Or—
perhaps the likeliest—something unlike any of our dreams."

Are these fanciful projections of any unknown future? Well,
the future is now. Here are the trends described by Dr. Philip
R. Cateora of the School of Business of the University of Southern
California, in what has been described as a landmark study (*An
Analysis of the Teen-Age Market*): "Basically, the family with one
or more teen-agers to feed, clothe, educate and entertain must
switch spending away from what adult members may want to
the needs and demands of the younger members of the family."
Among high school boys it is estimated that over 20% own cars.
Teen-age girls represent 13% of the female population, but they
buy nearly 20% of all women's apparel. "Who is responsible for
the auto boom? Young people. The auto industry leaders agree.
Young people tell their parents what to buy" (*New York Herald
Tribune,* July 21, 1963).

If this is our present and our future, it is no wonder that our
most sensitive spirits, our poets, artists, and thinkers, are being
forced to the conclusion that life is meaningless. T. S. Eliot writes
in his best known poem, significantly called "The Wasteland":

> "I cannot connect
> Nothing with nothing."

Modern music, art, poetry, and drama frequently arouse resentment among traditionally minded people who accuse the practitioners of decadence and lack of ability. As an amateur devotee of modern art, I am well aware that there are many motivations and insights involved in the techniques of modern art that must not be overlooked. Yet it remains true that these manifestations of modern culture are faithful representations of our modern lives. The dissonances of modern music echo the breakdown of the harmony of existence in a raucous and machine-made world. The severed limbs and disjointed objects which we often see in modern painting reflect the marred vision of a world in which patterns seem shattered. The advanced "theater of the absurd" seeks to express a vision of life as being without meaning. Thus the gifted young playwright Harold Pinter, in his play, "The Dumbwaiter," reveals life as ugly and dark, full of hazards, fear, and cruelty, in which a man kills his comrade without ever becoming aware that he did it.

A century ago, the German philosopher Friedrich Nietzsche triumphantly proclaimed, "God is dead!" and there were loud hosannahs of rejoicing. Today we know that it was the death of man that he was announcing. Are we, therefore, at the end?

Ours is an age of revolution—and revolutions are violent, destructive, chaotic. By their very nature they disturb the even tenor of life. But however unsettling the experience, there is one truth that we must keep in mind: a revolution is a beginning, not an end.

IV

This is the triumphant affirmation of Rosh Hashanah—*Hayom harat 'olam,* "Today the world is born." Rosh Hashanah is the world's birthday. It is the festival which proclaims the sovereignty of God. Since God is in His heaven, the report of man's death is, in Mark Twain's words, "greatly exaggerated," for God and man are co-partners in creation.

The Midrash tells us that on the first day of his life, Adam saw the sun grow weaker as the hours went by, finally disappear, and darkness descend. He had never experienced night, and he was stricken with terror, believing that he stood on the threshold of annihilation. Long and agonizing were the hours of that first dark night. Finally he saw the first rays of light in the east at dawn growing stronger and stronger, until the sun emerged again in all its glory. Thus he discovered that the night as well as the day were parts of the Divine plan.

A faith that is mature as well as genuine is no self-delusion, no whistling in the dark, no narcotic to dull the senses. *True faith is trust in things unseen, fed by the evidence from things seen.* This vast universe in which we live is indeed a mystery, but it is also a miracle, and it has a direction. Vast expanses of time were required to produce the solar system, which gave birth to the earth. Untold millions of years passed until that greatest of miracles called life emerged on this tiny planet. Hundreds of centuries saw the slow, painful climb upward of the life principle, beginning with the one-celled organisms to the evolution of multicelled beings, the fish and the reptiles, the birds and the beasts, culminating in the higher apes and, finally, in man. Even after man emerged, tens of thousands of years of unrecorded history passed by before any written records of history began. It is only during the last eight thousand years that we can trace man's unending struggle onward and upward. Again and again man has suffered an agonizing defeat, but he never has been permanently halted. If there is one lesson that we can learn from our understanding of the history of the universe and the earth, of life and man, it is the prophetic faith, *lo' tohu bera'ah lashevet yetzarah,* "God created the world not for chaos, but for human habitation" (*Isaiah* 45:18).

It is true that on Rosh Hashanah we address our prayers to God, our Father. We declare that He is King, Sovereign of the universe. But faith in God means trust in man, who is created in God's image, His co-partner in creating the world.

Over a century ago, Abraham Lincoln addressed a delegation of Negroes in words that apply to human beings of every race, color, and creed: "It is difficult to make a man miserable while he feels he is worthy of himself and claims kindred to the great

God who made him" (Address, August 14, 1862). The evils we men have engendered we can conquer, if we remain mindful that God rules His world, which He created not for chaos, but for human habitation.

In the next section of our Service we implore God to remember His creatures. It is equally essential that His creatures remember Him and His ways with the world and with man. That is why Moses, the peerless leader of Israel, speaking to his people shortly before his death, said to them, *Zekhor yemot 'olam, binu shenot dor vador,* "Remember the days of old. Consider the years of every generation" (*Deuteronomy* 32:7). If we turn to the record of man's history and read the record of his struggles and defeats, his frustrations and triumphs, we shall find new courage and new patience—new courage when we survey the progress he has made, new patience when we remember how long and hard has been the road he has traveled from his humble beginnings.

Our country today faces a crisis in race relations. You have heard the song, "We Will Overcome." We can overcome, if we remember. The white American must remember the kidnapping of thousands of Negroes from Africa, the horror of the slave ships, the two centuries of the slavemaster's whip, the degradation, inferiority, and discrimination of the hundred years after the Emancipation Proclamation, the brutality and cynicism with which they are murdered with impunity even today. There is only one thing in the twentieth century cheaper than the blood of the Jew —it is the blood of the Negro. If there are traits in our Negro brothers to which white Americans take exception, let us recall the wise words of Lawrence Hogben: "Persecution rarely makes for attractive personalities. That is one of the best arguments against persecution."

And the Negro American must also remember. He must remember that the white man of today did not kidnap or enslave him. If we try to visit the sins of the past upon the present, we destroy the future. Age-old wrongs cannot be set right overnight, and certainly not through the perpetration of new wrongs. This we all must remember, and from the fountains of memory will come new courage and new patience.

Patience, however, is not inactivity. In the third and concluding portion of the Rosh Hashanah liturgy, the *Shofarot,* we pay
tribute to the Shofar, Israel's clarion call to battle, the rallying
sound for action. *'Adonay bashofar yitka,* "the Lord sounds the
Shofar." In the words of the Torah, *ki lo' davar rek hu' mikkem,*
"This is no empty call to you—and if it be meaningless, it is your
fault that it has no meaning." Let us cease taking refuge in all
the excuses and alibis dredged up by philosophies of despair, by
religions of surrender, by the prejudices of scientism. To be sure,
we live in a world of massive perils. The threat of nuclear war
hangs over the human race. Mutual hatred, violence, overpopula-
tion, disease, and poverty—all these evils are all too real. But not
one of them is inherent in the world. In the words of *Job*:

> *Ki lo yetzei' mei'afar 'aven*
> *Umei'adamah lo yitsmah 'amal*
> *Ki 'adam le'amal yullad*
> *Ubhenei resheph yagbihu 'uf.*

> Not from the dust does evil grow,
>   nor trouble sprout from the earth.
> It is man who gives birth to trouble,
>   as surely as the sparks fly upward.
>   (*Job* 5:5-6)

The evils that man has made he can unmake. For he is fashioned
in the image of God. Today man is fighting to throw off the
shackles of slavery; he has yet to learn the art of freedom. He
has invented machines; he still has time to make them his servants,
and not his masters. Perhaps the automatic computers can solve
the most involved and complicated of problems, but it is man,
and man alone, who can ask the questions.

This solemn season of Rosh Hashanah is the birthday of the
world, the beginning of the year. May it inspire us to recapture
our faith in the future by recalling the record of the past! May
we be moved to reorder the present after the kingdom of the
Almighty! The faith of all the ages since Moses and the Prophets
speaks to us in the words of the modern Hebrew poet Saul
Tschernichowski:

Laugh at all my dreams, my dearest;
   Laugh, and I repeat anew
That I still believe in man—
   As I still believe in you.

For my soul is yet unsold
   To the golden calf of scorn
And I still believe in man
   And the spirit in him born.

By the passion of his spirit
   Shall his ancient bonds be shed.
Let the soul be given freedom,
   Let the body have its bread!

In that day shall my own people
   Rooted in its soil arise,
Shake the yoke from off its shoulders
   And the darkness from its eyes.

Though the time be dark with hatred,
   I believe in years beyond
Love at last shall bind the peoples
   In an everlasting bond.

Life and love and strength and action
   In their heart and blood shall beat,
And their hopes shall fashion for them
   Heaven and earth beneath their feet.
            (*Credo,* translated by Maurice Samuel)

The world is not dying. By this faith we shall triumph.

Night of Terror—
Day of Judgment

I

A few years ago, Premier David Ben Gurion of Israel created a storm in the Jewish world by his question as to who and what is a Jew. Actually, the issue was not a new one. It has been a moot question argued for nearly two hundred years, from the time when Jews emerged from the ghetto and took their place as citizens of the modern world. Countless answers have been suggested during these two centuries. Yet whatever Jews may be—a religious, a cultural, or a national group, or, as is far closer to the truth, a unique amalgam of all three—there is at least one more ingredient in this unique fellowship called Israel. Jews possess a sense of kinship, a feeling of family relationship, that links them together through a common ancestry. Perhaps that explains why Jews quarrel so passionately with one another—it is a family affair! We are all cousins, going back to Abraham, Isaac, and Jacob.

No wonder, therefore, that time and again on these High Holy Days and, for that matter, throughout the year, we invoke the honored name and the illustrious example of the Patriarchs. Each of them possesses a vivid personality, sharply etched in the pages of the Torah, and revealing the boundless variety of human nature.

Abraham, our earliest ancestor, bears the stamp of the heroic. It needed intellectual courage to break with the universal paganism that surrounded him on every side, and raise up the banner of the One Living God. It needed moral courage to shake off the dust of his native home and brave unknown dangers in an unnamed land at the behest of an unseen God. It needed physical courage for Abraham to do battle against the victorious armies of kings, not for the sake of glory or plunder, but only to rescue his nephew from captivity. Abraham is the hero among the Patriarchs.

And Isaac is the saint. As a mere child he is called upon to sacrifice his life for what is a test of his father's faith and love of God. Without flinching, the lad goes forth, lets himself be bound upon the altar, and waits for the sacrificial knife to descend. In his mature years, blindness overtakes him. His household is riven by enmity between his sons, but he bears all his calamities without complaint and retains his composure and serenity.

All of us can be inspired by the exalted lives of Abraham and Isaac, and we can conceivably become the better by contemplating their example. But most of us are neither heroes nor saints. Our prototype is the third of the patriarchs, Jacob, who is each of us— you, and I, our friend and our neighbor, and the man on the other side of the globe. For Jacob's character is neither lily-white nor coal-black, but a mixture of white and black with all the shades of gray in between. His entire career from the hour of his birth reflects the spectrum of strength and weakness, of nobility and baseness characteristic of human nature. He is Everyman.

II

Jacob is the younger of twins born to Isaac and Rebekah. At the very moment of birth he tries to push for his place in the sun— *Veyado 'ohezet ba'akebh 'Esav (Genesis 25:26)*—holding on to his brother Esau's heel, as though seeking to supplant him. What is denied him by nature Jacob tries to achieve by his wits. When, years later, his brother Esau returns from the hunt, tired and hungry, Jacob persuades him to sell him his birthright, the privilege of being the first-born. Later on, at the instigation of his mother, Rebekah, Jacob goes even further. When the blind Isaac calls in his older son Esau and arranges to bless him, Jacob disguises his appearance and steals the paternal benediction. These successful contrivances of Jacob do him little good. His actions arouse the bitter hostility of his brother Esau, who vows to kill him. Jacob must therefore flee, leaving home and family behind him, and seek refuge in a foreign land.

On the way, the young man falls asleep on a rock. He has a dream of a ladder reaching from earth to heaven with angels ascending and descending upon it. This is the vision of a young man with all of life before him. All of heaven and earth is seemingly within his grasp; the world is full of limitless possibilities.

After the dream comes the rude awakening. When he comes to his uncle Laban's home in Mesopotamia, he falls in love with Laban's beautiful daughter Rachel. But his cunning uncle is more than a match for Jacob, and he marries him off to his older and less prepossessing daughter Leah, before giving him Rachel. Laban exacts in all twenty years of labor from Jacob as a shepherd. The young, carefree Jacob turns imperceptibly into a middle-aged, worrisome *pater familias,* with four wives and a large household of children. He still has dreams, but now they are dreams not of angels and a ladder from earth to heaven, but of sheep and goats and ewes. He concocts schemes to outwit his wily and unscrupulous father-in-law and to extract the wages due him for his years of labor.

Jacob determines to go home to Canaan, and he undertakes the slow, cumbersome, perilous journey with his household and possessions. As he approaches his native land, Jacob learns that his brother Esau is waiting for him with a band of four hundred armed men. Jacob decides to try to placate him with gifts, but at the same time to protect himself as well as he can against violence from his impulsive, undisciplined, yet basically good-hearted brother. Jacob has his wives and children, together with all his possessions, carried across the stream Jabbok. Night falls, *vayyivvater Ya'akov lebhado (Genesis* 32:25), "and Jacob is left alone." As the dark shadows gather, he is filled with terror and foreboding. In the deep gloom, a mysterious figure appears and wrestles with

Jacob throughout the night. In the struggle, his opponent twists the hollow of Jacob's thigh. At dawn, Jacob's antagonist asks him to let him go. But Jacob refuses unless he bless him, whereupon the mysterious being says, *Lo' Ya'akov ye'amer 'od shimekha ki 'im yisra'el* (*Genesis* 32:29); "Not Jacob, the 'supplanter,' wilt thou henceforth be called, but 'Israel, Prince of God,' or perhaps *'yeshar 'El,* the one right with God.' " As the sun rises and the angel disappears, Jacob discovers that he bears the scars of battle on his person, for he is limping on his thigh.

This much the Bible tells us, and no more. It leaves it to us to ponder on the meaning of Jacob's mysterious encounter in the middle of the night. What did the Patriarch feel and think when he found himself in a desperate struggle with an unknown assailant? Who was the being who fought with Jacob? Being human like Jacob, we can reconstruct the state of his mind in the dark night. He was alone—his wives and children were on the other side of the river, and there, too, his implacable enemy was lying in wait for him. All kinds of fears assailed him, worries and anxieties, concerns about unknown perils that lurked in the vengeance of Esau.

Who did Jacob think his opponent was? What the Bible conceals, the rabbis reveal. In fact, the Midrash gives several answers. Rab Huna declares, *nidmah lo bidemuth ro'eh tson* (*Genesis Rabbah,* chap. 16), "The adversary appeared to him in the shape of a shepherd." Another view is that *archilestes nidmah lo,* "he appeared in the shape of a bandit leader." A third opinion has it that the opponent seemed to Jacob to be a *pharmakos,* "a magician or sorcerer." Actually, the rabbis tell us, this mysterious enemy who struck terror into Jacob's heart was neither a shepherd nor a bandit nor a magician. In reality, it was *saro shel 'Esav,* "the patron angel and protector of Esau." For, according to Rabbinic thought, every nation has its guardian angel—and this was Esau's patron angel who came to do battle with Jacob.

We can now understand Jacob's mysterious encounter when alone at night. It is his conscience which rises to torment him for cheating and outwitting Esau. For many years his conscience has been asleep—Esau is far away and long ago, out of sight, out of

mind. Now retribution is close at hand—Esau is waiting for him
in the morning. Jacob is terror-stricken, and all kinds of worries
and fears arise, taking on mysterious forms. He sees his adversary
in various strange guises, as a shepherd or a bandit or a magician.

But the truth is that this is no night of nameless terror, but a
day of moral judgment. He is confronted by his own conscience.
The rabbis declare that when Jacob finally recognized that his
real opponent was the guardian angel of his brother Esau, whom
he had wronged, Jacob called out: *Kevan she'attah saro shel 'Esav
lo' 'annikhekha 'ad shetimhol li min haberakhah sheberekhani
'abba (Midrash Aggadah ad locum),* "Since you are the guardian
angel of Esau, I shall not let you go until you forgive me for the
blessing with which my father blessed me instead of Esau."

Healing comes to Jacob only when he recognizes that the enemy
is no mysterious force from without, but his own sin, for which
he must make atonement, his own guile, for which he must offer
restitution. He is no victim of meaningless misfortune. He is the
architect of his own doom. When he learns this basic truth, Jacob
can be regenerated. No longer will he be *ya'akov* "the supplanter,"
but *yeshar 'El,* "the Prince of God, who is right with his Maker."
To be sure, scars of the battle will remain. Jacob ever after will
limp in his gait. In the ledger of life every debit and credit are
entered and must be accounted for. But henceforth Jacob can
walk on life's highway with new-found serenity and strength.

III

This is not the story of an ancient Patriarch alone. It is the life
of every man today. For our age has been described by many
epithets, but by none more appropriately than as "the affluent
society" and "the age of anxiety." On every side we are surrounded
by plenty, luxury, ease, unknown by earlier ages. But we are also
prey to worries and fears which earlier generations never knew.
These terrors we may see symbolized in the mysterious shapes
which Jacob thought he saw on that lonely night.

One of the foes that threaten each one of us takes on the guise
of a shepherd, who serves as the symbol of our economic worries,

our business woes. In our affluent society, most of us have comforts and luxuries unknown by kings a few centuries ago, but we have no serenity, no peace, because of our constant chase after economic "security." Even after we have established ourselves, the will-o'-the-wisp continues to escape us and we try to "provide" for our children and our grandchildren. We are oblivious of the fact that life is a perpetual hazard, and that only the dead are safe against peril.

We forget, too, that the mirage of security has a high price-tag on it. In a play produced on Broadway, dealing with the life of Sigmund Freud, called "A Far Country," Freud tells his earlier collaborator and friend, Dr. Breuer, about his new ideas. Dr. Breuer, who has become a very successful medical practitioner, withdraws from this exploration of the human spirit with these words: "Once we have security, we discover how many gifts of the spirit we can no longer afford, the freedom to think, the freedom to speak."

We today are no longer concerned, as was Jacob, merely with *lehem le'ekhol ubheged lilbosh,* "Bread to eat and a garment to put on" (*Genesis* 28:20). We have gone far beyond that primitive level. We have now developed the national pastime, now fast becoming international, of "keeping up with the Joneses." *We need more and more things we don't want, lest people think we can't afford the things we don't have.* All the resources of psychology and motivational research, all the impulses of greed and sex, all the mechanisms of installment buying and charge accounts are being mobilized to keep us perpetually dissatisfied, adding burden to burden and obligation to obligation.

Let me read to you from an advertisement which appeared in the newspapers not so long ago:

> "What became of the idle rich? They gave way to the busy rich—those energetic young women who are riding in Corvettes, driving Volkswagens, investing in blue chip stocks, hightailing it to Europe, buying hi-fi and high quality everything. Living high and aspiring high, they're the new carriage trade canny merchants are cultivating like crazy. For all income is discretionary and disposable to young women in their spree-buying twenties bent on a style of living."

For this, thousands of years of man's painful ascent on the ladder of civilization—all in order to attain this level of high living!

If we turn aside from our personal and family problems to the national scene, the mysterious adversary who robs us of peace appears as *archilestes*, "a bandit leader, an arch-criminal." Corruption and crime we have always had with us, but today they have penetrated the highest levels of government. Never has the line between respectability and corruption been so thin, so invisible. Corporation executives rob the companies which they head and are deterred by no sense of responsibility to the stockholders, whose executive officers they are supposed to be. Labor leaders flaunt their criminal connections and line their pockets, knowing that the rank and file will triumphantly return them to office. Politicians convicted of crime are elected by landslide votes to office while they are behind bars. Only results count—to get it and get away with it.

We read the mounting statistics of crime and delinquency, especially among our young, and we wring our hands in helpless horror—and ask, "What is happening to our youth?" The truth is both more disturbing and potentially more hopeful. As one expert put it, "What we are witnessing in the world today is a failing of standards generally, and our children are reflecting this. Delinquency is not the result of one or two world wars; rather, the wars were the result of moral deterioration to start with. Since the end of the last war, technology has advanced far more quickly than our spiritual values. There has been a growing irreverence toward the sanctities of life, and, as one Indian authority put it, 'an increasing tendency to mistake mere change for real progress.' "

Let me put it bluntly. Our youth are not maladjusted to society. They are all too well adjusted to a civilization that prates of ideals, but spawns selfishness, materialism, religious prejudice, racial animosity, class snobbery, and contempt for the life of the spirit.

If we avert our gaze from the national scene to the international arena, we find ourselves confronted by another source of peril, which is well symbolized by *pharmakos*, "the sorcerer, the evil magician." Today the all-powerful enemy that threatens us in our way of life is called communism. Its power seems limitless.

It has beaten us in space travel, in atomic explosions, in the
poisoning of the atmosphere, in the manufacture of devilish instruments of destruction that threaten to destroy the world. If
ever terror seems to be justified, it is in the face of the imminent catastrophe toward which we and the Russians are moving,
and dragging the world with us.

Listen to these words written in a letter to a newspaper by a
young girl on Long Island. She is more articulate than most of
her generation, giving voice to the unspoken fears of our children
and grandchildren living in a long night's journey of terror:

"I am one of the 16-year-old girls who sit and watch their world
slipping into the void of death. Every day I listen, hoping not to
hear the pounding of men's feet in their movement toward the
end of a world, a world I have just begun to touch and hear and
see.

"I know that when the time comes there will be no escape,
either from the bomb of merciful swiftness or from the slow agony
of pitiless radiation. I know the fearful insect, landing a thousand
miles away, can creep into the bones of my unknown children.

"I wait for the sign telling me that I will one day be able to
breathe and see without the smog of fear filling my throat and
stinging my eyes. I wait for the people who hold my world's fate
to tell me that I have the right to grow up, to marry and to have
children who will not live in such a place, who will not be afraid
of losing even this nightmare world before they have known it"
(Beth Susan Ingber in the *New York Times,* September 4, 1961).

In our homes, in our country, in the world—worries, worries
everywhere—no wonder we are frightened, frightened unto death.
About fifteen years ago a classic study was made of a typical
American town, Muncie, Indiana. Recently Muncie was surveyed
again, and the contrasts were revealing. There is a far higher
standard of living, and it is climbing ever higher. People are buying less and renting more. What they cannot afford to own, they
pay to hire. There is more and more installment buying, more
and more renting of cars and appliances. Said the local banker:
"Americans are extremely willing to mortgage their future." Per-

haps one fact is the most revealing of all. In 1946, 3% of all pre-
scription sales were tranquilizers; today they total 20%. Perhaps
we can drug ourselves into tranquility and drive away the demons
that threaten us in the dark night.

IV

But the truth is both more sombre and more reassuring. There
can come no healing for us until, like Jacob, we recognize that
it is our past errors and crimes that have emerged to plague and
torment us. It is *saro shel 'Esav,* "the guardian angel of Esau," the
spectre of our own individual and collective sins which now attacks us. There are our sins of commission and omission and the
sins we have permitted others to perpetrate in our name, through
our silence or inaction. If this were a series of causeless calamities,
there would be no defense. If we were suffering without rhyme
or reason, this would be a night of meaningless terror. But it is
the Day of Judgment that has come upon us. Therein lies the
challenge, the penalty, and the hope.

It is this message which Rosh Hashanah seeks to emphasize to
us again and again. Through the noble liturgy of the day, which
draws upon Biblical verse, ancient prayer, and medieval *Piyyut,*
Rosh Hashanah underscores the truth that this is *Yom Hadin*—
the Day of Judgment. It declares that God rules, that we live in
a world of justice and order. It reminds us that the law of moral
consequence, of reward and punishment, operates in the world
as surely as the law of gravitation in the physical world, more
slowly and subtly perhaps, but with equal universality and in-
evitability.

Yes, great economic problems confront us, but it is not because
the heavens give no rain and the sun no warmth. On the contrary, we have a glut of food and we are going bankrupt, while
millions are starving. No, we are going bankrupt, *because* millions
are starving. "A house divided against itself cannot stand." The
world cannot endure half slave and half free, half wallowing in
luxury, the other half groveling in misery. Millions are dying of

disease today in this age of antibiotics. Malaria in Africa takes every year thousands of lives which could be saved at the cost of one cent a day, and our affluent society cannot afford it.

It is true that Communist tyranny threatens our democratic order, but only because of our own follies and failures, and the thought is not pleasant to contemplate for any American. The ancient Roman emperors kept the hungry plebeian mobs quiet, if not contented, by the famous formula *"Panem et circenses"*— bread and circuses. Their modern counterparts behind the Iron Curtain have improved on the formula—they give them the circuses, but the bread they promise. Today there are parades of sputniks and space capsules, and as for the bread, the homes, and the clothes, these are sure to come—tomorrow and tomorrow and tomorrow. If communism is going forward, it is not because of its merits, but because of the failures of democracy.

When democracy was born in the United States over a century and a half ago, its great glory was its dynamism, its forward thrust in time and space. Tyranny and dictatorship, these stand still— democracy must be on the march. For a full century and more, the ideals of democracy continued to expand their frontiers. A greater measure of freedom came to more and more people in more and more countries of the world.

But in our day democracy has stopped in its tracks and is now on the defensive almost everywhere. In the nineteenth century we had a right to be satisfied with what democracy had accomplished, though it fell short of the fullness of the American dream. In the twentieth century we have a duty to be dissatisfied with what democracy has failed to accomplish, because it has fallen short of America's hope.

Instead of proclaiming the abundant life for all men, we find ourselves the allies of exploiters and tyrants from Spain to Saudi Arabia. We spend millions on foreign aid, but far too much of it is siphoned off to benefit the tiny group in the Orient who live in unimaginable luxury, while little or nothing benefits the masses who live in indescribable poverty. We repeat slogans in which we believe but which we do not have the courage to put into practice. We loudly declare that all men are created equal, but we give the world an unequalled example of segregation and discrimination at home, accompanied by brutality and wholesale contempt for law. One Philadelphia, Mississippi, is worth a hundred MIGS to the Russians in the war for the world.

It is time that we learned the facts of life. White men are the minority of God's children on this planet. The darker skinned majority have determined no longer to permit the white race to rule and oppress and exploit them.

There is nothing wrong with the ideals in which we believe, but there is a great deal wrong with our pretenses, upon which our enemies pounce. Though we are in mortal peril, the ills which we suffer from are no mysterious malady. They are not inherent in the nature of the world or in the nature of man. They are the consequences of our own sins—individual, communal, and national. Nothing in the stars above or on the earth below compels us to persevere in evildoing. For we live in a world in which, as the *Yigdal* hymn declares, *Gomel le'ish hesed kemif'alo, noten larasha' ra' kerish'ato,* "God requites the righteous man according to his deed; He punishes the evildoer according to his sin." This is a world of law, and God is its King.

But a world governed only by consequence, by the principle of retribution, would be a cold, dead, mechanical universe. Again and again we invoke God as *'Avinu Malkenu,* not only *Malkenu*—our King and Lawgiver—but also *'Avinu,* our Father who loves His children. He is *zokher haberit.* He remembers His covenant not only with Abraham, Isaac, and Jacob, with the land and the people of Israel, but with Noah, who was far from perfect, as well. God remembers His creatures and loves them. They have the power to repent and turn away from folly and sin. The world is governed by Divine Mercy as well as by Divine Judgment. But before God's mercy can come into play, we must show ourselves worthy of God's love, by the words we speak, by the sentiments we feel, and, above all, by the actions we undertake.

On Rosh Hashanah, the Shofar sounds a clarion call to regeneration and rebuilding. The remedy for our sins lies within us—to recognize our shortcomings and overcome them. Let us cease giving excuses and alibis for ourselves, whether they be ancient or modern, drawn from the myths of the pagans, the propaganda of tyrants, or the misreadings of pseudo-science. We are not helpless pawns of fate or of nature. We are not nameless cells in a Volk or a state or a class. We are not lifeless atoms at the mercy of social forces or blind instincts. We are not foam tossed about on the sea of life by an imaginary "wave of the future."

We are men—with immortal souls, capable of great deeds. We are free and therefore responsible. In the words of the Torah: *Re'eh, natatti lefanekha hayyom 'et hahayyim ve'et hatobh, ve'et hammavet ve'et hara'* (*Deuteronomy* 30:15), "This day I give you your choice. This day and every day you have the decision between the blessing and the curse, between good and evil, between life and death."

The remedy for the ills of democracy lies in more democracy. Let us proclaim our truth with sincerity, and no falsehood will be able to prevail against it. Let us take seriously the right of all men to life and liberty—liberty at home and life abroad, and men will not surrender the blessings of freedom and security for the allurements of circuses and the promissory note of bread.

These are the solemn, challenging, and hopeful truths of these High Holy Days—

> *The world is governed by God in accordance with justice.*
> *God rules with justice, but practices mercy.*
> *Man is free to rebuild his life and recapture his hope in the future.*

This is no night of meaningless terror, but a day of moral judgment. No unknown spectres threaten us, but our own shortcomings, that we can conquer and overcome. We face grave problems, but are not defeated unless we will it so. We are not condemned to disaster, unless we haul down the flag. Like the Patriarch Jacob, we can each wrestle with our memories of past evil and emerge stronger and purified as a Prince of God, right with our Maker.

Ours is not the first age when darkness enveloped the earth. Yet always men of character and courage can see through the gloom and look to the sunrise. One recalls the words of Thomas Jefferson written in a letter to John Adams in 1821: "I shall not die without a hope that light and liberty are on steady advance. We have seen, indeed, once within the records of history, a complete eclipse of the human mind continuing for centuries. And even should the cloud of barbarism and despotism again obscure the science and liberties of Europe, this country remains to preserve and restore light and liberty to them."

In our day, the *Hasidic* rabbi of Lubavitch restated this great truth in individual terms: "The evil deeds, not good ones, are only temporary, and they can, through true and honest repentance, be corrected and wiped away. This truth must arouse in the heart of every human being, no matter what his self-examination for the past year may bring forth, a spirit of encouragement and strong hope for the future. For he can know that his good deeds in the past year are eternal, and have brought light into his life, in that of his family and in that of all Israelites. . . .

"From this, it is more understandable that even if we at times see phenomena which point to a decline—not everyone becomes wiser, nor more pious—nonetheless, in truth and in depth, the good in the world becomes stronger every year, every day more powerful, every day greater. For each moment adds good deeds to the store, and even when the not-good seems to have the upper hand, this is only temporary. In the end the good must conquer, and the not-good completely be destroyed."

This is our faith, and by its light we can live, we can fight and emerge triumphant.

V

Alone in the World

I

Few and far between are the sons and daughters of our people who are not in some fashion conscious of Yom Kippur. The widespread observance of the day, the long fast inaugurated before sundown on Kol Nidre Eve and ending after sunset tomorrow, and the elaborate ritual of worship have their effect even upon the Jew who does not come to the synagogue and whose ties with Judaism are minimal.

Yet though Yom Kippur is undoubtedly impressive, it is not universally meaningful. Thus in the State of Israel Yom Kippur is the one festival that poses a stumbling block to the nonreligious elements of the population. They have succeeded in reinterpreting all other sacred days in nonreligious terms. But Yom Kippur is neither a nature holiday nor a national festival. It is concerned with the soul of the individual human being and his relationship to God, with sin, atonement, and divine reconciliation.

Not only those who are consciously antireligious, but also many Jews who adhere to Judaism, are uncomfortable with words like "sin," "atonement," and "forgiveness," that are sprinkled so liberally throughout the High Holy Day liturgy. What meaning do these terms really have for modern man living in the most scientific of centuries? Are they not vestigial remains of a dead past? Has not scientific truth made religious truth obsolete? The French philosopher Auguste Comte said that the day would come when

54

mankind would escort God to the door, bow politely, thank Him
for past services, and show Him out. Has not the day finally arrived with the space age?

Within a few short years the vast expanses of outer space have
been opened up not only to man's vision through the telescope,
but also to man's actual presence through the space capsule. In
the race between Russia and the United States, billions of dollars
are spent in duplication and in error that could be saved through
cooperation and the pooling of resources. Both we and the Russians have made solo and dual flights through space. The Russians
even sent up a female astronaut, perhaps in an effort to shatter
the deafening silence of interstellar space! There have been
rockets and missiles that stagger the imagination, all as prepara-
tory steps to an assault upon the moon.

Yet perhaps the most important scientific discovery from the
long-range point of view is the one that attracted the least attention. You may remember the passage in one of the Sherlock
Holmes detective stories. Holmes turns to his lifelong companion,
Dr. Watson, and says to him, "Watson, I call your attention to
what the dog did last night." "Why?" Watson answered, "the dog
did nothing." "That's what I am calling to your attention!" In
the summer of 1965, Mariner IV was sent up toward Mars and
brought back a collection of computerized photographs. When
these close and accurate pictures of Mars were studied by scientists,
they came to the definite conclusion that there can be no life
on Mars. For centuries the red planet Mars had exercised the
imagination of man. Its atmosphere, its polar caps, and, above all,
its "canals" inspired scientific speculation as well as fiction. The
belief was widely held that life existed on the planet Mars. Only
a few weeks before Mariner IV set out on its journey to Mars, a
panel discussion on a T.V. program entitled "Lamp Unto My
Feet" dealt with the question of the scientific break-through and
its impact upon man's notion of God. Walter Sullivan, science
editor of the *New York Times,* stated that "the universe *probably*
is the home of rational creatures who have achieved a higher
state of development than mankind" *(Italics ours) (New York
Times,* July 11, 1965). Then came the evidence from Mariner IV

that Mars, the only planet previously believed to be capable of sustaining life, was a dead world. We cannot speak of other universes millions of light years away, but in our solar system it is clear that the earth is the only planet which sustains life.

President Johnson, far from exaggerating the implications of this discovery concerning Mars, understated them when he said, "It may be, it just may be, that life as we know it with its humanity is more unique than many have thought. We must remember this."

I would go further. The voyage of Mariner IV may be much more than a scientific break-through. Its negative results may ultimately prove more significant for man's understanding of his place in the universe than the loudly acclaimed and widely publicized journeys into space and even the planned assault upon the moon. For it may help to halt the process of the degradation of man that has been going on for centuries, and may thus usher in his rehabilitation which has long been overdue.

II

For several hundred years the best minds of the human race have been engaged in pure and applied research, and have produced extraordinary results. No wonder that Western civilization made obeisance to the great god Science, from whom all blessings flowed or were promised very soon. There is a striking legend in rabbinic literature that King Solomon, the wisest of men, became conceited about his wisdom. Thereupon God cast him away hundreds of miles from his palace in Jerusalem and changed him into a beggar. Slowly and painfully Solomon, dressed in rags, had to make his way back to the capital city, laughed at as an impostor and a madman when he claimed to be king. For on Solomon's throne God placed Asmodeus, the devil, who looked and talked like the king, so that no one was the wiser.

So in our day men enter to worship in the Temple of Science, and often fail to notice that the god seated on the throne is a usurper. Or, if one prefers, the god on the throne has two faces, like the Roman deity Janus. One face is science, bringing man

food and shelter, health and ease. The other is scientism, a mass
of ideas claiming to be derived from science, presenting conclusions about man's nature and his place in the world. The face
of science is kindly and smiling, offering man its gifts. The face
of scientism is frowning, wearing a mask of scorn, deriding man's
hopes as fancies and his sense of worth as an illusion. Science has
showered comforts and pleasures upon man, but they have
brought him little pleasure and less comfort because scientism
has deprived man of his sense of significance. Science has filled his
life with things; scientism empties it of values. He lives better and
better, but he counts less and less.

Let me make the point clearer. In the ancient world, man was
the center of the universe. The earth was regarded as flat, surrounded by the great sea on all sides. Arched above the earth like
an inverted bowl was the sky, in which the sun, the moon, and
the stars had been placed to illumine man's path and to serve
his needs. God had created the world, the earth was its center, and
man was its crown and glory.

Then came the Copernican revolution in astronomy. An
obscure Polish monk in the seventeenth century demonstrated
what had long been suspected, that the world was heliocentric
and that the planets, of which the Earth was one of the smallest,
revolved around the sun. In the succeeding centuries more and
more galaxies came into the view of man's telescope, so that even
the solar system was now revealed as only one small element in
the vast expanses of space. The earth was a tiny clod, and man
a speck of dust upon it. The process of downgrading man had
begun.

In the nineteenth century came the Darwinian revolution. The
English biologist Charles Darwin assembled a mass of evidence,
much of which had been known before, which demonstrated that
all life was part of a single process of evolution and that man, far
from standing apart and above the lower animals, represented
only one more link in the evolution of species.

Centuries before, the Biblical sage Koheleth had speculated as
to whether man was more than a beast. Now science seemed to
have given the final answer: Man was simply an animal, a more

agile and certainly a more cunning ape than his brothers, the
baboon and the gorilla.

Then came the Freudian revolution in the twentieth century.
The father of psychoanalysis, Sigmund Freud, was a veritable
Columbus of the mind, discovering continents undreamt of before. He revealed unsuspected levels of consciousness in man and
their impact upon his behavior, during both his waking and his
sleeping states. In his psychoanalytic theories Freud emphasized
the power of irrational impulses and frustrated desires in molding
and at times perverting the human psyche.

The popularizers and the vulgarizers of Freud went further, and
declared that man was nothing but a collection of abnormalities,
with only a thin line separating the so-called normal from the
neurotic and the psychotic. The gift of reason, in which man had
gloried through the ages as the mark of his superiority over the
beast, was now discounted as a delusion. His conscience was no
longer the voice of God, but the mechanism of the super-ego.
Biology had demonstrated that man was no better than the beast.
Now psychology had shown that man was worse, for animals at
least were free from complexes and perversions. Then into the
halls of philosophy came existentialism, insisting that man could
never hope to grasp the essence either of the world or of his own
nature, and that the only thing he could know was that he existed,
and nothing else. Religion had taught that man was only a little
less than divine. Now philosophy insisted that he was much less
than human!

The world's greatest dramatist, William Shakespeare, had declared: "What a piece of work is man! How noble in reason! how
infinite in faculties! in form and moving how express and admira-
ble! in action how like an angel, in apprehension how like a god!
the beauty of the world, the paragon of animals." Now the contemporary theater of the absurd spoke in moving accents of the
total meaninglessness of life and of the absurdity of human
existence.

The attitudes of scientism, which found expression in philosophy and literature, did not long remain in the area of theory.
With the advent of the second third of the twentieth century, the

greatest mass movement of brutality was let loose on the world. To describe Nazism as the most horrible form of bestiality is an insult to the beasts, for no animal remotely approaches the cruelty that men had perpetrated upon their brothers. Racialism was thoroughly "scientific," with laboratories, experiments, and control data. And in the free world, the fine fruit of scientific research was the atomic bomb, which wiped out tens of thousands of human beings and maimed hundreds of thousands more for untold generations.

No wonder the greatest scientific mind of our age, Albert Einstein, in 1955, a few months before his death, wrote in a letter to his friend and fellow Nobel Prize winner, Max Born, that if he could start his life all over again he would not choose a profession that "has to do with the search for knowledge." According to Professor Born, Einstein's aversion to science developed after the dropping of the first atomic bomb, to which he had contributed with his knowledge. "He left the world without regret," Professor Born said (*New York Times,* July 1, 1965).

Thus the long process which had begun with man's degradation now brought in its wake the threat of his annihilation.

III

It goes without saying that during this process there were protests in various quarters, some voices declaring that man does count in the world. Here and there some scientists and philosophers objected to the perversion of the true role of science and its usurpation by scientism. The French philosopher Henri Bergson had opposed the mechanical view of evolution and insisted that the process of "creative evolution" demonstrated a vital spirit at the heart of the cosmos. The biologist Lecomte du Noüy had argued that the evolutionary process was neither slow nor blind, but that, on the contrary, it gave evidence of direction and meaning: "When we examine a process like evolution, which brought about such prodigies as human intelligence and conscience, we should, therefore, never take the rapidity or slowness of the event into consideration. What is 'rapid' to us in relation to the rhythm of our life . . . will be 'slow' for an ephemeral insect with a life span of only a few days. To an imaginary being with a life span of ten thousand million years, evolution would seem very rapid. To God, whom we cannot even conceive in relation to time, it may well be 'instantaneous.' " He and other scientists saw evidence of orthogenesis, of a direction in the evolution of species and of man.

Centuries ago the Hebrew prophet had declared, *Ki lo' mahshebhotai mahshebhotekhem, velo' darekheikhem derakhai ne'um Hashem,* " 'My thoughts are not your thoughts, nor My ways your ways,' saith the Lord" *(Isaiah* 55:8). We cannot hope to fathom the ways of God, but we sometimes can discover a glimmer of His purpose even with our limited power of insight. As we read the history of the cosmos which astronomy, geology, biology, and psychology increasingly reveal to us, however imperfectly, some conclusions emerge. Today it is clear on scientific grounds that the universe had a fixed point of beginning in time—in other words, it came into being from nothing, that it was created. Then untold aeons of years passed until the solar system came into being, followed by many millions of years until life had its humble beginnings. Thereafter, untold eras were required for the ascent from the one-celled protozoa to the higher animals.

If we read the record aright, it seems clear that the entire universe came into being for the creation of life. Size and significance are not synonymous. The earth may be one of the smaller planets, but it is the bearer of this most precious attribute of the cosmos— life. This line of thought, which I presented in the book, *A Faith for Moderns,* is now supported also by the conclusions derived from the voyage of Mariner IV. For even Mars, the one planet which was regarded as the most likely habitat for life, cannot sustain life.

Finally, the earth was the scene for the emergence of man, who alone is gifted with consciousness, conscience, and creative power. Man is linked to all life, and yet is unique. For man is the only creature who can laugh and can weep, who can be sad when he is not in physical pain and can rejoice when his body is in agony, who knows not only the present moment, but has a memory of the past and a vision of the future.

This great truth is taught in the Bible with matchless vividness when it declares, *Betselem 'Elohim bara' 'otho,* "In the image of God created He him [man]." It is no megalomania that emphasizes the importance of man. We are the bearers of God's purposes in this vast universe, the crown and purpose of creation.

From other quarters, too, the revolt against scientism—the illegitimate use of science—is growing. Dr. Vannevar Bush, who coordinated atomic research during the war and is now honorary Board Chairman of M. I. T., pointed out that science has gone far toward delineating the probable nature of the universe. It has even pried into the mechanism by which the human brain thinks. But beyond this, science cannot go. "It offers no proof," Dr. Bush declares, "It does not even produce evidence on the two vital realities of man's being, his free will and his consciousness. Those who follow science blindly come to a barrier beyond which they cannot see" (*Time Magazine,* May 7, 1965).

In August, 1965, a group of scholars and scientists met at Bowdoin College under the auspices of the Study Group on Foundations of Cultural Unity, under the chairmanship of Michael Polanyi, a distinguished physical chemist. The group issued a ringing declaration of war against what it called "reductionism." Reductionism may be explained in simple terms as "the fallacy of 'nothing but.' " Violin music is nothing but horse hair scratching on catgut. Love is only a physical pressure upon certain glands. A human being is only ninety-six cents worth of carbon, oxygen, nitrogen, and hydrogen. Perhaps with inflation today the figure is closer to a dollar and a half! Literature, music, and art, which Freud described as sublimations of the sexual impulse, are nothing but substitutes for sex. These are all examples of "reductionism."

At this conference in Bowdoin, it was argued that it is precisely this error that modern science has been committing for three hundred years. In strictly scientific terms the participants insist that it is a basic blunder to reduce all aspects of life, and especially its higher manifestations in man, to the level of chemistry and physics, which means to treat them in terms of inanimate nature. In a declaration issued at this Conference, these scholars and scientists said: "Since the 17th century the kind of knowledge afforded by mathematical physics has come more and more to furnish mankind with an ideal for all knowledge. This ideal also carried with it a new conception of the nature of things: All things whatsoever are held to be intelligible ultimately in terms of the laws of inanimate nature. *In the light of such a reductionist program, the finalistic nature of living things, the sentience of animals and their intelligence, the responsible choices of man, his moral and aesthetic ideals, the fact of human greatness seem all of them anomalies that will be removed eventually by further progress. . . . Since its ideal is fundamentally mistaken, the result has been to debase the conception of man.*" (Italics ours.) (*New York Times,* August 29, 1965.)

The voyage of Mariner IV and the revolt against reductionism are to be welcomed because they mark the beginning of the end in the conflict which has been waged against religion, not by science, but by scientism. It is not the task of science to demonstrate God or even to rehabilitate man. Its function—and it is glory enough—is to seek the truth and find the answers to the questions of the nature of reality. There the proper function of science ends. At this point religion and philosophy, utilizing the discoveries of science, begin to grapple with the great issues of the meaning and direction of the universe. Science is not expected to prove religion true; it makes religion possible.

Today we need not put our minds to sleep in order to hear the promptings of our hearts. God is as real as man. "Sin" and "atonement" are not only solemn words; they express great truths about man, because they remind us that man is important.

IV

These High Holy Days are a mighty declaration of man's dignity. He counts not only for himself and his fellows, but also for God and the universe. Throughout Yom Kippur we confess our sins and plead for forgiveness, promising to do better if God, in His mercy, grants us a new lease on life. We thus reaffirm the basic doctrine of man in Judaism. Man is endowed with reason, and is by that token free to choose. He is therefore responsible for his actions. As we are told in the Torah no less than three times: *Hahayyim vehamaveth natatti lephanekha hayom,* "Life and death have I placed before you this day, the blessing and the curse. Choose life, so that you may live, you and your children" (*Deuteronomy* 30:19; see also 12:26; 30:15).

It is true that the word "sin" is old-fashioned. But it can never become out-of-date, because it expresses a basic reality. Truth driven out through the door re-enters through the window. Modern psychology dismissed the idea of sin as meaningless, but then it found that it needed the concept. Wishing to avoid "contamination" with religion, psychologists avoid the term "sin" and prefer "guilt," because it is a basic element in human experience. What is guilt, as used in the jargon of our day? It may be defined, not unfairly, as an overpowering feeling that something is wrong, without any clear understanding of what is right! Religion calls a spade a spade, and a sin a sin.

What is sin? It is an act of rebellion against God and the laws of His world. Sin is man's failure to render obedience to God's law of righteousness in the universe. In Solomon Schechter's words, "Sin taints the divine in man, breaking all communion with heaven." Martin Buber adopts the Hasidic definition of sin as that which cannot be done with the whole being. It may therefore be possible for us to silence the conflict in our soul, but we cannot uproot it until the sin is overcome. "Integrity" means wholeness, health, and harmony; sin is conflict, within man and vis-à-vis the world, a disharmony and disease of the spirit.

The various Hebrew terms for sin have highly significant etymologies. Sometimes a man imagines that he can escape the law of consequence in the world and therefore commit a *pesha',* an act of rebellion against the Ruler of the universe. Or he may permit weakness and perversion to distort his conduct through *'avon,* an act of crookedness and deceit. The basic term for sin, however, is *het'.* It means "missing the mark," a goal for which man should have aimed and which he could have reached. It under-

scores the teaching of Judaism that when he misses it because of
his imperfections, he may still return to his Maker through the
power of atonement.

Here, too, it is noteworthy that the process of restoration is described not by the term "penitence," derived from the Latin
poena, "pain, punishment," but *Teshuvah,* which means "return."
There is a highway to God from which man strays all too often,
but toward which he may retrace his steps.

How is this return to be effected? In Judaism there are several
steps in the process. The first is *Haratah,* genuine regret and sorrow at one's failing. The next is *Viddui,* or "confession," the
straightforward recognition of one's weakness without alibi or excuse. The culmination of the process is *Teshuvah,* "return," which
includes restitution for such evils as can be undone and the solemn
promise to God to avoid repeating the offence.

V

If man counts in the universe, it means that you and I count,
for there is no mankind apart from individual men, from you and
me. It means that what we do, or fail to do, what we create or what
we destroy, what we fashion or what we pervert, matters supremely
to God and the world.

We can make no greater error than to offer the alibi, "What I
do doesn't really make a difference." Recently the *New York
Times* carried a story about the well-known philanthropist, Aaron
Rabinowitz, who is seeking to have the social worker, Lillian
Wald, elected to the Hall of Fame on the N. Y. U. campus. He
told that the single most important incident in his life took place
when he was a youngster on the East Side. He had been asked
by a boys' club in the Henry Street Settlement, of which he was
a member, to arrange for a party, and Lillian Wald made an appointment to meet with the lad to decide on the refreshments
to be served. In the interim, she was called away to Rochester.
She tried to reach him, but failed, since he had no telephone in
his tenement home. Lillian Wald took a train back to New York
to keep the appointment with this unimportant youngster, and

then went back to her important work. The boy never forgot the lesson. The entire direction of his public service in philanthropy was the result. He had been taught that he counted and should count for something.

Perhaps nothing quite so striking happened to us. Yet if we pause a moment to look back on our own lives, most of us will discover that we have been greatly helped by someone, be it a parent, a grandparent, a friend, a teacher, or an employer, or even by a total stranger.

Because we can count in the lives of others, let us search our hearts and actions, discover at least one weakness, and resolve to overcome it in the New Year. Let us pray for God's forgiveness, because we count for Him and His world. The Talmud says, *Kol hammekayyem nephesh 'ahath ke'illu' kiyyem 'olam male'* (*Sanhedrin* 4:5), "He who saves a single life is as though he has saved an entire universe." The first life we should try to save is our own.

Judaism does not exaggerate our virtues or overlook our weaknesses: *'Adam yesodo mei'aphar vesopho le'aphar,* "Man's foundation is dust and his end is dust." We know how often we miss the mark. But as Supreme Court Justice Oliver Wendell Holmes said, "We aim at the infinite, and when our arrow falls to earth it is in flames."

In the vast reaches of an infinite universe where only the earth has life we are not alone, for God is with us, He is *'Avinu Malkenu,* "Our Father, our King." If we are with Him, as His co-partners in building His world and fulfilling His inscrutable purpose, if we go forth to Him, He will reach out to us. If we seek Him in sincerity and truth He will answer us, *Ki bayom hazeh yekhapper 'aleikhem letaher 'etekhem mikkol hatoteikem liphenei Hashem titharu* (*Leviticus* 16:30), "For on this day will He forgive you, to cleanse you; from all your sins shall you be clean before the Lord."

VI

The Beginning or the End

On these High Holy Days we usher in the Jewish year 5727, which corresponds to 1966–67 in the secular calendar. In other words, the world is now entering the last third of the twentieth century. What a tragic change has taken place between its beginning and its end! How many of man's hopes have turned to ashes! In the year 1901 the nations of the West faced the future with confidence and hope. All signs pointed to the twentieth as the greatest of centuries. The progress of science in the nineteenth century had vastly increased man's understanding and control of nature. Thanks to science, the world was poised on the threshold of an age of plenty, which promised that want and hunger would soon be banished from the lives of men. Men were on the threshold of fulfilling the vision of the great prophets, philosophers and poets, who had dreamt of an era marked by justice, peace, and freedom for the world.

Freedom, to be sure, was not universal, but democracy was on the march everywhere. The greatest democratic nation in the world, the United States, had just won the Spanish-American War. It had liberated Cuba, Puerto Rico, and the Philippines, and had become a world power. In Europe there had been no major war for several decades. At the end of the nineteenth century Czar Nicholas II of Russia was instrumental in founding the Hague Court of International Justice for the peaceful adjudication of conflicts among nations.

In the opening years of the twentieth century, men's high hopes for peace seemed thoroughly justified. Early in 1914 the American steel magnate and philanthropist, Andrew Carnegie, surely no starry-eyed visionary, set aside a million dollars to organize the Church Peace Union, now called the Council on Religion and International Affairs. Its purpose was to utilize the forces of religion to strengthen the peace movement. So convinced was Carnegie that world peace was just around the corner that in the charter creating the organization he stipulated that as soon as world peace was achieved, the funds were to be used for the relief of the poor. Now, fifty-two years later, I can report as a Trustee for the Council on Religion and International Affairs that our treasury, by dint of judicious investment, has grown from one to six million dollars! But few of us expect that we shall soon be called upon to turn over the money to the poor because world peace will have become a reality! Quite the contrary, as we know to our cost.

Our century, which began with high hopes for peace, has seen the bloodiest conflicts in human history. World War I was horrible enough, but it pales into insignificance by the side of the Second World War. Not only were six million of our flesh and blood cruelly done to death, but thirty million human beings died as a result of the holocaust. And the Third World War may well be the last! All this would be impossible without the inventions of science: germ warfare, the submarine, the airplane, the atomic bomb, and the intercontinental missile.

Two-thirds of a century have passed—and today the forward sweep of democracy has been halted, if not reversed. Totalitarianism of all colors, black, brown, and red, has all but submerged the democratic ideal. Though Nazism was finally overthrown in Germany, Fascism is still very much alive, and Communism is on the march almost everywhere.

As our awesome physical might has grown greater, our moral capacity has become smaller. Ours is an age of giant power and pygmy leadership. In describing the chaos that would precede the advent of the Messiah, the rabbis declared, *Penei hador kiphenei kelebh* (*Mishnah, Sotah* 9:19). One commentator explains: "The leaders of the generation have the appearance of a dog." He points out that while it is true that a dog runs before his master, every so often he turn around to make sure that he is going where his owner is heading. So our leaders go in front of us, but instead of offering courageous and intelligent guidance, they keep their ears tuned to the television set and their eyes glued to the popularity polls in order to decide the course of action. Our elections are conducted like beauty contests.

What is most ominous is the breakdown of the sense of the common weal, the disruption of the feeling of community. Men have always been concerned with their own interests, but in the past there was also present an overriding sense of an obligation to the common good. Today society seems to consist only of bitterly competing pressure groups, fighting for their own advantage against the rest. There is little sense of responsibility, by men in high office, to their constituencies, be it the electorate, the stockholders, or labor union members. The *esprit de corps* of the professional is rapidly disappearing. Physicians, social workers, teachers, defend their interests like any manufacturers' association or trade union. People quote President Kennedy's famous words, "Do not ask what your country can do for you; ask what you can do for your country"—but more often in derision than in admiration.

Instead of the familiar *Mah Nishtannah* at the Passover Seder, men in our age have a new set of Four Questions: The first is, "What is there in it for me?" The second is, "Why knock yourself out?" The third is, "Why stick your neck out?" And the fourth, "Why be a sucker?"

The decay of character is accompanied by the decline of culture. A new god has arisen—the computer—who can answer all questions, solve all problems, meet all needs. Indeed, we are told by some educators that books belong to the horse and buggy age. This is the period of audio-visual aids, so that the process of learning has been simplified and mechanized. Teachers are required less and less. Perhaps, before long, we shall dispense with students as well!

The dean of an Eastern university tells the story of a distinguished professor on his faculty who received many government grants and was in great demand as an expert in various parts of the world. As a result of his expertise, he was less and less available for classroom teaching, until his load was reduced to one seminar course for fifteen chosen graduate students.

One day the professor came to see the dean. "You know, Dean, I am scheduled to be traveling to Latin America, Africa, and Europe a good deal during the coming semester. This will interfere with the course I am scheduled to give on Wednesday afternoons. The thought has occurred to me that I might dictate my sixteen lectures for the course and arrange to have a graduate student play the tape each week for the students, thus maintaining the continuity of the course."

The dean, having no alternative, agreed and the course was launched with the professor's lectures recorded on tape. A few weeks later, between two trips abroad, the professor found himself on the campus. Having a sense of dedication to his work, he decided to visit his class. As arranged, the graduate student was sitting at the desk in charge of the recorder and the lecture was coming over clearly. But facing the desk were fifteen tape recorders!

What is certain is that the art of reading is rapidly declining. The television screen pre-empts thirty to sixty hours a week in the lives of children, young people, and even adults. A small intellectual élite remains as the custodians of culture. For the masses, culture has been vulgarized and largely emptied of content. At best, it is a decoration, a hobby, a pastime, principally for women. Rarely is it the crowning glory of a man's life.

Reinhold Niebuhr summarized the conditions of our time in these brief words: "The realities of the twentieth century are war instead of peace, poverty and class conflict instead of justice, nationalistic passion instead of world government, and racial prejudice instead of world enlightenment."

Parallels in history are notoriously dangerous. Yet it is hard to escape the impression that our situation is very similar to that of the Roman Empire in the third and fourth centuries. Rome was mistress of the world, rich and powerful, ruling a vast territory from Britain to India. But the signs of its decay were already visible. The great historian Eduard Meyer declared there were three factors in the fall of Rome: the decreasing birth rate, a large class of economically uprooted men who had to be supported by the State, and a weakened sense of communal responsibility, particularly on the part of the intellectuals. Does this not read like a description of our times?

How did an ancient, cultivated Roman react when he looked upon the mounting chaos of his time? Undoubtedly he was troubled, but he was not perplexed, for he expected it. The ancient Greeks had two views of history, which the Romans shared. According to one view, all human experience runs in cycles that recur interminably and meaninglessly, so that nothing new, and surely nothing better, can ever emerge. The other Greek view of the world was even more pessimistic. It held that history runs downhill, so that each succeeding period in history is worse than that which preceded it. The Greek poet Hesiod spoke of the four ages of man, the age of gold, followed by the age of silver; then came the age of copper, and, finally, the age of iron, of chaos and war. For the ancients, the Golden Age of mankind lay in the distant past and could never be recovered. The present was bad, and the future would be worse. As the saying has it, "Cheer up. Things can be worse—and probably will be!"

It was the Hebrew prophets who reversed this concept of human history completely. No people had suffered greater disasters than the Jews, but none had resisted despair more effectively. The prophets insisted that in a world governed by God the end would be better than the beginning, and that the Golden Age of humanity lay in the future. For them, history was neither a static tableau nor a repetitious cycle, nor was it a toboggan running downhill. History was a great drama directed by God and moving to a predestined higher goal. The evil in the world would be used to destroy evil and usher in the good. The Golden Age of mankind, which the prophets foresaw, they called the Kingdom of God.

The prophets not only dared to dream of peace for all nations; they declared that it would come to pass through the acceptance of the universal moral law under God. They denied that man was doomed to suffer poverty and want in a world where all men were the children of God. They rejected the Greek notion that the vast majority of mankind was destined to perpetual slavery, and they insisted on man's inalienable right to freedom and justice.

From this faith Judaism has never retreated. In the face of the chaos and conflict of our age, Judaism still insists that history has meaning and direction. In the spirit of biblical religion, Judaism today rejects both the false optimism of automatic progress held at the beginning of the century, and the helpless pessimism of inevitable doom now being maintained as we begin to approach its end.

For the Jew, Rosh Hashanah is not the end of the year, but the beginning, when he triumphantly proclaims his faith, *Hayom harat 'olam,* "Today the world is born." If there is chaos in the world today, it is the *tohu vabhohu,* the chaos before Creation, the pain before birth, the confusion preceding a new order. Eras of change are always disturbing and even dangerous, the unfamiliar is always uncomfortable, but it is revolution, not disintegration, that we are witnessing.

A dozen years ago, Adlai Stevenson pointed this truth out in his book, *Call to Greatness:* "In the foreground is the mortal contest with world communism. But in the background are the opaque, moving forms and shadows of a world revolution, of which communism is more the scavenger than the inspiration."

Actually, it is a threefold revolution that is taking place in our day. The first is *the scientific revolution,* which has annihilated time and space. The adults in our generation can well remember when it took twice as long to get from New York to Chicago as it requires today to travel between New York and Paris. We may have not yet placed a man upon the moon, but we talk to one another via satellites in space.

The great tragedy of modern man is that he is a citizen of the world and does not know it. We talk of "foreign" nations and countries on the other side of the globe, and act as though they were really far away. We should never forget the truth proclaimed by Koheleth, that evil is not merely sinful, it is stupid. In his words, *Resha' kesel, vehasikhluth holleloth,* "Evil is folly, and folly is madness" (*Ecclesiastes* 7:25). In earlier ages, when distances were tremendous and men lived in isolation from one another, their power to injure one another was correspondingly smaller. Who is our neighbor today? This is best answered in the Jewish manner by another question: Who is not?

As a result of our folly and shortsightedness the blessings of rapid transportation and instantaneous communication have become a peril and a curse. Our jet planes and atom bombs threaten the annihilation of entire nations, if not of mankind. Our electronic means of communication, the radio and now television, made it possible for demagogues and madmen like Charles Coughlin, Adolf Hitler, and Joseph Stalin to control the thoughts and actions of millions.

It cannot be denied that the scientific revolution has thus far brought great perils in its wake. Yet there is nothing in its achievements that need be a curse. Mankind can make it a blessing, when we recognize the great truth that the Founding Fathers of our country understood two hundred years ago. In Ben Franklin's homely words, "We must hang together, or we shall hang separately." As surely as the thirteen colonies had to become the United States of America in order to endure, the 120 nations on the face of the globe must become the United States of the World in order to survive. It is true that science does not guarantee Paradise on earth, but neither does it condemn us to perdition. Science is an instrument at our disposal, for good as well as for ill.

The second revolution in our day is that of *rising expectations,* the far-flung and simultaneous revolt of the submerged groups in mankind. The most obvious aspect is the uprising of the people of color. Mark Twain once said, "God must love the poor, He made so many of them!" Whether or not this is true, it is certain that He must love the darker races, for He made most of mankind black, brown, and yellow. As soon as we travel away from home, whether to Asia, the Far East, or Africa, we discover that the white race is a small minority. With greater or lesser grace, the imperialist European powers have retreated from Africa and Asia, and colonialism is dead. The desire of the new, small, undeveloped

African nations to achieve independence with dignity may seem laughable at times, but they are establishing their legitimate position in the council of nations. It will not require centuries for them to attain to maturity—the process will be far more rapid in our time, however unsettling to our narrow self-interest and vaunted self-esteem.

Not only the "have not" nations, but also the "have not" individuals, are on the march. At home, the poor and the dispossessed will no longer remain contented with their lot. In what we like to call our affluent society there are millions still living in penury and squalor. Nor is it any comfort to point out that even the poorest of our time have access to conveniences, comforts, and amusements unknown to the kings of the Middle Ages. Poverty is relative, and in the face of boundless luxury, those who live on the edge of subsistence are roused to revolt. In his wise book, Koheleth tells us: *Metukah shenat ha'obhed*, "Sweet is the sleep of the toiler whether he has eaten little or much. But the full stomach of the rich man does not let him sleep" (*Ecclesiastes* 5:11). A commentator offers a witty interpretation of the last phrase: "The full stomach of the rich man does not permit *him* (the poor man) to sleep." He wants his share of the good things of this world. Neither at home nor abroad can this revolution of rising expectations be long ignored or suppressed. If the "have nots," nations and individuals alike, are to get a share of the world's goods, the "haves" will of necessity remain with less, but they will not suffer privation—there are enough of God's blessings for all.

Finally, the most widespread and far-reaching is the third revolution, *the breakdown of accepted standards of morality, in belief and conduct.* Elders today are wont to wring their hands at the behavior of the younger generation. The rise of promiscuity, the appalling growth of illegitimacy, the increase in abortions, the staggering statistics of the divorce courts, all point to the breakdown of family stability. Three years ago, a study in Britain pointed out that one out of every six births was illegitimate, and the percentage was much higher in London. Roughly, two out of three babies born to girls twenty years old or younger in England were conceived outside of marriage, Dr. Ernest Claxton, Assistant Secretary to the British Medical Association, declared. The trend probably has been accelerated in the interval.

Drug addiction is on the increase among children of high school age. Experimentation with the hallucinatory drugs, like LSD, by college youth, and the use of marijuana, which we are told is not dangerous in and of itself, are on the increase. There are many other marks of the new generation, like the beatnik morality. Youth is in revolt against the standards that have been preached, though not often practiced, by their elders. They are not impressed by the national goals enunciated but not implemented by our leaders.

What is the major foreign policy issue confronting our country today? Without question, it is the war in Vietnam. It is true that honorable men differ in their evaluation of this conflict. Nor do I doubt for an instant that President Johnson sincerely desires peace. There is no gainsaying the fact, however, that no war has ever been fought with less enthusiasm at home and with less support by our friends and allies abroad. We were told that all we needed was 100,000, then 300,000, now 400,000, later 700,000 and still later 1,000,000 men to "stop Communism" in Southeast Asia. In spite of the barrage of propaganda, it is increasingly clear that no one wants us in South Vietnam except a handful of profiteers and generals who are battening on the woes of their unhappy country and are ready to fight until the last American.

Lest they be thought unpatriotic, millions of Americans are loath to speak out. Lest we "lose face"—an Oriental doctrine that has become a cornerstone of American policy—we prefer to lose lives, with thousands of casualties on both sides, in a constantly escalating war.

France fought for seven bloody, costly years to retain her Asian and African empire. Finally she withdrew from Vietnam and from Algeria, unable to "save any face" or any of her national interests in either country. Yet today General Charles De Gaulle has been able to build up the prestige of France to an all-time high, because he had the courage to take the unpopular course when he recognized that it was best for his country.

President Johnson has constantly proclaimed his willingness to negotiate, except that he would not meet with the enemy we are fighting—the Vietcong. Ambassador Arthur J. Goldberg's speech on September 22, 1966, before the United Nations seemed to suggest a change in American policy in the direction of greater flexibility. But on the same day, almost at the same hour, Secretary of Defense Robert S. McNamara announced that orders for two hundred eighty more jet fighters than had originally been planned had been placed. I know no more striking fulfillment of the New Testament injunction, "Let not your right hand know what your left hand is doing."

To be sure, the Communists in Vietnam are bitterly opposed to us. But so are the masses of the people who are heartily sick of war, the Buddhist majority, the farmers, the small people who want to be let alone and allowed to make their own mistakes and pay the price for their own errors. This includes the millions of South Vietnamese who, however mistakenly, shelter and support the Communist guerillas in the South.

There is, in addition, the agonizing question as to whether China will be drawn into the conflict and let loose the Third World War that will bring about the annihilation of civilization. But quite aside from the possibility of China's active participation in the conflict, the choice is not whether we shall win or lose. With all due respect to our official spokesmen, the choice before us is how heavy the cost of our ultimate defeat or stalemate will be, whether we shall lose twenty or two hundred billion dollars and suffer thousands or tens of thousands of casualties, and whether we shall fight five or ten or twenty years in a never-ending war.

On the solemn Day of Atonement, the truth must be spoken. There is a good deal of complacency here at home about the conflict, on the assumption that it is the source of our prosperity. If a few thousand American soldiers die, but billions of profits are racked up, there are some who are quite content to pay the price —especially if it is not their own sons who are doing the dying. Signs are multiplying, however, that one cannot build national well-being upon human blood. We may have begun with a pros-

perity based upon war; we may end with a depression derived
from a defeat or a frustrating stalemate. *There must be peace or
we perish.*

What is our major domestic issue? It is the struggle for civil
rights, which is now entering into a far more dangerous period
of violence and conflict. Ever since 1954, when the United States
Supreme Court decision outlawed racial segregation, we have sat
by complacently, feeling very moral about the decision and un-
troubled about our failure to implement it. Negroes continue to
be killed, and their murderers are acquitted in Southern courts.
The schools in the North show little improvement and less integration. Now the Negroes are talking of "black power"—a form
of racialism in reverse. The riots in Harlem, in Los Angeles, in
Chicago, in Omaha, in a dozen other cities, pose a very genuine
threat of civil insurrection.

The Western world has always drawn its ethical ideals and
moral standards from religion. Now the fundamentals of religion
are under attack. Today there are Christian teachers who declare
that "God is dead." They are accused of being enemies of religion
and are called atheists and misleaders of the young. On one level
this entire agitation in Christian circles is irrelevant to Jews—
since our God was never born, He cannot die. Christianity believes that God died for men's sins. For Judaism there is a God
who lives eternally for man's redemption.

In a deeper sense, however, the idealistic and sensitive men,
like Gabriel Vahanian, Thomas J. J. Altizer, Paul Van Buren, and
Wm. Hamilton, who are proclaiming "the death of God," are
simply using a striking phrase to attract attention to a great truth
which is no novelty in Judaism. Untold numbers of men and
women have discovered that for them a certain conception of God
is dead. God is not the manager of a celestial department store,
duly filling orders for prosperity, health, well-being, and peace of
mind sent up to Him by His worshippers each Sunday. Nor is God
a benevolent grandfather with a long white beard, to whom we
come to confess our sins by means of a few pious words and who,
actuated by a senile love, forgives all our scrapes and wipes the account clean, every time we begin to whimper.

For Judaism, God is not dead because He is *melekh chai vekayyam,* "the eternal and ever living King." In the liturgy of the High Holy Days time and again we hail God as king, sitting in judgment upon His creatures who are fashioned *betsalmo,* "in His image." What are His attributes which He asks us to emulate? The Psalmist gives the answer: *Tsedek umishpat mekhon kis'ekha, hesed ve'emet yekaddemu phanekha,* "Righteousness and justice are the foundations of Thy throne; love and truth go forth to meet Thee" (*Psalm* 89:15).

The first pillar of God's throne is justice. Because God is righteous, He has created and governs a law-abiding universe. In the words of the Mishnah: *Hehanut petuhah vehahenvani makkiph,* "The store is open and the owner gives credit. The ledger is open and the hand writes. Whoever wishes to borrow may come and borrow, but the collectors go about continually, exacting payment from man, whether he is aware of it or not, and the judgment is a judgment of truth" (*Abot* 3:16).

There is a law of righteousness operating in the universe which can no more be violated with impunity than we can defeat the law of gravity, the doctrine of the conservation of matter, or any of the other great laws discovered by the natural sciences. In the words of *Proverbs: Tsedakah teromem goy, vehesed le'umim hattat,* "Righteousness exalts a nation, but sin is the disgrace of peoples" (*Proverbs* 14:34). Men are always tempted to try to defeat the law of retribution, but the consequences are inescapable.

As has so often been the case, from the days of Abraham who smashed his father's idols, and Job who challenged God, the true friends of religion have been those who attacked it in the name of truth and justice, and its real enemies have been those who defended it by suppression and soulless conformity. From the days of the Prophets, the test of religion has always lain in the area of conduct. It is an index of its decay that people define "religious" today not in terms of ethical behavior, but as "having faith" or being punctilious about rituals.

What God demands of us is righteousness, just dealing with men and nations, especially with those who differ from us in color or creed, or in their concept of life.

But the throne of God rests not only upon justice—its second foundation is love. What does this mean? It means that because God loves His children, He has endowed us with the capacity to rebuild our lives if we have the will. Man possesses an immortal soul, with the stamp of freedom upon it.

The Torah emphasizes that we have the power to determine our destiny. Judaism declares that man is not powerless, because the creative power that is the hallmark of God exists in man, who is fashioned in the image of his Maker.

What does the demand to love mean for us? It means that we are called upon to remember that God is judge and not man, and that where a slight or an offence, real or imagined, is committed against us we must strive to forgive what we cannot forget, and try to forget what we cannot forgive.

And we should understand what love is not. Our young people at college and elsewhere are often told that the Old Testament is a religion of justice, while the New Testament is the higher religion of love. Both judgments are false, for the God of justice in the Hebrew Scriptures is also the God of love, and even the New Testament could not deny its Jewish heritage sufficiently to forget that the God of love is also the God of justice.

But even if we were to admit the distinction, we need not be ashamed of it. Today the word "love" has become a cant term. It is used for the lowest manifestations of lust at one extreme, and at the other, it has been virtually emptied of all content.

The Spanish Inquisitor, Tomás de Torquemada, burnt hundreds of men and women at the stake, out of his love for them. Some of the leading Negro spokesmen, like Stokely Carmichael and LeRoi Jones, call for violence against the whites, which is bad enough, but they do it in the name of love, which is worse. Early in the summer of 1966, the Students Non-Violent Coordinating Committee went on record as favoring the expansion of "black power"—all in the name of nonviolence. Months before, its then chairman, John Lewis, who was replaced by more extreme leaders, prepared an address for delivery which included the following passage: "We will march through the South, through the heart of Dixie, the way Sherman did. We shall pursue our own (scorched earth) policy and burn Jim Crow to the ground—*nonviolently*."

(*N. Y. Times,* August 28, 1965) (Italics mine). Can hypocrisy or, if you prefer, self-deception, go any further?

How wise is the observation of the English writer, F. L. Lucas: "If I am asked to love all mankind from China to Peru, I can only confess that I do not feel equal to it. It takes long arms to embrace the globe. And indeed to use the word 'love' so promiscuously seems to me only to profane it. It does not often make men become better: it merely makes the word 'love' become weaker." To love all mankind is impossible, but to strive for justice, to practice *tsedakah* in our relations with them, that is both possible and indispensable.

Finally, the seal of God, our Sages tell us, is *'emet,* "truth," and that attribute He demands of us as well. The great besetting sins of our society are hypocrisy, pretense, dishonesty. A story is told of the famous European rabbi, Samuel Mohilever. One day a group of his close associates were bemoaning in his presence the growth of disbelief and irreligion in the community. "No wonder," said the rabbi, "this is what we must expect; the truth always conquers." "What are you saying, Rabbi?" his friends asked, aghast. "You call their heresy and *apikursus* the truth?" "Yes," said the rabbi, *"Zei meinen zeyer sheker mit an emes. Mir meinen unzer emes mit a sheker."* "They regard their lie as a truth. We treat our truth as a lie."

Let us not rush to condemn our young people, for there is one great virtue underlying all their errors and confusions. Whatever their mistakes—and they are many and often costly—they are dedicated to honesty and to truth. If they rebel against accepted standards, it is because they recognize the patina of hypocrisy which covers our civilization. An outstanding American philosopher, Abraham Kaplan, writes: " A society which ceaselessly stimulates sexuality while condemning its gratification, that rewards competitiveness while extolling benevolence, that values ends for which it denies the means—such a society might be expected to generate conflicts, guilt, and anxiety to its members."

Our young people today are suspicious of ideology; they are by no means bereft of idealism, as the success of the Peace Corps and the civil rights movement demonstrates. Fine phrases, moralistic pronouncements, high-flown calls to duty, find little echo in their hearts, because they see the widespread spectacle of corruption and self-seeking on every level of society and in every walk of life.

We need no new and better principles; we need only to fulfill those proclaimed by the prophets and the sages, so that all men may enter into their inheritance from God. We need no improvement on the ideals of democracy; we need only give them a grip on our consciences and implement them in our society.

You may have heard these definitions. An optimist is a man who believes that this is the best of all possible worlds; and a pessimist is one who is afraid that the optimist is right! The real issue before us is not whether our world is the best or the worst, but how to go about making it better.

Long before he was Senator from New York State, Robert F. Kennedy set forth the goal of America, which might well be a blueprint for mankind: "It is an unfinished society that we offer the world—a society that is forever committed to change, to improvement, and to growth, that will never stagnate in the certitudes of ideology or the finalities of dogma. A hundred years from now there will be new ways of making life better, of giving man fuller opportunity to fulfill his hopes. We have no infallible party, no iron creed, no all-purpose blueprint; we do not propose to chain mankind to a system of false logic. We have, instead, faith in human intelligence, human will and human decency; and we know that, in the long run, these are the forces which make history" (N. Y. Times, August 28, 1962).

If it is an unfinished society that we offer the world, it is an unfinished world that God offers us, for in the words of the Talmud, man is *shuttapho shel hakadosh barukh hu' bema'asei bereshith,* "God's co-partner in the work of creation" (B. Shabbat 119b).

Hayom harat 'olam, Today, every day, the world is being born anew, in suffering and in pain, but with hope and promise, too. The night may be long and agonizing, but the dawn will come, if we remain awake and alert. With this faith let us go forth to meet the dawn: *Kumi 'ori ki bha' 'orekh ukhebhod Hashem 'alayikh zarah,* "Arise and shine, for thy light is come, and the glory of the Lord has risen upon thee" (Isaiah 60:1).

ISRAEL

VII

Jewish Existence—
Mystery and Miracle

I

It is on Passover, at the Seder table, that our children ask us, *Mah nishtannah halaylah hazeh mikkol haleilot,* "Why is this night different from all other nights?" That question we might, with even greater justice, ask ourselves tonight. For Kol Nidre Eve is unique among all the nights of the year in making every Jew conscious of his Jewish existence, and reminding him of his share in the life of his people. Even the most estranged of our brothers, if he possesses the tiniest spark of loyalty to his people and his God, wishes to be in the synagogue on the night of the Sabbath of Sabbaths.

• Every aspect of the Day is designed to heighten our sense of awe and wonder at the pathos and the glory of Jewish survival. Every member of the congregation draped in the Tallit, the white curtain on the Holy Ark, the white robes worn by the rabbi and the cantor—all speak to the sensitive spirit.

• Above all, it is the Kol Nidre prayer that stirs the heart of even the most indifferent Jew. Christians as well as Jews have been deeply moved by this outstanding prayer in our liturgy. The famous German general Helmuth von Moltke loved to have the Kol Nidre melody played for him by the well-known violinist,

Joachim. The best-known setting of the Kol Nidre is that of Max Bruch, himself a non-Jew. No more beautiful tribute to the Kol Nidre has ever been written than that of the gifted German poet and dramatist, Nikolai Lenau:

"Closer to my heart than 'the Marseillaise' is a third melody, which is entirely enveloped in sorrow. It is a night-song of those seeking repentance, broken children of men who regret their sins. This prayer of grief is called *Kol Nidre*.

"I heard it many years ago in my native town. The eve of Yom Kippur had arrived. I hid myself in a corner of the synagogue, so that the pious Jews might not be distressed by the presence of a Gentile lad. Big, thick wax candles were aflame. The people stood with heads bent low in broad, snow-white garments which looked like shrouds.

"Suddenly the cantor, with a deeply earnest, heartrending melody, rich in awe and supplication, began to sing. I had to struggle with a rare feeling of emotion. Feverishly I sighed. Hot, burning tears pouring from one's eyes cast a wondrous spell and at the same time purified. I fled into the night and came home. In that unforgettable hour, no black speck defiled my soul.

"Who had created this melody? The old people do not know. They have received this song from inheritance from their ancestors. Such grief-stricken songs, it seems to me, are never created by individuals. Yes, it is a mysterious melody which undoubtedly has surged up from hundreds of souls" (translated from the German).

Lenau was right. The plaintive notes of entreaty in the Kol Nidre speak of man's weakness and sin, and the soaring crescendo expresses the strength of man's faith in God's love and forgiveness.

So much for the music of the Kol Nidre. What of its words? Like so many other manifestations of the Jewish spirit, the Kol Nidre had been slandered and maligned through time. It has been argued by anti-Semites that its purpose has been to free the Jew from the obligation to honor any commitments to other men into which he has entered.

Only the ignorant and the malicious could believe this, for one of the great Biblical commandments is, *motza' sephatekha tishmor*,

"Thou shalt keep the utterance of thy lips" (*Deuteronomy* 23:24).
So high is the honor of the plighted word in Judaism that in
Talmudic law a witness in a law suit did not normally need to take
an oath, because he could be relied upon to testify truthfully
without it.

The intent and meaning of the Kol Nidre belong to an altogether different dimension of human experience. The Kol Nidre
asks for the abrogation, not of the oaths which we take in our
every-day business affairs, but of those oaths and promises which
we made in the presence of God that involve no other human
being except ourselves. Whether out of fear or anger, or because
of passion, hatred, or a lust for vengeance, we may have made
some promise to ourselves unworthy of being fulfilled. When the
eve of Yom Kippur is ushered in, we wish to free ourselves from
this incubus of unworthiness, which weighs upon our conscience.
Hence we pronounce the Kol Nidre, and ask for God's forgiveness.

How did the Kol Nidre originate? The mysterious and solemn
introduction intoned by the rabbi before the Kol Nidre, which
originates in the dim past, has suggested one answer. The formula reads: *Biyeshivah shel ma'alah, uviyeshivah shel mattah,
'al da'at hamakom ve'al da'at hakahal, 'anu mattirin lehitpallel
'im ha'abharyanim,* "With the permission of the Court on High,
and the permission of the Court on earth, with the consent of God
and the approval of this congregation, we hereby declare it lawful
to worship with the transgressors."

Who are these "transgressors"? Scholars have suggested that this
refers to one of the many periods in Jewish history when Jews
were threatened with massacre or expulsion, or the expropriation
of their property, unless they adopted the dominant faith of the
particular country in which they lived. In spite of these perils,
many Jews clung bravely to their faith and their religion, and paid
a heavy price for their loyalty. But others were too weak or the
temptations were too strong, and so they adopted the faith of the
majority. Throughout the year they professed alien rites and pronounced alien prayers.

Came Yom Kippur eve, and the moment of truth had arrived
when their whole being cried out for the forgiveness of the God

of Israel, and for fellowship with the household of Israel. And so in stealth and trembling they made their way to the synagogues, and the rabbis gave permission for them to enter, using the formula which we have already quoted. When these penitents intoned the Kol Nidre, they were asking to be forgiven for all the unworthy vows of loyalty to alien creeds, which they had spoken out of their weakness, because of their inability to resist the threats or the blandishments invoked against them.

Where did the Kol Nidre arise? The traditional explanation sees its origin in Spain, where thousands of crypto-Jews, or Marranos, professed Christianity outwardly while seeking to remain loyal to the God of Israel. Some scholars have traced the Kol Nidre further back to Babylonia, where the fanatical sect of fire-worshippers compelled Jews to accept their faith, and where there were also untold numbers who lived outwardly as Zoroastrians, and inwardly as Jews.

Probably the origin of the words of the Kol Nidre, like that of its moving melody, will remain forever sealed. Precisely for this reason, the Kol Nidre will continue to be the matchless and eternal expression of the miracle of Jewish survival, a miracle which is also a mystery, deepened by two thousand years of exile and persecution, of spoliation, and massacre.

Babylonia and Spain, as we shall see, represent two radically different types of Jewish community, yet in both Jewish existence was an epic of struggle and sacrifice, crowned by tragedy as well as by triumph.

II

In any particular age most Jews were neither heroes nor weaklings—they were ordinary men beset by economic hardships, family difficulties, illness, and death. Yet beyond their own troubles they were the bearers of the eternal Jewish destiny and the instruments of Jewish immortality.

The world has never been able to make its peace with this miracle which remains a mystery, and has attempted to probe the secret. Arnold Toynbee, the well-known contemporary philoso-

pher of history, found that the Jewish people alone did not fit
into his neat categories, and tended to upset his schemes. As a
result, he gave vent to his exasperation by calling Jews "a fossilized
relic of Syriac society"—surely the liveliest fossil on record anywhere!

Long before Toynbee, Christian piety had invented its own
explanation of why the Jew had survived through the centuries—
he was fated by God to live on as a wanderer, as an outcast, never
to know rest, because he had rejected the Savior of Christianity.
Even more sinister than the legend of "the Wandering Jew" was
the explanation invented by a modern anti-Semite. An obscure
Russian concocted a forgery called "The Protocols of the Elders
of Zion" which could be laughed off as childish, were it not being
circulated in millions of copies and fomenting hatred and persecution to the present day. According to this lurid product of a dis-
eased imagination, there were secret Jewish leaders throughout
the world who met periodically in the dead of night in the Jewish
cemetery in Prague, in order to take over the conquest of the
world! Only recently the "Protocols" appeared in Japan, as they
previously had in Europe, in the United States, and throughout
the Arab world.

For the Jew, the survival of his people is no sinister mystery. It
is a miracle founded upon a divine promise, reiterated by all the
Prophets: *ki 'ani 'adonai lo' shaniti, ve'attem b'nai yisra'el lo
khelithem*—"For I, the Lord, have not changed, and you, O children of Israel, have not been destroyed" (*Malachi* 3:6). It is true
that no other nation in history has ever survived the loss of land,
government and language, let alone experienced ageless and deep-
seated hatred and persecution. The reason lies in the fact that the
Jew is like no other group in society. This truth the Gentile
prophet Balaam understood at the very dawn of Jewish history.
When our ancestors were wandering in the wilderness under the
leadership of Moses, Balaam declared: "Behold, here is a people
living apart, not to be reckoned among the nations" (*Numbers*
23:9).

The contemporary Jewish thinker, Martin Buber, expressed
this truth in the idiom of our own age when he declared, "We are

not one other example of the species 'nation'; we are the only example of the species 'Israel'."

Even miracles have an explanation. How is it that the boon of eternal life was conferred upon us? The answer is that the Jews were not really exiled, because they were never exiled from Torah. The Torah goes to great pains to explain that it is not due to any innate superiority, or greater virtue, or the larger numbers of the Jewish people that they were singled out for God's love. Certainly, throughout history, the Jew was not more powerful than his neighbors.

√ The secret of the uniqueness of Israel lies in the familiar Hebrew phrase: *Barukh 'elohenu . . . 'asher natan lanu torat 'emet vehayyei 'olam nata' betokhenu.* "Blessed be God who has given us a Torah of truth, and planted in our midst eternal life." The Jew has lived eternally, because he has loved an eternal Torah. Wherever he has gone or been driven, he has carried his "portable Fatherland" with him. Synagogues can be burnt, and often were, cemeteries can be desecrated, scrolls can be torn, but the Torah remains indestructible in Jewish hearts and minds. It was the Jew's love for an eternal Torah that nourished his love for eternal life. The great Jewish toast has always been *L'hayyim,* "For life."

When other nations were driven into foreign lands, their exile always spelled annihilation. For as the individual integrated into the dominant society, the group from which he came disintegrated and disappeared. That happened to the ancient Egyptians and Greeks, who were conquered and dissolved into the melting pot of new ethnic groups.

This absorption has taken place within the last one hundred years in America, where each immigrant group to these shores has assimilated. And the longer it has lived here, the more unrecognizable it has become. What is there that is Dutch about Roosevelt, or German about Truman, or Swiss about Eisenhower? The Irish and the Italians are more recent arrivals, and discrimination has kept them more conscious of their background. The third-generation Irish-American may still like an Irish jig more than a hora, and the third-generation Italian-American may prefer pizza to potato pancakes. Nonetheless, the process of assimilation is inexorable and unmistakable—individual integration means the loss of group identity.

III

There has been only one exception to this universal law—the Jew. Throughout his long and tragic history the Jew had somehow learnt how to maintain the tension between integration and isolation, between a genuine and deep involvement in the life of the larger community, on the one hand, and an equally deep and genuine commitment to Jewish values and interests, on the other. Sometimes the first factor predominated, at others the second was more marked. But never did one tendency prevail to the exclusion of the other. It was like the systole and diastole of the human heart without which life cannot go on.

Whether one or another tendency would predominate depended on the type of society in which the Jew found himself, whether it was an "open society" or a "closed" one. When Jews lived in an environment marked by a high cultural level, they were inspired to share in the life of the group around them, and contributed richly to its advancement. In turn, they were challenged and stimulated by the culture which they encountered, and their Judaism was deepened and enriched in the process. But when Jews lived among people of low culture, where there was neither challenge nor stimulation to be derived from the outside environment, Jews were driven inward to their own spiritual resources. Their Jewish life remained deep and intense, but essentially it became narrower in scope.

Like the alternation of day and night, of summer and winter, of the ebb and the flow of the tides, the history of the Jewish people reveals an alternation in the centers of Jewish life between "open" and "closed" societies. It cannot be sufficiently stressed that the greatest periods of Jewish creativity, when the genius of the Jew produced its noblest fruits, were the ages of integration, when Judaism and the world interacted upon each other through challenge and response.

The first great center of Jewish history was, of course, the land of Israel, which lies at the crossroads of the ancient world. Palestine is a bridge linking Asia, Africa, and Europe, traversed for centuries by merchants, conquered by armies scores of times. Here in the very center of the ancient world our ancestors were exposed to the cultures of Babylonia and Canaan, Egypt and Persia, Greece and Rome. Some features they accepted, others they modified, still others they rejected. What emerged from this interaction of the spirit were the two greatest products of Jewish genius, the Bible and the Mishnah—the first, the charter of man's humanity; the second, the foundation of Jewish group-existence to the present day.

Then came a new center in Babylonia, where there was little stimulation that could be expected from the backward, superstitious and fanatical native population. Here the genius of the Jew produced the Babylonian Talmud, a massive monument of Jewish creativity. But the Babylonian Talmud was the product of a society closed in upon itself, acute and deep but essentially limited in its horizons. There is little evidence of the surrounding culture in the pages of the Talmud of Babylonia.

After Babylonia came a new center, medieval Spain. Here the Arabs produced a rich and flourishing culture, and Jews participated actively in the enterprise. The Golden Age of Spain in Jewish history was golden both for the Jews and for Spain. Within a few hundred years, a galaxy of genius appeared amongst Spanish Jewry, second to none. An unbroken line of statesmen and generals, philosophers and poets, grammarians and geographers, historians and commentators, Talmudists and translators, opened new and wider horizons for Judaism, and brought Judaism into the mainstream of world culture. Finally the light that was Spain was extinguished by the fanaticism of the Inquisition and the cruel decree of the Expulsion in 1492. It was the year which marked the discovery of the New World that was to prove, in God's Providence, a haven of safety and freedom for the children of Israel in centuries yet unborn.

However, even in the dark days of the Expulsion from Spain the lamp of Jewish life did not go out. It was rekindled in Germany and in Poland in the sixteenth and seventeeth centuries. Eastern

Europe became the new center of Jewish life, culture, and faith. Here again ignorant peasants, fanatic priests, and greedy noblemen could offer little stimulus to Jewish creativity. Hence a new chapter of intense Jewish activity was written. It lacked, however, the breadth and scope, the wide interests and the humane sympathies of Spanish-Jewish culture. Now, Talmudic studies became more and more subtle and involved, increasingly removed from life and its real problems.

IV

Then came the modern revolution symbolized by the French Revolution in Europe. The Jewish people was catapulted from the Middle Ages into the modern era overnight. A great inner schism developed, a cleavage in the soul of modern Jewry. Two types of Jews now emerged. Those who were at home in the modern world, who knew the culture of the age, its philosophy, science, and art, knew nothing about Judaism and therefore cared even less. On the other hand, those who knew Judaism, and lived by it—and their ranks were constantly growing less—knew nothing about the modern world. Thus with all too few exceptions, the modern Jew was a house divided against itself. No longer are integration and Jewish identity to be found in creative tension with one another. Humanity and Judaism seem to be enemies instead of allies in building human civilization.

This is the basic problem confronting the Jewish people in the two remaining centers of creative life open to it today—in Israel and in America. In Israel an entire generation of sabras has grown up who have no genuine contact with the Jewish past and little sympathy with world Jewry. Though they speak Hebrew, Jewish tradition is so alien to them that the government has felt it necessary to introduce courses into the schools on *toda'ah yehudit*, "Jewish consciousness," so that they may develop a sense of identification with their ancestors in the past and with their brothers in the present, as well as an appreciation of the ethical and cultural values of the traditional heritage of Israel. On the other hand, we have Jews living in Israel who are spiritually in the Middle

Ages, whose hostility to progress makes their counterparts here in America seem like modernists.

How create one people from both these elements, each of which has much to contribute and much to learn? More important still, how make the Israelis, Jews and the Jews, human beings, who will be conscious of their links to their people everywhere and to all mankind?

If the problem is intense in Israel, here in America it is literally a question of life and death. For a de-Judaized Israeli is an Israeli still, and some day may be redeemed, but a de-Judaized Jew in America ceases to be a Jew, and is altogether and irretrievably lost. The reason is obvious. Ours is a free society and each man is free to go his way, nor would we wish to have it otherwise. As a result, the perils of Jewish dissolution in our "free society" are real and omnipresent. At the extreme end is the rising number of conversions for which no figures are available. Intermarriages already approach ten per cent of all Jewish marriages in the United States. Even when there is no formal break with the Jewish community, there is widespread defection from Jewish ranks, indifference nourished by ignorance, and ignorance growing because of indifference. All too often, this affects our most creative and potentially valuable young people.

Where are our American Jewish poets and playwrights, our novelists and musicians? How often our most talented actors and directors glorify every culture, every people, and every religion but their own, finding nothing to inspire or move them in the history of Jewish piety and sacrifice? We have musicales dealing with the South Seas and the Old South, with Hawaii and Siam, with Ireland and Scotland. But the epic of the rebirth of Israel in our day, the record of Jewish heroism and Jewish martyrdom in the past, the nobility of Jewish idealism, both past and present—of all this our creative sons and daughters remain blissfully unaware, flaunting their ignorance as a banner.

In a now famous symposium *Commentary* magazine, which is published by the American Jewish Committee, revealed the same pattern of Jewish self-alienation and self-hatred. It invited some thirty young men to discuss the theme of "The Jewish Intellectual and Judaism." With only three exceptions, these writers, gifted artists, scholars, scientists, and men of affairs revealed in their contributions their estrangement from Jewish values, their contempt for the Jewish community, their ignorance of Jewish culture, and their lack of concern for the Jewish future. To berate these young writers is useless—they are a symptom of our age, when the ancient warning of the Torah is being realized before our eyes: *Banekha uvenotekha netunim le'am 'aher, ve'einekha ro'ot vekhalot 'aleihem kol hayom, ve'ein le'el yadekha* (Deuteronomy 28:32). "Thy sons and thy daughters will be handed over to another people, and thine eyes will look on and pass out with longing for them all the day, but thou canst do nothing."

V

How shall we meet the perils to the Jewish future which arise from the opportunities of the free society, the temptation to alienation and defection, to disloyalty and self-hatred? Answers are not lacking. The first response is *retreat*. If the present is dangerous, go back to the past. If modern ideas threaten, shut out modern ideas. If contact with the world about us poses problems, cut off those contacts. In one word, if the free society is perilous, let us withdraw into a ghetto. It may be the isolated urban ghetto of Williamsburgh, or the new-style suburban ghetto near Nyack, or the spiritual ghetto which is being preached in many a pulpit today on the ground that the new is sinful, for only the old is sacred.

The effort is therefore being made to build replicas of Polish, or Roumanian, or Russian villages here in America, to imitate their habits of thought and patterns of behavior. When this does not work—and it cannot—we pretend to do so. We talk as though New York in 1966 is identical with Wolin, Shnipeshuk, or Czernovitz in 1866. Thus, young and impressionable minds are filled with hostility to all who diverge from their pattern, or dare to tread new paths.

Psychology teaches that the effort to revert to the past is a form of pathology. A clockmaker will tell you that if you turn the hands backwards on a clock, time still goes on, and all that is likely to happen is that the mechanism will be damaged. History teaches that if we seek guidance from the Jewish communities of the past, we should turn not to the closed societies of eastern Europe where the general environment had nothing to offer, but to the open societies of Spain and Palestine, where Jews learnt and taught, where they contributed to and were enriched by contact with the rich cultures and dynamic civilizations all about them.

Retreat is no effective answer to the perils of life today. The only solution is to *advance*. Undoubtedly Jewish life faces a crisis today, but in Chinese the concept "crisis" is expressed by two ideograms, "danger" and "opportunity." We can meet the dangers of a free society—and they are real—only if we take hold of the opportunities—and they are equally genuine.

There is a lesson for us in the art of the tentmaker, to whom the Prophet turned, when he said, *Ha'arikhi metharayikh vithedothayikh hazzeki,* "Lengthen your cords, and strengthen your stakes" *(Isaiah* 54:2). The longer we build the tent cords, the stronger must be the stakes, if the tent is not to collapse.

Here in America, a broad, rich culture beckons to us and to our children. They will not be denied their opportunity to drink deep of these modern wells. But they need to learn that their stakes in Judaism must necessarily be deepened as they lengthen their cords. Our Tree of Life remains the Torah, knowledge of Judaism, of the Hebrew language, of the Bible, the Talmud, our rich medieval and modern literature, of the entire treasurehouse of Jewish philosophy and poetry, music and art. Jewish ignorance is the one luxury American Jewry cannot afford.

At this solemn season there are two resolutions that each of us should make. First, we should resolve that next year we shall know more Torah than we do today. Second, we must vow that our children will be given adequate opportunities, far more than were granted us, to learn Judaism so that they may love it and live by it.

The year we spent at the Center for the Study of Democratic Institutions in Santa Barbara, California, reenforced my conviction that Judaism's race is not yet run, because its work is not yet done. The leaders in modern life and thought who met in Santa

Barbara were interested, eager, and grateful for whatever insights and ideals could be gleaned from the rich storehouse of Judaism bearing upon the critical problems of democracy and world order, and upon the perils that threaten the survival of justice, peace, and freedom in the world.

It is true that we Jews gave the Bible to the world. Today, however, new applications of these ancient truths need to be derived, new ideas need to be formulated and, above all, new actions need to be undertaken, in order to make the teachings of the Prophets and the Sages serve as the foundation of human society. Our primary concern must be not how to preserve Judaism against the world, but how to preserve the world through Judaism.

The essence of Judaism is captured in the words of the Zohar: *Kudsha berikh hu' 'Oraitha v'yisra'el had hu.'* "God, the Torah, and Israel are one." A Jewish mystic added this comment: "Israel is the wick, the Torah the oil, and God the candle." May we be the wick and the Torah our oil, to light the candle that will banish the darkness. As we make the light of God manifest in His world, the miracle of Jewish survival will be revealed in all its glory, the mystery disclosed in all its meaning. Every succeeding generation will be able to echo the joyous words of the Psalmist: *Lo' 'amut ki 'ehyeh va'asapper ma'asei Yah*—"I shall not die, but live, and declare the works of the Lord" (*Psalm* 118:17). As we become conscious of our destiny, Jewish courage, Jewish wisdom, and Jewish character will not perish from the earth.

VIII

The Pursuit of Excellence

I

According to Jewish tradition, the High Holy Days are dedicated to *heshbon hanefesh,* "the stocktaking of the soul." It is during Rosh Hashanah and Yom Kippur that we have an opportunity to contemplate our lives, to consider our errors, to repent of our sins, and to make plans to reorder the pattern of our existence. That is why we pray to God for a new lease on life, a reprieve, an extension of our time on earth, a chance to do better.

The High Holy Days in general, and Kol Nidre in particular, may also be described as a period of spiritual inventory for the Jewish people as a whole. On what other occasion do such multitudes of Jews gather as Jews? When else do we lay aside our personal concerns and mundane pursuits, abstain both from work and from play, and dedicate ourselves to our common goals and aspirations as a people?

More than twenty years have elapsed since the end of World War II, which marked the destruction of our would-be destroyers. Today the Jewish people is, thank God, still alive, but never in its long and tragic history was it so close to death. When Hitler began his dastardly work, there were sixteen million Jews in the world. When his bloody career ended, only ten million remained alive. The six million men, women, and children whom he destroyed represented *robh minyan* and *robh binyan,* the finest quality as well as much of the quantity of world Jewry. Those whom the Nazis exterminated constituted the noblest, the most loyal and creative elements in our people.

But, as the Psalmist tells us, *Hinneh lo' yanum velo' yishan Shomer Yisra'el,* "The Guardian of Israel neither slumbers nor sleeps." We were brought to the gates of death, but they did not close upon us. We were grievously stricken, but we were not destroyed. Two decades later, the physical ruins are still considerable, but much has been rebuilt. Even the Jewish population has recovered about two million of its losses, and it now stands at about twelve million souls.

Before we go forward into a new era, we ought to take inventory of our situation. What is the condition of the Jewish world today, and what are our prospects in the future?

II

Like Caesar's Gaul, the Jewish world today may be divided into three distinctive parts. One-third of the Jewish people, widely scattered over five continents, is fighting a desperate struggle for survival against superior odds, and the outcome is in grave doubt.

This group includes over two million of our brothers in Soviet Russia who, we are told, are physically safe. What is obvious is that they are being spiritually done to death. All religions suffer grave liabilities in Russia, but none is as persecuted as Judaism. Hebrew has the melancholy distinction of being the only language that cannot be legally taught to children. Yiddish, technically permitted, is not taught in a single school in the Soviet Union. Hebrew and Yiddish books may not be imported, nor are they being printed in any significant quantity in the Soviet Union. Over three hundred synagogues have been closed in the past few years. Jewish cemeteries are closed down everywhere. The unrelenting anti-Israel, pro-Arab policy of the Soviet Union remains unchanged.

Yet even here we may continue to hope. New winds may begin to blow even in the Kremlin. Moreover, the vigor of this persecution of Judaism testifies that *dos pintele Yid,* "the spark of the Jew," has not yet been extinguished among our brothers in the

Communist world. Perhaps we shall yet welcome back the lost children of Israel to their father's house.

Elsewhere in Central Europe, we have a half dozen small Jewish communities. Austria has with regard to the Jews a post-war record which is far worse than that of West Germany. It has not paid a cent of reparations for the spoliation of Jewish property in the Nazi era. The once proud and creative Jewish community in Vienna, which we recently visited, is marked by almost total intellectual and moral decay.

In Denmark and Sweden, a few dedicated rabbis and a handful of loyal laymen are battling heroically to strengthen Jewish life, intensify Jewish education, and halt the alarming trend to intermarriage and conversion.

In West Germany, an aging Jewish community finds itself impaled upon the horns of a paradox. This is well described in an article in the German periodical *Der Spiegel,* which quotes the German Jew as saying, "For the Jews in the rest of the world, we are Germans; for the Germans, we are Jews. Nowhere are we at home."

In South Africa, the superbly loyal Jewish community is sitting on a powder-keg. When the repressive policy of *apartheid* explodes, as it must, they will be in mortal danger from both directions, from the Boer oppressors and from their dark-skinned victims.

In South America, and particularly in Argentina, its largest community, anti-Semitism is vocal and powerful. Jewish spiritual resources are all but non-existent. There is not a single native-born rabbi in all of South America. One of our younger rabbis, a graduate of the Jewish Theological Seminary, now stationed in Argentina, recently organized a pre-theological seminary where a group of promising young men are being prepared, so that they may ultimately be admitted to the Seminary in New York and then return for spiritual leadership in Latin America.

What is clear from our survey is that this scattered third of world Jewry has a desperate struggle on its hands. Its survival is dependent on the help, the encouragement, and the inspiration which it will receive from the other two great centers of Jewish life—Israel and America.

Each succeeding visit to the Holy Land makes it clear that Israel is not a miracle—it is a miraculous succession of miracles. The reclamation of the desert has proceeded apace, and green has replaced yellow and brown over thousands of acres. The cities of Haifa, Tel Aviv, and Jerusalem, each unique in character, are also expanding in housing, education, industry and commerce. In addition, new urban centers, Eilat, Ashdod, Lachish, and Nazareth, are rising throughout the land.

Living standards everywhere in Israel are higher. Literature, music, art, the dance, the theater, opera, are flourishing. Perhaps the most significant index of the material improvement in Israel is that this summer 180,000 Israelis, nearly one-tenth of the population, traveled abroad for their vacations!

Meanwhile, immigration continues from North Africa, and also from behind the Iron Curtain, as well as from South America and South Africa. The old Ma'abarot, the temporary dwelling places for new settlers that defaced the landscape in the past, are almost all gone. The new settlers are transported directly to one of the new cities or settlements, given a job, a plot of land, and are trained and encouraged to become productive and self-sufficient citizens.

Have you ever watched a skillful magician, whose hand is quicker than your eye? Israel is a wonder-worker, but the wonders are real. As the people persevere in their own peaceful progress, they have the additional energy, wisdom, and idealism to extend help and guidance to the underdeveloped nations of the world. The Technion in Haifa, the Weizmann Institute in Rehovot, the Hebrew University in Jerusalem, now crowned by the Hadassah Medical School and Hospital, are acting as hosts to hundreds of students from every continent, who represent every race, color, and creed.

At the same time, as recent incidents on the border have indicated, perpetual vigilance cannot be dispensed with. But there is no fear, no hysteria—only a realistic assessment of the situation and a readiness to defend the life and honor of Israel against its five hostile neighbors. Just as Southern politicians use the shibboleth of "white supremacy" to remain in office, the tyrants and

misrulers of the Arab world shout the slogan "Death to Israel"
because they have no real interest in bringing life to their own
people. Israel is not only our pride and glory; it is the miracle
of the twentieth century!

What of the third part of the Jewish people, the American
Jewish community? By all the usual statistical standards, Jewish
life is forging ahead steadily. Synagogue membership in all groups
is at an all-time high, with at least three million of the five and
a half million Jews in the United States affiliated with Orthodox,
Conservative, or Reform synagogues. Between 1948 and 1954, the
enrollment in Jewish schools grew about three times faster than
the Jewish child population. While the rate of progress has become
slower since the last decade, it still continues to be most encourag-
ing. Campaigns for federations of charities and welfare funds, for
Israel Bonds, for the U. J. A., as well as for specific institutions,
continue to increase their quotas, and even their collections, each
year. The building of colossal edifices from Maine to California
for synagogues, centers, and philanthropic institutions continues
apace. Everywhere, growth, expansion, and progress are in the air.

III

If this survey is sound, the future seems safe. Granted that the
first scattered third of the Jewish people has a desperate struggle
on its hands; Israel and America, the other two great centers, are
secure. The present is prosperous, the future seems rosy.

Israel's progress has been phenomenal, but its problems are
equally massive. Nor am I thinking of the military or economic
issues that confront the State, which it is tackling with energy and
intelligence. The basic spiritual problem of Israel is that of unity
—forging a united people in Israel and maintaining a united people throughout the world.

On the most obvious level, there is the problem of the gap
between the Oriental Jews, on the one hand, and on the other,
the Jews from Europe and America, who have been trained to a
different sense of values and outlook on life. All Israeli leaders—
Zalman Shazar, Levi Eshkol, and David Ben-Gurion—are aware

of the grave danger that the Oriental tide may inundate Israel and make it a Levantine country. The government and the army—the great educational agency of Israel—are laboring with might and main to elevate the social, educational, and ethical standards of the Oriental Jews. It is my conviction that they are meeting with a substantial measure of success, and that the problem will find its solution.

The unity of Israel is gravely imperilled by the problem of religion and the state. Newspaper headlines are made by various extremist groups, like the *Neturei Karta* in Me'ah Shearim, who, like the Arabs, refuse to recognize the State of Israel. They do not hesitate to violate Jewish law, let alone ordinary decency, when they attack people and property that do not conform to their ideas. But even the official, so-called moderate religious leadership in Israel grows constantly more militant as the gap between it and the rest of the population increases. Their cry is "Freedom of religion," by which they mean full freedom of religion for themselves, and the total denial of freedom of religion to others.

Since the dominant religious authorities in the country have succeeded in making religion appear irrelevant, if not repugnant, to most Israelis, and since there are more pressing practical issues, there is no widespread active concern about the issue among the people. But the simmering problem of the relationship of religion and the state must and will eventually be solved in the spirit of freedom.

Unfortunately, the third and most important aspect of the problem of unity is one that cannot wait. I refer to the relationship between Israel and world Jewry, which becomes ever more acute. If the Jews in Israel are Jewish only by virtue of the Hebrew language and their Israeli citizenship, and have little concern for the Jewish religion and world Jewry, while the Jews of the Diaspora are citizens of the various lands in which they live, and know little Hebrew and express themselves Jewishly principally in religious terms, it is obvious that the bond between them is dangerously slight. A young Israeli diplomat stationed in Paris, who is more sensitive than most of his fellow Sabras, confessed that he was taken aback when he went out on a date with a young lady. In the course of their conversation she asked him, "Tell me, are you an Israeli or a Jew?" "I didn't know how to answer," he candidly confessed.

To be sure, there is kinship between Israeli and world Jewry. This factor is indeed very important, but it, too, will recede with time. How powerfully will the tie of blood survive with the passing generations, when brothers become first cousins and then cousins of the second, third, and fourth degrees? Pride in the achievements of Israel, loyalty to its interests, contributions to its needs—yes! But, can this build an *'am 'olam,* an eternal people, a world people?

The danger of division goes even deeper. In the wide spectrum of opinion and practice among Israeli Jews, there is only one article of belief which they all seem to share. It became clear at the Ideological Conference, in which I participated in 1957, and was reiterated with even greater sharpness at the Dialogues held each summer under the auspices of the American Jewish Congress. This article of faith, shared by virtually all Israeli Jews, is that *there is no future for Jewish life outside of Israel.*

There are both objective and subjective reasons for this passionately held faith. Virtually every Jew in Israel is a direct victim, either in his own person, or through his immediate family, of the Nazi persecutions. His own eyes have seen the most civilized nation in Europe become a pack of beasts in human form. He has seen the rest of the civilized world, including the so-called free world, stand by unconcerned. As one British general put it, "The Germans are doing our work for us. Why interfere?" The Israeli Jew, therefore, bears indelible scars not only on his body, but also on his soul.

Moreover, the superhuman exertions and sacrifices that are called for by life in Israel become tolerable only if the Israeli believes that there is no other way—that there is no other place in which he can live as a Jew. His martyrdom and heroism can be justified only if Israel is the Jew's last hope upon earth. Hence Israeli Jews believe that, no matter how secure Diaspora Jews consider themselves to be, they are in perpetual danger.

The motivation may be psychological, but the analysis is no

mere figment of the imagination. However unpleasant the diagnosis may be, the important question is, Is it true? Are American Jews threatened by ultimate extinction?

IV

As to the possibility of the physical destruction of American Jewry, no man alive can offer an iron-clad guarantee that "it can't happen here." But the chances are strongly against it. It is more than a pious hope to believe that America is different. America is not Germany, either in the character of its population, in its tradition, or in its history.

In Germany, the Jew was the most conspicuous minority in a homogeneous Teutonic majority. America, on the other hand, is, in Walt Whitman's words, "a nation of nations, a people of peoples." We have no uniform and compact majority—in fact, *all* Americans belong to one minority or to several. Even the Roman Catholic Church, the largest Christian denomination in the United States, is a minority within a Protestant majority. Anglo-Saxons, Swedes, Irish, Italians, are all minorities.

Moreover, America was founded upon the principles of liberty, to which its basic documents, the Declaration of Independence and the Constitution, are dedicated. Our greatest conflicts, the Revolution, the Civil War, and the two World Wars, were fought for the principles of freedom, either at home or abroad. Our great American heroes, Washington, Jefferson, Lincoln, Roosevelt, are heroes of liberty.

Germany has no such tradition or history of dedication to freedom. Germany cannot boast of a single great national hero who was a liberator. On the contrary, whenever democracy came to Germany, it was in the wake of defeat, with the stigma of defeat upon it.

To be sure, as the Huey Long and the McCarthy episodes indicate, Americans may temporarily lose sight of their tradition of liberty, but it cannot be permanently obliterated. Sooner or later sanity and decency reassert themselves. So long as Americans are free, American Jews will be safe. If, Heaven forbid, America loses

its freedom, Israeli Jewry itself will be in mortal peril. But unless
all signs fail, the physical safety of American Jewry is assured.

The danger that threatens us is of another, subtler order. The
Bible tells that two sons of the high priest Aaron, who violated
the holiness of the sanctuary, were suddenly stricken and died in
the Tabernacle. Commenting on this mysterious tragedy, the
rabbis say that their destruction was *serephat neshamah veguph
kayyam,* "Their souls were burned, while their bodies remained
intact" (*Sanhedrin* 52a). This is the crucial danger for American
Jewry—that it may survive physically but perish spiritually. The
capital of the past is running out; we need new sources of interest
or we shall go spiritually bankrupt.

Today 70% of American Jewry are native-born, and the percentage is rising steadily. We can no longer count on memories
of a European *shtetl* to preserve Jewish group feeling. So, too, the
great Jewish neighborhoods of yesteryear, the East Side of New
York, the West Side of Chicago, the South Side of Philadelphia,
where the very streets breathed a Jewish atmosphere, belong to
the past.

Jews are fanning out into suburbia, smaller towns and villages
throughout America. Jews are now living in close proximity to
their non-Jewish fellow citizens, going to the same schools, participating in the same activities, sharing the same interests. What
is more, the apparently unimportant phenomenon of name-chang-
ing by Jews to Anglo-Saxon cognomens speeds the process of
assimilation and intermarriage. All too often, a Jewish boy or girl
begins a friendship in all innocence with a pleasant companion
of the opposite sex, unaware of the difference of religious background. The friendship ripens into love, until the point of no
return is reached.

Recent studies bear out the conviction which I have long held
that the rate of intermarriage among American Jews is now substantially in excess of 10%. What is most tragic is that the percentage is highest among our most gifted, creative, and ambitious
young people, whose Jewish roots are weak or nonexistent. What
is ominous is that it is considerably higher among our college
graduates. A hundred years ago the Reform Jewish leader Abra-

ham Geiger declared, "Every intermarriage is a nail in the coffin of Judaism." That judgment still stands.

It is true that there is a revival of interest in religion in the United States, on college campuses and among many intelligent men and women. Yet even this has its danger for Jewish survival. As all comparative tests reveal, Jews are the most irreligious group in America today. Their degree of attendance at services, the level of their personal observance, their knowledge of the Bible and the fundamentals of their religion, are far lower than is the case with Catholics and Protestants of the same social, economic, and educational level.

When, therefore, a Jewish youngster at college becomes interested in religion, it is often not to his own religion that he turns. Judaism is for him only an empty burden, a meaningless label, without value or appeal. What little he recalls about Judaism relates to a few practices and phrases—most of it either unimportant or wrong. What self-respecting Jewish father and mother would send their son or daughter off to college without a substantial wardrobe of shirts and skirts, slacks and sweaters, and much more? But how content we are to see them off to a new world with no spiritual wardrobe at all, or with a few rags and tatters left over from childhood. Our Jewish collegian, in the vast majority of cases, suffers from "pediatric Judaism," possessing the "Jewish knowledge" of a Bar Mitzvah youngster—or less. Now that he is grown up and, he believes, mature, it is not difficult for enterprising advocates of other faiths to wean him away and win him over to the more attractive creeds of the majority.

As a result, some of our youth are formally converted, more are led to intermarriage, and many more, who do not formally break the ties that bind them to their people and their tradition, are effectively and permanently alienated. Their hostility to Judaism, its institutions, its ideals, its way of life, is unmistakable.

To be sure, the Jewish community is not sitting idly by in the face of these spiritual perils. We are engaged in a vast building program. Magnificent centers and synagogues have been erected everywhere, with the avowed hope that they will attract and bring back the young and the lost sheep of the House of Israel.

Unfortunately, even this massive countercampaign has several grave disadvantages. First and foremost, it is expensive. Many young families, in particular, find it beyond their means to contribute proportionately. Feeling themselves outside of the "inner circle," they are all too often led to alienation and estrangement. The problem of making people of moderate means feel at home in Judaism and within the organizational pattern of American Jewry is a major issue with which we have scarcely begun to grapple.

Nor is the inner situation with regard to our synagogues and temples all that it should be. Unfortunately, many of them are best described as "catering establishments with chapels attached." They are large institutions, if one measures their area. They are petty, if one evaluates their program. Yet how few Jews or, for that matter, even members and trustees of congregations, stop to inquire what their Temple is doing with its income from its social functions, besides paying the charges on the mortgage which it would not have had, if it had not built the catering facilities in the first place? What are the quality and content of its religious service? How intensive and successful are its schools for the children? What cultural and educational activities does it carry on for young people and adults? What guidance does it offer for the personal problems of the youth, the middle aged, and the senior citizens? How rarely are these questions raised, let alone answered.

A social center as an adjunct to a house of prayer and of study can be a blessing, helping to maintain and expand the program. A social center which swallows up and dwarfs the house of study and the house of prayer is a travesty and a peril.

Thousands of years ago, the Talmud prophetically saw the dangers inherent in an empty synagogue, a hollow mausoleum pretending to be a center of Judaism. We read in the Talmud (*Baba Kamma* 60b): *'Al yikkanes 'adam yahid lebhet hakeneset shemalakh hammavet mafkid sham kelav, vehanei milei hekha dela karei beh dardekei vela metsallei beh 'asarah,* "A man should not enter alone into a synagogue because the Angel of Death places his instruments there. This refers only to a synagogue in which the Torah is not studied and where prayer is not offered." Here is the voice of truth—a warning in the present and guidance for the future!

We American Jews are blessed more than any other Jewish community in history. If we are to avoid the spiritual decay which is worse than outright death, we need to emphasize the obligation of every Jew to attain to an increased knowledge of his heritage. The Jew who is Jewishly ignorant is in greater spiritual danger if he is generally cultured, for he is like a luxuriant tree that has no roots. He is led to countless forms of subtle deception or gross distortion, as he struggles to deny his true background and invent an imaginary one. In James Baldwin's words, "To accept one's past, one's history, is not the same thing as drowning in it. It is learning how to use it. An invented past can never be used. It cracks and stumbles under the pressure of life like clay in a season of drought."

The notion that anyone is too old to learn is refuted not only by all the latest discoveries of psychology, but by two thousand years of Jewish experience. A Jew studied as long as he was alive, and looked forward to continuing to study in Paradise—with even greater teachers! Only a learning people is a living people. What we *know* may be dead, inert, all but buried. What we *learn,* no matter what the level of our knowledge, is alive, compelling, active. It is noteworthy that in Yiddish the word for scholar is the Hebrew word *lamdan,* which means not a "knower" but a "learner." While we continue to learn, the Torah remains a living inspiration.

Every Jew who is sincere in his loyalty to his people and takes pride in his heritage must take steps to discover his heritage *for himself,* because that which is a joy to carry is never a burden to bear. The Bible, the Hebrew language, Jewish literature, Jewish history, Jewish religious ideals and practices, contemporary Jewish life and its problems—all these must become part of the spiritual baggage of the modern Jew.

Torah means not only learning, but faith. It is not enough to have a body of information from the past. It must be alive, related to the world of which we are a part. Judaism is a world view that warms our hearts without insulting our minds. The faith of Judaism cannot be demonstrated mathematically—nothing really important can—not even mathematics. But it does offer the most adequate and satisfying interpretation of the miracle and the mystery of life and the universe. The way of life inculcated by Judaism disciplines our nature without shackling our freedom. The Jewish tradition is a never-failing fountain of faith rooted in knowledge, chastened by reason, enriched by human experience.

Faith and knowledge are expressed by a single Hebrew term, *Torah*. The cultivation of Torah as learning must become the major enterprise of the adult American Jew, not merely of children before Bar Mitzvah. But Torah includes even more. Torah also means "guidance, discipline, law." It includes practice as well as study, living as well as learning. There are those who mistakenly imagine that Conservative Judaism means a moratorium on the Sabbath, a surrender of Kashruth, a whittling away of the Festivals. No view could be more tragic or more mistaken.

There are two basic principles in Conservative Judaism— *Growth is the law of life, and the Law is the life of Judaism.* One without the other spells stagnation or chaos. The evidence is abundantly clear that Judaism was never fixed, immovable, unchanging, but never did it abandon its fundamental emphasis upon Torah as learning, lore, and law.

These two aspects of the philosophy of a living Judaism I find superbly expressed in two statements, one by a jurist, the other by a poet, neither of them a Jew. The first statement is by Judge Learned Hand: "If we must not change too quickly, at least we must not refuse to change at all." The other is by T. S. Eliot: "Only by acceptance of the past, can you alter it."

"God, Israel, and the Torah are one," Jewish mysticism declares in words which we have emblazoned upon the walls of our Temple. And Jewish rationalism emphatically agrees. "We are a people only by virtue of the Torah," said the great philosopher Saadia. Without God and Torah, there can be no Israel—not even in the land of Israel, surely not in the Diaspora.

But we are not merely Jews; we are also Americans. What have we learned from our experience in the United States? America has contributed to the world the concept of pluralism, the ideal and the practice of men of different outlooks and backgrounds living in mutuality and cooperation, respecting each other's right even to be wrong. The right to differ and to be respected was always implicit in Judaism. The passionate dissent of the Prophets created the Hebrew Bible, while the Talmud is a massive monument to argument and free discussion. American democracy has made the ideal of freedom of the spirit explicit in the lives of men. This great principle is embodied in the great American doctrine of the separation of church and state, and is expressed in the First Amendment. Though this doctrine is now under widespread attack, it may well prove to be the greatest American contribution to the free society of the future.

The history of America underlines the possibility and the importance of the great moral virtue of genuine tolerance and mutual understanding. Tolerance is no pale, colorless, negative virtue, as some would have us believe today. Without this quality, other ethical virtues turn to gall and wormwood. The roots of tolerance are humility of spirit, openness of mind, and respect for differences. Its fruits are the advancement of truth and the blessings of liberty. To quote Justice Learned Hand once again: "The spirit of liberty is the spirit which is not too sure that it is right; the spirit of liberty is the spirit which seeks to understand the minds of other men and women; the spirit of liberty is the spirit which weighs their interests alongside its own without bias; the spirit of liberty remembers that not even a sparrow falls to earth unheeded."

We need the spirit of good will and tolerance not only with regard to our fellow men, be they Catholics, Protestants, or non-believers, but vis-à-vis our fellow Jews, be they Orthodox, Conservative, or Reform. Yet I do not regard it either as essential or as beneficial to have all Jews share a single outlook—only that they respect the right of others to differ from them. The trouble today is not that some Jews are Orthodox, others Conservative, and still others Reform, but that the Orthodox are not Orthodox, the Conservative not Conservative, and the Reform not Reform. That is why, all too often, Jews express their loyalty to their specific group not positively, but negatively, not by adherence to the practices and tenets of their school of thought, but by hostility toward the others. Each group, Orthodoxy, and Reform, as well as Conservatism, has important values to contribute to Jewish life if its adherents will be sincerely and intelligently loyal. The truth is that no group has a monopoly on the truth—for the whole truth is with God alone.

On this, the holiest night of our year, let us recognize that important as it is, it is not enough for us to support Judaism—we must be supported by it. Our temples need our tangible loyalty if they are to carry on their God-given tasks. But our concrete aid is not enough to guarantee the life of our people and its role in the world. The longest journey begins with a single step. Each of us must resolve to take the first step to build his personal life on the firm foundations of faith and knowledge, learning and living, loyalty to the truth as we see it and tolerance for those who see it otherwise. We would do well to remember always the old Yiddish song, *Vos mir zeinen, zeinen mir, ober yiden bleiben mir,* "Whatever we are, Jews we remain." Only as we deepen our love for God, for Israel, and for Torah will we be worthy of having our prayer answered: "Inscribe for the good life all the children of Thy covenant."

IX

What Is Worse than Death?

I

We are met on the evening of the most solemn day of our year, our Sabbath of Sabbaths. Being as old as the Jewish people itself, Yom Kippur has naturally undergone many changes in observance. Today Yom Kippur is not only a day of fasting, but also a day of prayer, when Jews everywhere crowd into the synagogues in order to be at one with their brothers and their God.

Now, Yom Kippur was always a day of fasting, but in ancient days when the Temple stood on Zion's hill, its ritual revolved essentially around one man, the High Priest of Israel. It was he alone who was charged with the awesome responsibility of pleading for his people. On Yom Kippur the High Priest would lay aside his gorgeous vestments of purple and array himself in the white linen robes of an ordinary priest. After offering up the sacrifices ordained for the day, he would cross the courtyard of the Temple. Passing through the chamber called the Holy, he would enter into the Holy of Holies, that one room which no man ever entered from the day the structure was completed. Only the High Priest, and he only on Yom Kippur, dared to enter its precincts. In awe and trembling he would pronounce the Divine name and plead for God's forgiveness. First he would confess his own sins and those of his family, then he would pray for the entire tribe of Levi and finally for the whole household of Israel. Outside in the Temple courts, the masses of the people would stand in rapt silence, waiting for him to emerge unscathed from this encounter with the Divine. When they saw the High Priest standing once again at the entrance, they would see it as a sign that his prayers had been accepted. A joyful shout would go up from the people in the happy consciousness that a New Year of happiness and well-being had been granted them.

The preparations of the High Priest for this ordeal began long before the holy day itself. The Mishnah *Yoma* tells us that seven days before the Day of Atonement he was taken into special chambers and separated from his family, so that he might concentrate upon his great task. By holy exercises, meditation, and study, he would prepare himself to be a worthy spokesman for his people. The ritual of the sacrifices ordained for the day was carefully reviewed. On the eve of Yom Kippur, he was not permitted to eat much, because food induces sleep. Throughout the night, he and the elders who were his companions studied Scripture. They would read with him out of three books of the Bible, *Job, Ezra,* and *Chronicles.*

We know from ancient sources that no ritual was more impressive than the Yom Kippur service conducted by the High Priest. Aliens as well as Jews were deeply stirred by the solemnity and awe of the occasion. Described in the Mishnah, it is recapitulated in the *Avodah,* a central feature of the Yom Kippur morning service.

Today no Temple stands on Zion's hill and no High Priest serves as intercessor for his people in the Holy of Holies. The Jewish people itself must plead for its life in the future, for, in the words of the Torah, *Ve'attem tihyu li mamlekheth kohanim vegoy kadosh,* "You shall be for Me a kingdom of priests and a holy nation" (*Exodus* 19:6). The solemn assembly of men and women of Israel gathered in synagogues throughout the world will help determine life or death for our people.

II

From the beginning of our history, from the days of Abraham, Jews have always been concerned—if you will, obsessed—with children, because of a passionate desire to preserve their identity, their way of life, their world view. Nothing mattered to our father Abraham except the desire for a son to carry on the truths he had discovered about the living God. And because the future is always unknown and often dark, and the Jewish people more exposed to danger than most, men in every age have asked, as did the prophet Isaiah, *Shomer mah milaylah,* "Watchman, what of the night?"

Sometimes our ancestors were threatened by physical extinction. Thus Pharaoh sought to drown all the male children in the Nile River, and Haman plotted a one-day massacre of all the Jews in the Persian Empire. In other ages, it was the subtler threat of spiritual disintegration and the death of Judaism that confronted them. This was the goal of the Syrian king Antiochus IV, who sought to force Greek religion and civilization upon the Jews of Palestine, and three centuries later of the Roman Emperor Hadrian, who forbade the study of the Torah and the practice of Judaism.

But it is our age that has the melancholy distinction of being exposed simultaneously to both perils, physical destruction and spiritual extinction. No wonder that this fear of tomorrow, this concern for the future, has grown increasingly acute in our own day. The physical disaster is all too evident. Before our eyes, yes, before our folded arms, six million of our brothers, the best, the wisest, the most loyal of our people, were cruelly done to death.

As for the remnants of European Jewry who reached the State of Israel, even they cannot relax their vigilance. They must stand perpetual guard against a far-flung alliance of vicious and bloodthirsty foes who have vowed, "Come, let us destroy them from being a people, so that the name of Israel may be mentioned no longer" (*Ps.* 83:5). And even now, twenty-five years after Hitler's massive blood bath, the United Nations and the free world remain silent as the Arab states trample the Charter of the United Nations under foot in their repeated calls for the destruction of Israel.

But our peril goes further. We are exposed to a subtler, impersonal, less dramatic form of extinction as well. In the recent past, *Look Magazine* published a sensational article that attracted widespread attention. It was called "The Vanishing American Jew." Basing itself upon a significant study by an American sociologist, Erich Rosenthal, the *Look Magazine* article suggested that the American Jewish community was steadily moving toward total disappearance through intermarriage. Rosenthal's painstaking research was conducted principally in two areas. The first was Iowa, where the Jewish population is small and thinly scattered, so that the rate of intermarriage is as high as 37%. His second field of inquiry was Washington, D. C., where the government services have attracted a very high concentration of mobile, intellectualized, and often alienated Jews. Here he found that no less than 13.1% of all Jews, more than one out of eight, had intermarried. Even more disquieting is his statistical evidence that intermarriage grows with each succeeding generation. The first generation of foreign-born Jews has a rate of 1.4%; the second, 10.2%; and the third, 17.9%.

No sooner was the *Look* article published that defenders of American Jewry rushed into the fray to deny the thesis of "The Vanishing American Jew." Rosenthal's study was attacked as pessimistic and exaggerated. Obviously, Iowa and Washington are not typical of all communities. The over-all figures for American Jewry are undoubtedly lower. But they are dangerously high. I have long maintained that intermarriage has made far greater inroads into the Jewish community than was generally recognized. At a time when most students cited a figure of 6%, I felt that the rate of intermarriage was closer to 10%.

It is scant comfort to point out that intermarriage among Catholics is nearly four times as high. When Catholics intermarry, they still marry Christians. When Jews intermarry, the vast majority of the children, at least 70%, are lost to the Jewish people. Intermarriage represents a major threat to Jewish survival in America and it is on the increase.

Nonetheless, the sensational thesis of the *Look* article on "The Vanishing American Jew" is an exaggeration. There is little danger that American Jewry will vanish in the foreseeable future. The natural reproduction of Jewish families guarantees that for generations to come there will be large numbers of men and women in the United States who will be recognized by others and by themselves as Jews. The numbers may stand still or even decline, but, barring some unforeseen catastrophe, American Jewry is here to stay.

Having reached this conclusion, we may be tempted to breathe a sigh of relief and sit back in contentment. An astronomy professor was once lecturing to a large class of students. Suddenly he noticed a student in the last row excitedly raising his hand. "Professor, Professor, I would like to ask a question. Did I hear you say that a giant meteor will crash into the earth and destroy it in fourteen million years?" "No," said the professor, "what I said was 'forty million years.' " "Thank you!" said the student, with a sigh of relief, "I feel better now!", and he settled back into his slumbers.

III

Death does not threaten us, but a worse fate does, and its name is decay. The Jewish identity is not likely to disappear. What threatens us is a steady attrition, a loss of vitality, a stripping away of our finest, most gifted, and most creative spirits.

The phenomenon of intermarriage is sensational, but actually it is not the most extreme form of de-Judaization. Far too little attention has been paid to the process of outright conversion to Christianity by American Jews. We have no reliable figures, but I suspect that they are by no means negligible. Qualitatively, conversion to Christianity is particularly dangerous because it has caught up many of our most gifted, creative, and successful Jews. Many causes are at work. Undoubtedly many converts are seeking an easy way out. They may want to avoid the various forms of anti-Jewish discrimination, to remove obstacles to their personal advancement, to be socially accepted. But by no means all. There are some who sincerely sought a religion for themselves. They were attracted by the glamor of the dominant faith, as they saw it beautifully presented to them on college campuses and elsewhere. Its ideas are available in books, its advocates are skillful and determined. As for Judaism, all they remember are some childish notions, more likely than not mistaken, and a few rituals which they never understood. In such an unequal struggle for a human soul, which contestant will emerge victorious?

Often intermarriage is the cause of conversion, but not always. At times intermarriage is the effect. Not infrequently, both husband and wife are converts, to Catholicism, to Episcopalianism, to Unitarianism, to Quakerism, to Christian Science, even to the Jehovah's Witnesses, which is strongly anti-Semitic in its theology. An impressive—and depressing—list of famous Jewish converts to Christianity in the United States can all too easily be drawn up. It can also be augmented by many young people on the college level and beyond, who never attain fame, but whose defection weakens us tremendously.

Far more widespread than intermarriage or conversion is the phenomenon of alienation. These are the numberless Jews who have not formally cut their link with the Jewish people but who are effectively estranged from it, sharing none of its ideas, ideals, hopes, or loyalties. Here again they run the gamut from the famous to the unknown.

This estrangement of our creative sons and daughters from the sources of their Jewish existence is a threefold tragedy. It robs the Jewish community of some of its potentially most valuable human resources. It deprives these creative spirits of the insights and values of the Jewish heritage that could help and enrich their own work and thought. And, by the same token, it impoverishes the life of humanity, which could benefit enormously from the outlook of the Jewish world view—at once wise and humane and courageous.

IV

Intermarriage, conversion, alienation—these perils threaten from without. What about those of us who are within the fold, the leaders and members of our Jewish institutions and organizations, the men and women and young people who are active in Jewish affairs and contribute to Jewish life? Their loyalty and zeal cannot be honored too highly. It is due only to their devotion and concern that the structure of Jewish life has been reared and the agencies for Jewish survival created and maintained.

Yet on the solemn eve of Kol Nidre, the truth must be spoken. Even within the ranks of the faithful all is not well. Today the gleaming temples and Jewish centers from Maine to California, resplendent in chrome and aluminum and glass, are the last word in modern architecture—and sometimes a little beyond that! They are symbols of the growing self-respect of the American-Jewish community, of the sense of at-homeness which American Jews have in their various communities, of their vastly improved social and economic status.

But what do these institutions reveal about the religious depth, the ethical commitment, the cultural concern of modern Jews? Even to ask the question is embarrassing. Speaking of the English people today, Alastair MacIntyre writes: "The difficulty lies in the combination of atheism in the practice of the life of the vast majority, with the profession of either superstition or theism by that same majority. The creed of the English is that there is no God and that it is wise to pray to Him from time to time." I know no better description of the spiritual status of American Jewry.

Nor is there any comfort in the knowledge that the situation is equally tragic among our Christian brethren. Nonbelief and superstition—what can seem further apart? Yet such are the intricacies of the human soul that for untold thousands of Jews and non-Jews both lodge in the same breast! One of my friends, a distinguished historian at an American university, who is personally deeply committed to Judaism and observant, once said to me, "Judaism is in grave danger from two directions today—from the *goyim* and the *meshugoyim!*" The evidence for this judgment is all too abundant.

Another source of peril is the growth of rampant and extreme denominationalism in Jewish life and the rabid hostility between one group and the other. Let me not be misunderstood. There are significant differences in the philosophies of Orthodox, Conservative and Reform Judaism. Never has Judaism been more desperately needed than today—never has it been more difficult to maintain. In the face of the massive, unprecedented problems that threaten Judaism in the mid-twentieth century, only the blind and conceited can claim to have the one and only true answer everywhere and always. There are values and insights and emphases to be found in every group and every philosophy of Jewish life.

As the reader may suspect, I believe that Conservative Judaism represents the mainstream of the living Jewish tradition. Because of its capacity for continuity and growth, I am convinced that it has within itself the greatest measure of life-giving truth for our people and its heritage. But I do not lament the fact that not all Jews are Conservative and that there are many who are affiliated with Orthodoxy and with Reform. What is tragic is that these designations are empty labels, devoid of meaning for many Jews, who use their affiliation as a sword against their brothers. The Talmud says that the Temple in Jerusalem was destroyed because of *sin'ath hinnam,* "causeless hatred." Our Sages exhaust their ingenuity in emphasizing its heinous character. They declare, *Kol hason'e lahavero k'illu harago,* "Whoever hates his brother is regarded as his murderer." *Shaani sin'ath hinnam dehamir tefei me'avodah zarah,* "Causeless hatred is far worse than idolatry" (*Kallah Rabbati,* ed. Higger, p. 237).

Instead of a fruitful dialogue between the various groups in Jewish life, which would stimulate and benefit them all, we have slander and mud-slinging, half-truths and total falsehoods, and the lowest forms of competition and envy, bigotry and insult, "all in the name of God." A wise Jewish teacher pointed out that in the long catalogue of sins contained in the great Confessional *Al Het,* only one of the fifty-two offenses is attributed to the *yetzer hara,* "For the sin which we have committed against Thee through the evil inclination." All the other fifty-one sins against our brethren and ourselves we commit in the name of lofty ideals.

It may seem strange to speak of the magnificent edifices built by American Jewry as a source of spiritual peril. After all, these are our centers for worship, for education, for community life. They make possible the maintenance of the activities without which we would cease to be a recognizable community. Undoubtedly, many of these buildings serve excellent purposes and are indispensable. Yet all too often these resplendent structures stand as monuments, nay, as mausoleums, to Judaism, elaborate, expensive, and almost empty of content. The synagogue becomes debauched as it adopts the standards of commercialism and competition of the market place, and all its authentic functions are relegated to a corner.

What is more, these new structures represent capital investments of many hundreds of millions of dollars. As a result, families of limited income and particularly young people, who are beginning at the bottom of the economic ladder, find themselves unable to meet the dues and assessments and therefore remain outside of organized Jewish life. Human nature being what it is, these families tend to rationalize their non-affiliation and justify it by developing a hostility to the goals and ideals of Judaism as a whole. They cannot have what they want. They end by not wanting what they cannot have. They are strangers in what should be their spiritual home. What a tragic irony that the buildings erected in order to attract the youth become effective barriers to their meaningful participation in Judaism!

V

Is there then no future for our heritage—only a past? Are we doomed either to vanish or, what is far worse, to decay? Fortunately, there still remain great resources for spiritual health and rebirth in our people. The Jewish toast *Lehayyim,* "For life," has been the watchword of the ages. Judaism has survived through the centuries because of the amazing fecundity of Jewish genius and talent, coupled with the extraordinary capacity of Jewish leadership to evaluate a new situation and take active steps to meet the challenge.

If we wish to avoid the perils of decline and disintegration—and they are real—we may find a clue and a direction in the practice of the High Priest on the threshold of the Day of Judgment. The

Mishnah tells us that his companions would study three books of
the Bible with him on the eve of Yom Kippur: *Chronicles, Job,*
and *Ezra.*

The book of *Chronicles* narrates the history of mankind and of
Israel from Adam almost to the High Priest's own day. Before
the High Priest could effectively intercede for his people, he
needed to know its entire history and recall the experiences
through which his ancestors had gone. The first basic necessity for
a rebirth of Jewish vitality is a knowledge of our past, a familiarity
with Jewish history in depth, with the great men and movements
of our people, with the basic ideas and ideals which they proclaimed to the world and the great books and institutions they be-
queathed to mankind. There can be no hope for American Jewry
until it is universally recognized that the major problem confronting us is education, more and better education, at every level,
for both sexes, for every segment of the community, for girls as
well as for boys, for the rich as well as for the poor, for adults and
adolescents as well as for children.

It is true that there are more Jewish children attending Jewish
schools today than ever before in America. Unfortunately, these
figures give a misleading picture. The vast majority of them attend an institution called the Sunday School, which was borrowed
from our Protestant neighbors and which they themselves have
long discovered to be totally inadequate. If the Sunday School is
unsatisfactory for Christians, it is catastrophic for Jews. A Sunday
School education may suffice to keep alive, on however inadequate
a level, the Christian culture of a dominant Christian population.
But for Jews who are a minority group in a majority culture, a
smattering of half-baked notions carried over from childhood is
often worse than useless.

A recent survey of Jewish education in America described it as
a mile wide and an inch deep. Without sufficient hours and without enough years of study, the finest teachers and the best equip-
ment are powerless to reverse the march to Jewish "know-nothing-
ism." We need a broadly based program of education, from the
nursery and the kindergarten through the elementary school. We
need more and better day schools, finer and more intensive Hebrew

schools. Above all, we need greater emphasis on Jewish education at the high school level. For this is the period of adolescence, of searching, the opening up of new horizons and the confrontation of new challenges. We need to extend the scope of Jewishly oriented camps, like Ramah and Massad, for the summertime. Thousands of youngsters now experience the joys of contentful, natural Jewish living during July and August. Their ranks should be increased, ten, twenty, fifty fold.

Adult Jewish education, which in so many communities is conducted by a minyan of faithful souls, must become a major enterprise on the part of all our institutions and movements, whatever other purposes they may have, be it religion, Zionism, social service, or civic defense. In our practical civilization, we have tended to define a good Jew as one who does and one who gives. We need to add a third test—one who learns, who, whatever his present level of Jewish knowledge, is not content to stand still, but adds to his information, his appreciation, his participation. We need to use all available devices, so that every Jew may open the book of *Chronicles* and read and learn and be inspired by the past to build the future.

The second book that the High Priest would study on Yom Kippur Eve was the book of *Job*. This, the most profound book in the Bible, revolves about a righteous man who is plunged from the apex of prosperity and well-being to the depths of degradation and misery. Stripped of his position, robbed of his possessions, bereaved of his children, stricken with a loathsome disease, Job remains steadfast in his faith in the God of righteousness. So strong is his trust in his Maker that he rejects with scorn all the conventional answers spoken by others in defense of God. Finally he himself is vindicated when God recalls to him the mystery and the harmony of the world and thus gives him the faith that even the inexplicable has its place in the cosmic order. The book of *Job* is a flaming protest against a religion that is merely respectable, against piety that is only conventional. It calls for us to wrestle honestly with the problems of existence and to reach out for God, who sustains our every waking moment.

Rabbi A. Alan Steinbach has spoken of "faucet-Judaism," the

widespread feeling that when a tragedy comes, we can turn on
faith like a faucet and the waters will begin to flow. The truth is
that there is no shortcut to religion, no superhighway to faith. It
must be achieved through agony and suffering, through blood,
sweat, and tears. But when we reach the mountain peaks of faith,
we shall be raised up and exalted above all the events and acci-
dents that befall us. We shall be able to bless God's name and
exult in the miracle of life. *Our religion will no longer be an
exercise in respectability, but an adventure in discovery.* Our
home will again become a sanctuary, the Sabbath will be a beloved
island of refuge, and the Festivals, fountains of inspiration, beauty,
and joy.

Finally, the High Priest spent the solemn eve of Yom Kippur
reading the book of *Ezra*. This book is the record of the life and
the struggles of one of the most misunderstood figures in Jewish
history. Ezra lived after the period of the Babylonian Exile. In
many respects, conditions then were similar to our situation today. The Persian King Cyrus, as part of a farsighted policy, permitted those Jews who so desired to return to their homeland and
establish an autonomous community once more. Some forty thousand Jews took the long journey back from Babylonia, with high
hopes for the grandiose restoration of the Jewish people, as the
Prophets had foretold. They soon discovered, however, how far
short reality fell of their hopes. The Jewish community in Jerusalem was a tiny island in a Gentile sea. They were surrounded
by neighbors who hated them, slandered them to the Persian home
government, and prevented their growth and progress.

Moreover, the inner fiber of the small Jewish community was
also decaying. Intermarriage was practiced on a wide scale. Even
the high priestly families had taken foreign wives to themselves.
The children were being raised in foreign cultures and spoke alien
tongues.

During this long and protracted crisis, which lasted for a century or more, a Jewish scholar, a *Sopher* or Scribe, named Ezra,
came from Babylonia to teach and guide the struggling Jewish
community in Jerusalem and its environs. He saw the signs of
decay and imminent disaster everywhere. Ezra did not make the

mistake so common today of calling for a return to the past, of trying to turn the clock of time backward. Instead, Ezra undertook the far more arduous and creative and life-giving task of conserving the values of the old in new forms, and of extending the insights of the past to meet the needs of the present and the future. Together with his co-worker, Nehemiah, the Jewish governor of Jerusalem, he declared war on intermarriage, because it meant the death knell of Judaism, the total extinction of the tiny Jewish community living in a great non-Jewish sea.

Ezra was concerned not only with the physical survival of his people. During the days of the First Temple, the religious leadership in the Jewish community, as among all nations, was vested in the hereditary priesthood, who handed down the functions and the emoluments of their office from father to son. Ezra realized that if Judaism was to meet the challenge of new and unknown conditions, it needed the qualities of flexibility, responsiveness to the present, and the capacity of growth in the future. He did not remove the Kohanim, the priests, from their role as officiants at Temple sacrifices and the other rituals, which was ordained in the Torah of Moses.

But by the side of the Temple in Jerusalem, which continued its time-honored role, he introduced from Babylonia a new and modest institution of recent origin. It was the Synagogue, with a threefold function, as the house of assembly, of prayer, and of study for all the people. In this new institution leadership was vested not in one class or clan, nor was it dependent upon economic position or social prestige. Whoever possessed the requisite character and scholarship, no matter how humble his origins, could become a *Sopher,* a master of the Book, a Rabbi, a teacher of his people. As a result of the activity of these *Sopherim* there grew up, by the side of the written Torah of Moses, a vast additional body of doctrine and law that we call the Oral Law, embodied in the Mishnah and the Talmud. Even more than the written Torah, it was the Oral Torah which made Judaism impregnable to the assaults of all its enemies from within and without.

According to the Talmud, Ezra took another great revolutionary step. The Hebrew Bible, like all West Semitic literature, was written in an archaic and difficult alphabet. Ezra did not hesitate to replace this *kethabh 'ivri,* "ancient Hebrew alphabet," by a new and easier one, the so-called *Kethab 'ashuri,* or Aramaic script. This each Jew could learn to read and write and thus make himself a "Master of the Book."

One wonders how many of those who today glorify Ezra would have possessed his courage to innovate and his understanding of the needs of the hour. Ezra was a revolutionary, not because he wished to destroy the old, but because he wished to give it new life. He was a conservative, not because he clung to the outworn, but because he wished to conserve all that was vital in the past.

VI

On the eve of Yom Kippur, the High Priest of old studied the books of *Chronicles, Job,* and *Ezra.* On the threshold of the Sabbath of Sabbaths, in the hour of decision when life or death for his people hung in the balance, we who are the high priests today must prepare ourselves through a similar threefold program. We must undertake the study of our people's history and culture. We must immerse ourselves in the depth of our religion and rise to the height of its ethical insights. We must embark upon a program of action geared to the new age—and this is the call not to our neighbor, but to each one of us—here and now.

Education, religion and creative action—nothing less can save us today.

On this most solemn day of our year, as we pray to be written and sealed in the Book of Life, let us fight not merely death, but decay, not merely extinction, but degeneration, not only defection, but alienation. Let us go forth and bring back the lost sheep of the house of Israel to their Father in Heaven, through knowledge, faith, and action.

X

Seeking the Secret

I

For perhaps the first time in living memory, the complacency of American Jewry has been shaken to its foundations. For years American Jews have had a strong feeling of self-assurance in the present and confidence in their future. With the overthrow of Hitler and the steady decline of overt anti-Semitism, most Jews have been convinced that under the Stars and Stripes the destiny of the Jewish community is secure.

Now this age of complacency has suddenly come to a close. It is true that no ugly cloud of anti-Semitism has arisen to darken the horizon. Anti-Jewish prejudice has not a shred of respectability in America, as it had in Germany for a half-century before Hitler came to power. Jewish names figure prominently in government and public affairs, in commerce and industry, in science and education, in literature and the arts. It is a striking sign of the times that when the first Catholic pope in history to visit the Western hemisphere came to these shores, he was scheduled to meet the President of the United States, who is a Protestant, in the home of a Jew bearing the typical name of "Goldberg." American Jewry is externally safe, secure, and respected.

It is no enemy from without that threatens American Jewry: the peril is from within. American Jews now recognize that intermarriage is a major threat. They have only to look into their families and those of their neighbors to see how widespread intermarriage has become. In the words of the Torah, *Ein bayit 'asher 'ein bo met* (*Exodus* 12:30), "There is scarcely one house in which the disease has not struck."

The situation grows steadily more acute. There is scarcely a week in which some distraught father or mother, or a confused youngster, does not come to my study with a problem of intermarriage. As for those young people who have already passed "the point of no return," they naturally avoid any possible contact with a rabbi.

In Europe, it used to be said, a baptismal certificate was the passport to Western society. In America, deserting Judaism rarely takes the form of outright conversion. But as one reads the story of Jews who attain to prominence, one finds very many who have intermarried and have raised their children as non-Jews. It seems almost that intermarriage is the necessary stepping-stone to public advancement and success.

It is clear that in an open society, where young people of varying religious and ethnic backgrounds meet freely in business and in the academic world, intermarriage cannot be totally eliminated. Intermarriage is part of the price which American Jewry must pay for living in a free society. But the price is distressingly high, and getting higher. It threatens to undermine the vitality of the American Jewish community, because it robs us of our ablest, most ambitious, and most creative spirits.

Intermarriage is only the most obvious form of assimilation which is eating away at the vitals of American Jewry. Never have we had a community of Jews as well educated generally and as abysmally ignorant Jewishly as in our day. No other segment of the American people remotely compares with American Jews in their devotion to a college education. When our young people on college campuses are exposed to the corrosive acids of modern thought and hear attacks on religion that are announced in the name of philosophy and science, legitimate or illegitimate, they are helpless before the challenge. When they see Christianity attractively presented to them in class, in chapel, and by their classmates, they are totally unequipped to defend their heritage. Their resources consist perhaps of a few Jewish phrases and food preferences from home, and some childhood memories of what they had learned in Sunday or Hebrew School before Bar Mitzvah, notions that are generally incorrect and always childish.

Even if they escape the perils of intermarriage, and marry within the Jewish fold, they fall victim to total alienation from anything Jewishly meaningful, be it religious, cultural, or national. When they set up their own homes, they demonstrate the truth of the melancholy observation of Professor Mordecai M. Kaplan: "The Western world gives the Jew the freedom not to be Christian without the power to be Jews." In a word, they become practicing "nonsectarians."

The tragedy goes even further. It is not merely that American Jews are assimilating, but that they are assimilating to the lowest practices and values of the general environment. Throughout America we witness the breakdown of moral standards. What used to be regarded as elementary honesty and a sense of responsibility is all too often lacking among government officials, corporation executives, labor leaders, and others in high authority. In a cynical moment, I once defined democracy as that system under which the poor are free to imitate the vices of the rich. In the lower echelons, too, stealing, loafing, malingering, and other forms of cheating on the job are common. Jews today are not at all backward in any of these activities, proving that they are thoroughly American.

For thousands of years the family has been the bedrock of civilization. It has virtually broken down in these United States. Nearly one marriage in every four now ends in divorce. One is staggered by the mountain-mass of misery, recrimination, hatred, and pain which precedes as well as follows every divorce.

The breakdown of marriage is prepared for by other practices that are widespread today. Extramarital relations are glorified in our books and magazines, films, and on the stage. Premarital intimacies, in which even youngsters participate, are today, we are told by competent authorities, almost the rule. One of our finest young men, married a few months ago, told me after his *Aufruf*, "When my fiancée and I stood on line at City Hall to get our marriage license, I felt there was something wrong with us. Prac-

tically all the other girls on the line were pregnant!" Time was
when a childless Jewish couple, wishing to adopt a baby through
legal channels, had to wait a very long time. Now, thank God, the
waiting period has all but disappeared. There is an ample supply
of Jewish children available for adoption. The moral—or the
immorality—is obvious.

In days gone by, delinquency was regarded as the consequence
of poverty. While, to be sure, poverty is still its major cause, we
have today developed a new variety, affluent delinquency, as the
various outbursts of rowdyism at Southampton and Westport
clearly indicate. Drunkenness, drug addiction, promiscuity, and
sexual perversion are no longer restricted to the fringes of society.
They can almost be described as respectable, were it not that respectability is itself under a cloud.

As Senator Margaret Chase Smith said: "Many years ago the
word 'square' was one of the most honored and respected words
in our vocabulary. A 'square' deal was an honest deal. A 'square'
meal a good and full meal. It was the 'square' shooter rather than
the 'sharp' shooter who was admired. When you were financially
'square,' you had paid all your debts. What is a 'square' today?
He's the fellow who never learned to get away with it—being the
one who volunteers when he doesn't have to—who tries to do
better than others—who has to be reminded to go home because
he's so lost in his work . . . He is the man who says: 'I am my
brother's keeper.' "

It is true that we American Jews have not quite caught up with
the procession—alcoholism is still somewhat lower among us—but
we are straining every muscle to get to the head of the parade!

II

No enemy threatens American Jewry from without. Yet its survival, physical, intellectual, and moral, is in grave jeopardy. Where
can we find guidelines to the future? Our Sages tell us: *Ma'asei
'abhot siman labanim,* "The deeds of the fathers serve as a guide to
the children." Particularly on the High Holy Days when we invoke again and again *zekhut 'abhot,* "the merit of our fathers,
Abraham, Isaac and Jacob," we have only the past to teach us.

What can the American-Jewish community of today learn from the great Jewish communities of yesterday? It is true that they have been physically destroyed, but their spirit lives on in the cultural, religious, and ethical riches they have added to the treasure house of Judaism, and in the newer communities their survivors have helped to build.

When we turn to the past we naturally think first of the great East European Jewish community, which is closest to us in point of time. Most American Jews are descended from the Jews of Russia, Poland, Hungary, and Roumania. Many in our congregation were themselves born and spent their earliest years in Eastern Europe. It is no wonder, therefore, that so many Jews today look back with nostalgia to the *shtetl,* the tiny village where they were young. They remember the intense dedication to Jewish life, the warm sense of fellowship, and the strength of faith that prevailed there. The march of time has blotted out the harsh lines of the reality of yesterday and left only the gentler lineaments of an idealized and even an imaginary past.

No wonder that in so many quarters we are told that only East European Judaism is true Judaism. Most American Jews find it impossible to isolate themselves physically from American society. If only for economic reasons, they must live in the great urban centers. The advocates of nostalgia Judaism urge them to erect an invisible ghetto of the spirit. They insist that the modern world must have nothing to do with Judaism, and Judaism must have nothing to do with the modern world. They strive to reproduce in America the *Yiddishkeit* that their grandparents knew in Galicia or Hungary, in Roumania or Poland.

Their ideal is lofty and their intentions are noble. But in the long run they are doomed to failure. It is impossible to re-establish in twentieth-century America, or in twentieth-century Israel, for that matter, a facsimile of the isolated Jewish communities of Eastern Europe. Our grandfathers were not confronted by our problems and therefore they have no solutions to offer us. Their religious faith was not challenged by the discoveries of science or the insights of philosophy. Their religious practice could be maintained without any modification because they had virtually no meaningful contact with non-Jews.

The story is told of two Jews who met on a train in Poland. After an exchange of the usual amenities, the first said to the other, "Where do you come from?" He replied, "I come from a small village." "How many Jews in your village?" "Oh, about five hundred families." "How many Gentiles?" "About a hundred." "Very good," said the first Jew, "five hundred Jewish families really require a hundred Gentile families for Shabbos goyim." "And where do you come from?" "From Warsaw." "How many Jews?" "One hundred thousand!" "Wonderful, wonderful, and how many Gentiles?" "About five hundred thousand." "Tell me, why do you need so many Shabbos goyim?"

Our grandparents found neither competition nor challenge in the general environment about them. The study and cultivation of the Torah was confronted by no rich general culture demanding attention and cultivation. The ignorant Polish peasant, the illiterate Russian *moujik,* could contribute nothing that might either enrich the pattern of Judaism or challenge any of its assumptions.

In spite of the dangers of pogroms and the exactions of tyranny, our parents and grandparents in Eastern Europe lived in a closed society and therefore enjoyed the advantages of a static, self-contained community. As a result, there was an intense attachment to Torah and a warm sense of Jewish fellowship. These qualities we wish to revive and preserve in the modern world, but we are unprepared to go back into a closed ghetto society. *We would not if we could, and we could not if we would.* With all our reverence for the precious qualities of soul which lived among our ancestors in Eastern Europe, they cannot supply the answers which we, their grandchildren, need today to make Judaism live under radically new and challenging conditions.

III

There was another great Jewish center in modern times from which many of us derive, the German Jewish community. Here the conditions of life were far closer to those under which we live. Within the short space of one hundred and fifty years, from the

French Revolution of 1789 until the Nuremberg Laws of 1935, the Jews of Central Europe, whose language and culture were basically German, produced the greatest galaxy of genius and talent in modern history. The number of Jewish Nobel Prize winners was ten to twenty times as large as their proportion to the general population. The four seminal minds of modern times whose influence for good or ill is enduring were Charles Darwin, Karl Marx, Albert Einstein, and Sigmund Freud. Of these four, three were of the seed of Abraham. When, in the heyday of his power, Hitler declared that the Jews were poisoning the wells of German culture, he was paying a perverted tribute to the extraordinary contribution that German-speaking Jews made to the national life, and which made Germany the mistress of modern civilization.

This is not all. German-speaking Jewry constituted the great laboratory of the Jewish spirit in modern times. Here the Jewish tradition and the Jewish community first encountered the challenge of the modern world, with all its power, its peril, and its promise. It was in the German *Kulturkreis,* which included Austria, Hungary, and Bohemia, as well as Germany, that there emerged virtually every aspect of the problem of Judaism and Jewish identity in the modern world. Here every conceivable solution was proposed and every approach tried. As all roads were explored, some led to dead ends, while others opened into fruitful vistas. With relatively few exceptions, every significant movement in modern Jewish life—Orthodoxy, Reform, Conservatism, the Science of Judaism, even Zionism and modern Hebrew literature— had its origin or found its expression within German-speaking Jewry.

In spite of the widespread existence of anti-Semitism, German-speaking Jews, unlike their East European brothers, were living in the modern world in what was in most respects an open society. They came into close contact with non-Jews in their personal lives, and were challenged and stimulated by the riches of modern culture, to which they themselves contributed so amply. The various movements in Jewish life, religious, national, and cultural, were the result of cross-fertilization of the Jewish tradition by

modern life and thought. Their problems and their solutions were
not radically different from our own. As George Santayana said,
"He who forgets the past is doomed to repeat it." There is much
that we can learn from the problems confronting German Jewry,
its achievements, and even its failures. Not to do so is to court
disaster.

Nonetheless, even German Jewry cannot offer us ready-made
answers. It is of the nature of the adventure of living that we must
run the risks and reap the rewards ourselves. There was one fatal
defect which the German Jews could not overcome. They often
spoke of a German-Jewish symbiosis, that is to say, a mutual creative relationship between their Germanism and their Judaism.
But very few of them succeeded in achieving this harmony. The
greatest lyric poet of Germany, Heinrich Heine, was deeply and
profoundly Jewish in spirit. Yet he felt it necessary to be baptized.
Only later did he discover the sad truth expressed long after his
time by the American writer, Robert Nathan: "It isn't being kept
out that hurts, it's being *let* in, and made to *feel* out." Ever afterwards, Heine was plagued by this inner conflict:

> Sie haben mich gequaelt,
> Geaergert blau und blass,
> Die einen mit ihrer Liebe,
> Die andren mit ihrem Hass.

> "They have tormented and pained me deeply,
> Some with their love, others with their hate."

His famous contemporary, Germany's greatest journalist, Lud-
wig Boerne, wrote in his twenty-sixth letter from Paris, dated
February 7, 1832, after he, too, had been converted to Christianity:
"One attacks me for being a Jew, another forgives me my Jewishness. A third even praises me for it, but all think about it. They
stand as though transfixed in this magic Jew-circle, and none of
them can emerge from it."

One of the most profound German novelists of the twentieth
century, Jakob Wassermann, sought to explain his dual relationship in his book, *Mein Weg als Deutscher und Jude,* "My Way

as a German and as a Jew." In 1933, when Hitler came to power, Wassermann's world collapsed and he died of a broken heart.

Intermarriages and conversions were widespread—and there was worse. In his important work, *Jüdischer Selbsthass,* "Jewish Self-Hate," Theodor Lessing, who was murdered by Nazi assassins, adduced untold numbers of examples of gifted and creative Jews who committed moral and even physical suicide because they could not make peace with their Jewish background.

German Jewry did point the way toward a synthesis of Jewish tradition and modern culture. But only a few of its members succeeded in establishing a viable pattern. For most of them, the German and the Jew were at war within their breasts. This inner harmony cannot be taken over ready-made. Each community, indeed, each human being, must labor to achieve it for himself.

IV

There is a third great creative Jewish community to which we can turn for insight and for guidance—the medieval Spanish-Jewish community. In the summer of 1965 the World Council of Synagogues, the international affiliate of the United Synagogue of America, organized a tour to Spain, Portugal, and North Africa. It was more than a trip to a fascinating area of the world. It was a voyage of rediscovery of the Jewish past, indeed, an adventure in self-recovery, because no other Jewish community in history, after the days of the Bible and the Talmud, produced a Golden Age comparable to that of Spain.

As we walked the old streets of Seville, Malaga, Cordova, Granada, and Toledo we could hear the footsteps of the great giants of the spirit who had lived, created, struggled, and suffered in these centers. The medieval Jews loved Spain intensely. They called it *Eretz Hatzevi,* "the land of delight." They gave it their wholehearted allegiance and served it in peace and war. They participated in its political life, fought on its battlefields, helped create its science and philosophy, and were the mainstay of its commerce and industry.

But their centuries-old love affair with Spain, both under the

Moslems and under the Christians, was no honeymoon. They were
exposed to countless dangers, both physical and spiritual. They
suffered defections from their ranks, some of their most pernicious
enemies being converts or the descendants of converts. The persecution of the Jews in Spain, now by the Christians, now by the
Moslems, continued throughout the thousand years and more of
Jewish life on the peninsula. It began with the Visigoths in the
seventh century and reached its climax in the bloody massacres of
1391. Then came the tortures of the Inquisition "for the greater
glory of God." The last act in the tragedy was the Expulsion of
the Jews from Spain in 1492. It was as though the destiny that
watches over Israel had decreed that the bloody extinction of
Spanish Jewry would coincide with the discovery of the new continent which would prove a home and a shelter for the storm-
tossed children of Israel.

Spanish Jews were confronted by all the perils and the temptations that threaten American Jews. Yet the vast majority of them
succeeded in loving Spain while remaining deeply attached to
their Jewishness. How were they able to achieve this inner
harmony?

Spanish Jews possessed three attributes. *The first was their personal involvement in Jewish learning,* not as a philanthropic enterprise for the poor, or as a public campaign, but as a vital activity of every Jew. And because Jewish learning was the concern
of even the most important and the most gifted Jews, Spanish
Jewry came upon another life-giving secret—*the road to Jewish
identity lies in Jewish creativity.* Spanish Jewry did not merely
maintain Jewish culture, but enriched it through the achievements of hundreds of men of genius and talent. It was creative,
not merely preservative; it was striving after the new, not merely
repeating the old. They studied the old books, but they also wrote
new ones. They cherished the old disciplines, but they also discovered new horizons of culture.

It is here that those who wish to preserve Judaism today by
going back to the past are doomed to failure. For they bring all
sacrifices to keep it unchanged, but changelessness means petri-

faction and death. Only a Judaism with new fruits can bring the sap of life to the old roots.

This life-giving secret Spanish Jewry knew. There were great Jewish statesmen in Spain who attained to positions of supreme importance. At the same time, they were deeply committed to Judaism, practiced their religion, and knew its culture. In fact, they contributed to its greatness. Hasdai ibn Shaprut was the vizir of a caliph. He did not hesitate, as part of his foreign affairs, to send emissaries to Russia where he had heard of an independent Jewish kingdom called Chazaria on the Volga. He supported Talmudic scholarship at its beginnings in Spain, and was the patron of the first scientific Hebrew philologists, who were also among the earliest medieval Hebrew poets.

Samuel Hanagid, "the Prince," was a redoubtable general on the field of battle and an astute political leader. He was the author of a first-rate introduction to the Talmud, a prolific poet, and a dedicated leader of his people. Abraham Zacuto produced the geographical and astronomical tables used by Christopher Columbus. He also wrote a history of the Jewish people in Hebrew.

The list could be extended indefinitely. It would include the august name of Moses Maimonides. Born in Cordova, he was the physician of the sultan of Egypt and of his court and the author of medical books still of value today. At the same time he was the greatest rabbinic authority and the mightiest philosophic genius produced by medieval Judaism. There was Solomon ibn Gabirol, born in Malaga, the greatest religious poet of Spanish Judaism. At the same time he was the author of a profound philosophic work, *Fons Vitae,* which was of such great influence on Christians and Moslems that it was not suspected that its author was a Jew.

Jewish culture in Spain possessed one other outstanding trait— a widespread, almost universal knowledge of the Hebrew language in which its greatest treasures were written. When, for practical or scientific reasons, Spanish Jews wrote in Arabic, they quickly translated their books into Hebrew.

It was the creative blending of Torah and Hokmah that dis-

tinguished Spanish Jewry. It characterized the proud grandee at
the royal Court, the Talmudic scholar in the hall of learning, the
philosopher meditating on the riddle of the universe, the scientist
measuring the stars or drawing his maps, the poet pouring out his
heart in human or divine love.\They were not satisfied merely to
posssess an awareness of Jewish identity or even a pride in their
Jewish background. As we have learned from the experience of
the last century, Jewish consciousness may be a source of bitterness and frustration, and Jewish pride is all too often an empty
and meaningless symbol. It was their personal cultivation of Jewish learning that kept them loyal.

The second great attribute of Spanish Jewry was *piety*. Spanish
Jews shared a personal commitment to Jewish law. In spite of
their close and intimate association with non-Jews, they held fast
to the Sabbath and the Festivals, the dietary laws, and the other
great practices of Judaism. By and large, the scholars at the universities, the ministers at the courts, and the generals in the field
were scrupulous in the performance of the Mitzvot. All the explanations, alibis, and excuses which we give nowadays for trampling Jewish observance under foot were available to them, but
they were not invoked to justify disobedience to the Torah.

The attachment to Jewish piety flowered in *Jewish morality*.
The Mitzvot include not only "the commandments between man
and God," but also "the commandments between man and man,"
ethics as well as morals. The ritual laws safeguarded the ethical
teachings and moral standards inculcated by Judaism. When we
read the history of medieval Spain we find the chronicle of the
courts, the nobility, and the clergy replete with incidents of conflict and treachery, immorality and cruelty perpetrated by the
ruling classes. Distinguished Jews, like Hasdai ibn Shaprut, Samuel
Hanagid, Judah ibn Ezra, and Samuel Halevi Abulafia, came into
close contact with all these manifestations of Spanish life. But
there was an invisible shield protecting them—their adherence to
Jewish ethical teaching. We do not hear many tales of Jewish
aristocrats practicing torture, treachery, drunkenness, and adultery,
which were rife in the courts of the Spanish kings, both Moslem
and Christian.

These three attributes of learning, piety, and morality produced a deep sense of unity with the Jewish people the world
over and an attachment to the land of Israel. Spanish Jews redeemed Jewish captives, intervened through diplomatic channels
on behalf of Jewish communities everywhere, and supported Jewish needs wherever they arose. They made it crystal clear that
the land of Israel was their spiritual center, the goal of all their
hopes.

We have surveyed the three great creative Jewish communities
which arose in the nineteen hundred years since the burning of
the Temple in Jerusalem and the exile of our ancestors by the
Romans. Closest in time is East European Jewry, whose passionate
and intensive loyalty to Judaism we must strive to recapture and
preserve. From German Jewry we should try to learn the secret
of openness to the world, so that Judaism may not merely be pre-
served as a dead fossil, but grow and put forth fruit like a living
tree. But it is in Spanish Jewry that we can hope to find the
innermost, life-giving secret. Here we may learn how to build integrated personalities in whom the Jew and the human being will
be in harmony with one another. Our goal, like theirs, must be
twofold—*to have the culture and civilization of the world enrich
the content of Judaism, and to have the faith and ethics of Judaism help to save the world.*

In every age authentic Judaism could be recognized by one outstanding characteristic—a deep sense of its distinctiveness. Every
generation of Jews was reminded by the Torah: *Hen 'am lebhadad
yishkon ubhagoyim lo' yithashabh (Numbers 23:9)*, "Behold a
people dwelling apart, not to be reckoned with the nations." Far
from obliterating this Jewish uniqueness, we should understand
it, accept it, and glory in it, making it our instrument for advancing the well-being of mankind. It is the duty, and not merely
the privilege, of the Jew to remember that he is a descendant of
the Prophets. He is called upon to proclaim to his fellow men
their sin, and to his brothers their transgression. Like Jonah in
the Bible, we are being sent to Nineveh, a city inhabited not only
by aliens but even by enemies, with a call to return to the fundamental principles of a truly human society.

There is, however, a wise and homely saying in the Talmud: *Keshot 'atzmèkha ve'ahar kach keshot 'aherim (Baba Metzia* 107b), "Correct yourself and then correct others." This saying has a deeper meaning as well. As we strive to heal others, we ourselves are healed. We have permitted our Jewish distinctiveness to be eroded, in order to conform, to run with the pack, to be in the swim, to keep up with the Joneses, without asking whether our keeping up with them is good either for them or for us.

How shall this Jewish distinctiveness express itself since we are not seeking to erect a wall against the world, but a window to let the air and the sunlight in? Spanish Jewry gives us the answer. We need to recapture the attributes of Jewish piety, Jewish learning, and Jewish morality.

V

This is the message of the threefold blast of the *Shofar* this day. We need to recapture a vivid sense of the presence of our Father, our King, who has made us, His children, the instruments for the fulfillment of His will. We must demonstrate our love and loyalty to Him by our lives and actions, by raising the level of our Jewish practice at home and abroad, in the Temple and in the school, on the Sabbath and on the Festivals.

We must also dedicate ourselves anew to Jewish learning. The German historian Leopold von Ranke declared that Jews are "the most historical of nations." We need to remember the past, not in the spirit of blind ancestor-worship or self-deluding nostalgia, but because the past is prelude to the future. A Jewishly ignorant community is not only a dying community; it is far worse, it is unworthy of life.

The Jew has left behind no monuments of stone, no temples or triumphal arches. Even the stone tablets that Moses carried were important only because of the words written upon them. *We are the people of the Book, and without the Book we are no people.*

No philanthropic contribution, no communal activity, can atone for or replace the greatest Jewish Mitzvah of learning. The

millions we pour out for hospitals and old age homes, for inter-
faith relations and goodwill activities, praiseworthy as they may
be, will not avail to save us until we make Jewish education for
our children and Jewish learning for ourselves a major enterprise
of Jewish life.

Finally, we need to re-establish the principles and practices of
Jewish morality for ourselves and our children. We need the
courage to make it clear to ourselves and to them that we are indeed a unique people. Whatever may be fashionable elsewhere,
we must insist upon the traditional Jewish virtues. From their
earliest years our children and our grandchildren need to be
taught the Jewish code of conduct, of personal integrity, the love
of peace, the sense of justice, a feeling of compassion for all suffering humanity, a sense of responsibility to our fellow Jews. We
need the moral courage to resist the trends to drunkenness and
drug addiction that are regarded as signs of modernity, and we
must stigmatize them for what they are, as disgraceful. We need
to inculcate standards of personal modesty and chastity. We must
battle against the inroads of promiscuity and immorality, both
before marriage and outside of the marriage bond, for marriage
is *kiddushin*, "the state of holiness." When these evils raise their
heads among us, we need to say to ourselves and to those we love,
"This is not the Jewish way."

Will our adherence to these standards of Jewish learning, piety,
and morality guarantee our survival? The history of our people
makes it clear that we are not the sole architects of our destiny,
that mightier forces play upon us. Jewish communities as radically
different as those of Eastern Europe, Germany, and Spain all rose,
flourished, suffered, and died. But we have a right to hope that
America is different, that in the new and greater society of free
America this tragic end may not come upon us. But though we
cannot guarantee our physical survival, which lies in the lap of
the unborn future, we can make sure that our present will have
meaning and content, and that come what may, we shall face our
destiny with dignity and courage.

The task is great, but not insuperable. In the Book of *Nehemiah*
we are told that when our ancestors returned from the Babylonian

Exile and found themselves a tiny Jewish island in a great sea of enemies, the redoubtable Jewish governor, Nehemiah, commanded the building of the city wall. The task loomed as impossible for the small, dispirited Jewish community. But Nehemiah was not daunted. He issued orders that each man was to build only a tiny section of the wall, *'ish neged beito* (*Nehemiah* 7:3), "each man opposite his own house." When each householder had erected his own rampart, the city of Jerusalem was safe.

Let us each resolve to build our threefold citadel of Jewish piety, Jewish learning, and Jewish morality. Like all that is best in the world, let us begin at home. Then, in truth, we shall be worthy of being inscribed by our Heavenly Father *besefer hayyim tobhim,* "in the book of a good life."

XI

The Perils of Victory

In a few moments we shall all rise and listen intently to the blasts of the Shofar. It is perhaps the oldest musical instrument still in use, difficult to blow, harsh in its sound, and limited in its range. Yet no other musical instrument, however mellifluous, can speak with equal power to the heart of the Jew, for it spans the ages. In its quavering notes we hear the *Shofar shel mattan Torah,* the ram's horn that was sounded on Sinai at the giving of the Torah, man's charter of humanity. And in its triumphant sounds we have a forecast of the great *Shofar shel mashiach,* the clarion that will be sounded at the end of time, proclaiming the great redeemer who will bring freedom to Israel, justice and peace to the world.

This Messianic faith has been one of the great fundamentals of Judaism for twenty-five centuries and more. The Prophets and Sages, the mystics and philosophers, the heroes and martyrs, as well as the masses of the people, interpreted its Messianic ideal in various forms. But they held fast to the faith that all history was moving to a Divinely ordained goal, when Israel would be restored to its homeland and all mankind would attain to justice, freedom, and peace.

Who can fathom the ways of Providence? Assuredly, the Messiah has not yet come, but our generation, far beyond its power to deserve, has been privileged to witness the *'athalta dige'ulah,* "the beginnings of the redemption," the footsteps of the Messiah. It

141

was in the modern age that at least one authentic prophet arose. His name was Theodor Herzl, the founder of the Zionist movement. When Herzl died of a broken heart at forty-four in 1904, Zionism was the chimerical dream of a handful of enthusiasts, and its goal seemed further away from realization than ever. Yet before his death Herzl declared that within half a century he foresaw the establishment of a Jewish State in Palestine. Forty-four years later, in 1948, the independent State of Israel came into being. In 1966, through the grace of God, Israel marked its *Chai* anniversary—its eighteenth year of life.

The Passover Haggadah tells us that several ancient rabbis spent the entire Seder night until dawn recounting the miracles associated with the redemption of our ancestors from Egypt. This entire day would not suffice if we sought to describe the miracles heaped upon miracles that constitute the creation, defense, and achievement of the State of Israel during these eighteen eventful years.

Merely to list the various elements in the progress of Israel is breath-taking. Two million Jews have been saved from death, discrimination, and degradation, and are today free and upstanding citizens of the State of Israel. The *Luftmensch* of the ages, the Jew who had no roots anywhere, who was accused of lacking the capacity for honest labor, has demonstrated his creative gifts and has produced a flourishing civilization almost overnight, in commerce, industry, and agriculture, in science and in technology. After two thousand years of neglect, the land of Israel has begun to blossom like the rose. In the words of Solomon Goldman, "The land without a people waited for the people without a land."

With the revival of the soil has come the rebirth of the Jewish soul. The Hebrew language, one of the most ancient of human tongues, has taken its place among the most modern of languages, capable of serving all the needs of literature, journalism, art, music, scholarship, and scientific research.

All this would be miracle enough even if it were not true that, poised on the borders of the State of Israel, there are five enemy nations, with a population twenty times as large, who make no secret of their determination to destroy the State of Israel root and branch, and drive its inhabitants into the sea.

It is no wonder, therefore, that this extraordinary progress has been accompanied by a series of major problems not yet solved. In the economic sphere, the government is wrestling with the difficulties of inflation. Unemployment, though slight, is a cause of growing concern. The standard of living is far higher than Israel can afford. Thus tourism has become a major industry, bringing sixty million dollars annually into the country. Yet the Israelis spend forty million dollars annually on travel abroad!

Integration is another basic problem. Today over 50% of the Israeli population come from the Oriental countries where Jews were kept in medieval subjection. The human material is excellent, but it will take time, skill, and patience to build the various fragments of the house of Israel from the East and the West into one vigorous and progressive nation.

Finally, the status of religion in Israel is a chronic problem, which grows increasingly more acute. There is a great chasm between the minority, which calls itself Orthodox, and the vast majority, which is at times hostile, and generally indifferent, to the religious heritage of Judaism.

Far worse than the problems are the perils confronting the State of Israel. The worst, already referred to, is the Arab threat. Bitterly divided among themselves, with no genuine unity among them, the Arab dictators and monarchs have only one slogan in common, one shibboleth, "Death to Israel!" which they trot out instead of confronting problems at home. It is therefore a matter of life or death for the State of Israel to expend a tremendous portion of its national income and its human resources on defense.

When the day comes that Israel and its Arab neighbors are able to replace the present uneasy armistice by a genuine peace, the entire Middle East will begin to flourish. Until that day dawns, the Arab menace is a major threat that cannot be lost sight of for an instant.

Thus the State of Israel is an extraordinary amalgam of progress, problems, and perils, but the greatest danger of all is both more subtle and more far-reaching. The Talmud tells us that while our ancient sages looked forward passionately to the advent of the Messiah, several of the scholars were wont to say, *Yetei vela' 'ahminei*, "May he come and I not see him!" (*B. Sanhedrin*

98b). Why this reluctance to see the Messiah? In part this may be
due to the Jewish tradition that declares that before the advent
of the Messianic age there will be *habhlei mashiah,* "the birth-
pangs of the Messiah," a period of chaos, war, and mass suffering.
But the rabbis in their wisdom may have had another reason. It
seems to be a law of life that anticipation is always more thrilling
than realization. The dreams which men conjure up are always
more glorious than the reality that follows. The ancient psalmist,
looking forward to the redemption of his people, had declared:
Beshubh Hashem 'et shibhat tziyyon hayinu keholemim, "When
the Lord restores the captivity of Zion, we shall be as dreamers"
(*Psalm* 126:1). Yet in the very hour when the dream has become
a reality, the Jewish future is more uncertain than ever before.
For the first time in nineteen hundred years of exile, world Jewry
as a whole is in danger of being stripped of the loyalty and unity
that kept it alive. In the very moment of national triumph, the
Jewish people is confronted by the spectres of degeneracy, decay,
and death.

Nineteen hundred years ago the Temple was destroyed by the
Romans, the city of Jerusalem was leveled to the ground, and
our ancestors were scattered over the face of the globe. Persecuted,
expelled, robbed, and massacred again and again, our ancestors
carried everywhere the double shield of unity and loyalty. There
were, to be sure, minor variations in the status of Jews in the
various lands of the Dispersion, but basically they felt themselves
to be *'ahim letsarah,* "brothers in affliction, comrades in adversity."
Because they shared the sense of a common destiny, extraordinary
human qualities emerged in them which helped to safeguard their
present and assure their future. In the words of a contemporary
editorial writer: "Even war and depression, for all their horror,
tend to bring out in sharp relief the human values of individual,
family and national integrity, of liberty and other things worth
living and dying for. On the other hand, their absence tends
toward discontent, disillusion and undue self-absorption. Perverse
it is that the achievement, in large measure, of the goals for which
men have striven through the ages brings its own disenchantment
with the achievements. For such time as material fortune smiles,

then, what is to replace adversity to solace the soul?" (*Wall Street Journal*, December 31, 1964).

The sense of a *common destiny* was re-enforced by the sharing of a *common legacy*. Jews everywhere, in Europe, Asia, and Africa, under the heel of the oppressor or in relative freedom and security, had a tradition that they cherished in common. In Solomon Schechter's fine phrase, all Jews possessed "a portable fatherland," the Torah. Wherever the Jew might go, he was at one with his brethren, with his way of life, with his tradition. Physically the Jew might be in exile, but spiritually he was at home everywhere.

Two centuries ago, with the rise of the Enlightenment and the advent of the French Revolution, there came the Emancipation. Jews were now permitted to leave their ghettos and become citizens of the various lands of their sojourning. The unity and loyalty which had bound them together were now shattered for many and weakened for most Jews. The modern world, with its blandishments, opportunities, and temptations, dealt Jewish loyalty and unity a body blow, but it did not succeed in destroying them completely. Even now, enough remained to keep the sense of Jewish consciousness alive in the hearts of most members of the Jewish people. Weaklings, traitors, and careerists deserted their people, in goodly numbers to be sure, but most Jews cherished the sense of Jewish identity in their hearts.

> Loyalty—where can it be found
> And what is the source of unity?

The first of these factors making for Jewish unity and Jewish consciousness was *anti-Semitism*. The Hebrew writer Peretz Smolenskin had spoken of *mastemat 'olam le'am 'olam,* "an eternal hatred for an eternal people." In the modern age massacres were barbarous, medieval, out-of-date, or so it seemed. Instead, anti-Semitism became scientific and spoke in the name of race and blood. It became genteel and took on the forms of economic disability, academic discrimination, and social exclusion. In addition, various sensational cases stretching throughout the nineteenth century, beginning with the Damascus Affair in 1840 and ending with the Dreyfus Case in 1894, served to remind all

Jews that they shared a special destiny which linked them to their brothers everywhere.

Then came the high point of anti-Semitism in the twentieth century, the foulest depth of human degradation: Nazi mass brutality. The free world stood by unconcerned in the face of Hitler's systematic campaign of extermination, in which he all but succeeded in sending to their death six out of seven Jews on the European continent. But as Nazism tortured and murdered six million Jews physically, it served to revive the Jewish spirit of millions of other Jews, making them conscious of their identity, and sending many of them back on a voyage of rediscovery of their heritage.

Today anti-Semitism is no longer respectable. While pockets of prejudice, discrimination, and ill-will still remain everywhere, anti-Semitism is universally recognized as the hallmark of the beast, the prelude to tyranny and mass destruction. As a result, the battle against anti-Semitism no longer creates Jewish loyalty and unity that can safeguard the Jewish future.

At the farthest possible remove from the dark force of Jew-hatred is the bright, shining light of *Zionism*. For seven decades and more, the Zionist ideal has brought to Jews of all backgrounds and outlooks a new sense of purpose, direction, and hope. Zionism has quickened every aspect of Jewish life. It stimulated the rebirth of the Hebrew language; it produced a new and significant literature; it revitalized Jewish education; it created Jewish music and the dance. Many of us in our childhood remember the blue boxes of the Jewish National Fund, the Tag Days and Flower Days, when we would go into the subways and in the streets and ask for the gifts of our fellow men, to help redeem the land of Israel for the people of Israel.

As the Balfour Declaration was issued and the Jewish community in Palestine began taking on more and more of the lineaments of a people, Zionists developed a far-flung political activity in the United States and in the United Nations, which brought to untold numbers of Jews a sense of Jewish self-fulfillment.

Then came the tragic yet heroic days of struggle against British tyranny in Palestine. Many Jews were caught up in the thrilling work of supplying men, means, and matériel for the Haganah, the Irgun, and the Stern group, who differed violently among themselves but were united in the contention that Jews had to fight the enemy in order to survive. When an American rabbi, Dr. Abba Hillel Silver, addressed the United Nations in an eloquent plea that led to the creation of an independent Jewish state, it was Zionism's shining hour.

Now the State of Israel is a reality, jealous of its prerogatives, independent in its policy, as it should be. Zionist organizations in the United States and throughout the world continue to perform very valuable, indeed indispensable, functions for the State of Israel. But the *élan* of Zionism is gone, its dynamism, its sense of ever widening horizons, of ever loftier goals. In a word, the most dynamic movement in modern Jewish life has become another organization.

> Loyalty—where can it be found
> And what is the source of unity?

In weary or cynical moments one is tempted to say that American Jewish life is overorganized. The truth is that, with few exceptions, these various causes in the fields of civic defense, culture, education, rehabilitation, and philanthropy are among the most positive aspects of contemporary life. Jewish life would be infinitely poorer without them. Yet all these organizations, valuable as they are—ZOA, Hadassah, B'nai B'rith, ORT, the American Jewish Congress, the National Council of Jewish Women—do not create a reservoir of Jewish loyalty; they draw upon it. The difference is fundamental. It makes all the difference in the world whether the resources in one's bank account are growing through deposits or are being diminished through withdrawals. Neither anti-Semitism nor Zionism nor organizational activity can generate Jewish loyalty and unity.

Neither anti-Semitism nor Zionism nor "organizational activity" is sufficient to safeguard Jewish loyalty and unity in the future. But is there not something new and glorious that has been added to the arsenal of Jewish survival? Ours is the first generation that has witnessed an independent Jewish state, that has shared in its

rebirth, and that can take pride in the roster of its achievements.
Cannot the State of Israel supply the *sam hahayyim,* the elixir of
life, the double shield of loyalty and unity? This was the hope,
nay, the conviction of the creators of Zionism, like Herzl and
Ahad Ha'am, who differed on so many other issues.

Unfortunately, the reality is different from the vision. In Israel
a secular society is developing which prevails in the government,
in culture, and in all other sectors of national life. To be sure, the
leaders of the Orthodox political parties are able to extract various
concessions from the government. Nevertheless, the chasm between them and the mass of the population continues to grow.
Most Israelis, confronted with only two choices—medieval religion
on the one hand, and no religion on the other—choose the second
alternative. Most Israelis find Talmudic law as interpreted by the
Israeli rabbinate highly unattractive. Traditional Judaism is associated in their minds with the *Galut,* the Exile, that the Israelis
are struggling to forget as though it had never been. Even so
scholarly a Jewish leader as David Ben-Gurion does not hesitate
to say: "We who have come to settle in the Jewish state have
taken a leap in time which makes us feel closer to David, Uzziah,
and Joshua bin Nun than to the *shtetl* in Cracow or to the nine-
teenth-century ideologists of Warsaw."

It is no wonder that the sense of unity binding the Israelis to
world Jewry is slight and gives every indication of growing slighter.
Studies of the behavior pattern of Israeli college students in the
United States and elsewhere demonstrate that they often prefer
to fraternize with Christian rather than with Jewish fellow students. This is not due to a perverse streak in their character. The
eighteenth anniversary of the State of Israel reminds us that an
entire generation has now grown to maturity who never lived
anywhere else but in Israel, or under any other system of government but that of Israel's independence. It is not that they are
consciously seeking to remove their sense of unity with their
brothers—they never possessed it. Commenting on the passage in
Deuteronomy (4:25) in which Moses exhorts the Jewish people to
remain faithful to God, one of the commentators puts these words
in the mouth of the great leader: "I am not worried about the

fathers who experienced slavery and beheld the works of God and His miracles. It is for their children who never knew the iron of slavery and the miracle of redemption, since they were born in freedom, that I am concerned" (*Hazkuni ad locum*).

Today most Israelis declare that the Jewish religion may be needed by the Jews in the Diaspora who have nothing else, but is superfluous for Israel, where Hebrew culture is pervasive, vital, and creative.

Moreover, what is there in Jewish life in the United States to lead them to change their opinion, to stimulate them to a new sense of unity with their brothers? What is there in the Jewish religion as practiced in America to attract them to a new feeling of loyalty to Judaism? Israelis respect the achievements of American, British, or South African Jews in business and industry, in science and technology, and even in literature, music, and art. They are happy for the economic support that the Jews of the Diaspora are giving the State of Israel in greater or lesser measure. But Israeli visitors find the level of Jewish knowledge, the character of Jewish education, and the quality of Jewish religious life in the United States abysmally low. They see little sense of commitment to Jewish living on the part of Jewish leaders and of the Jewish masses who are loud in proclaiming that they are "good Jews."

At the risk of oversimplification the situation may be described as follows: *Our brothers in Israel have everything Jewish but religion. The Jews of the Diaspora have nothing Jewish but religion, and of that, much is empty and superficial.*

> Loyalty—where can it be found
> And what is the source of unity?

Is there not one last factor left, perhaps the most important, linking Israel and world Jewry: the sense of kinship, the ties of family and ethnic loyalty? Are we not all the children of Abraham, Isaac, and Jacob? The Jews of Israel have relatives throughout the world whose pride in the State of Israel is strengthened by the feeling that we are not only members of one people, but of one *mishpahah*. Even in this day of dissolving loyalties, family kinship is still a mighty factor, thank God, among Jews.

Without question, this is a powerful force for which we may be grateful. But as each succeeding anniversary of the State of Israel comes, this element will play a less significant role. Consider two brothers leaving Czarist Russia in 1905. One becomes a pioneer in Israel, the other comes to the United States. A strong bond of affection links them together across the expanse of distance. Their children are first cousins to each other, still conscious of the bond of blood uniting them. The children of these children are cousins of the second degree; the next generation, of the third. After a few decades the sense of kinship will be largely dissolved.

It is therefore no figment of a morbid imagination that raises grave questions about the unity of the Jewish people and its loyalty to the Jewish heritage in the years that lie ahead. If these fears were to be realized, it would be a calamity for all. The prophet called the Jewish people *'am 'olam,* which means both "an eternal people" and "a world people." If our unity and loyalty were to disintegrate, we would cease to be both.

It would be a tragedy for our Israeli brothers. The State of Israel would become a small Levantine nation, clinging precariously to a thin strip of land along the Mediterranean coast, surrounded by an Arab world and limited in its perspectives and in its capacity for service. Its impact upon the civilization of the world would be no greater than that of the Bulgarians, the Iraqis, or even the Egyptians. If this were to come to pass, the State of Israel would demonstrate the truth of the sardonic observation that nothing fails like success.

And it would be a tragedy for the Jews of the Diaspora, who would cease to be *'am 'olam,* "an eternal people." For we would have no incentive to creativity, no confidence in the future, and we would be doomed to rapid decay and ultimate destruction.

It is late but, fortunately, not yet too late to rebuild the unity and universality of the Jewish people. We still have the power to make the miracle of the establishment of the State of Israel not a prelude to disaster, but a preface to greatness.

As our brothers in Israel observe with us the two days of Rosh Hashanah they, too, will be listening to the sounds of the Shofar. God grant that both they and we penetrate to its threefold message.

The *Malkhuyoth*, which proclaim the sovereignty of God, stress *the centrality of religion* in the constellation of Jewish life. Our brothers in Israel, both the so-called religious groups and the non-religious elements, need to recognize the true role of religion in Jewish life. Those who adhere with scrupulous fidelity to the great observances of the Jewish religion have all too often forgotten the great ethical principles and religious ideals which underlie the ceremonial. Concerned with ritual minutiae, they engage in political jockeying and are content to suppress freedom of thought so long as they preserve their preferential position.

There are, to be sure, great reservoirs of health in Israeli Orthodoxy. In the spring of 1966 Dr. Ephraim Urbach, Professor of Talmud at the Hebrew University, a staunch Orthodox Jew and a man of scrupulous ethical character and great learning, organized an all-inclusive movement called *Yahadut lema'an Hatorah,* "a Judaism for the Torah." Its purpose was to create a nonpolitical religious group dedicated to Judaism that would welcome all who accept the authority of the Torah, allowing each man freedom of interpretation. In spite of the violent barrage of attack and calumny let loose upon him, one cannot permanently halt an idea whose hour has come.

Reform, too, has a part to play in Israel. Having established a foothold in Israel, Reform, quite properly, is demanding fair and equal treatment from the government. Nonetheless, the basic defect of Reform, its surrender of the authority of Jewish law, is highlighted in Israel even more strongly than elsewhere. For Israeli Jews, and indeed for any Jew who is at home in the Jewish tradition, Judaism without law is not authentic Judaism.

If the vast majority of Israeli Jews are to rediscover the Jewish religion, it is Conservative Judaism that can achieve this goal, because it alone combines loyalty to Jewish tradition with responsiveness to the modern world. Judaism can live only if it recognizes that tradition is nothing cut and dried, but a dynamic process of interaction between the past and the present, between the heritage of the ages and the insights and needs of the age.

For a decade and a half, outstanding Israeli leaders have both publicly and privately called upon Conservative Judaism to establish itself in the homeland. They have been confident that they would find an echo in the lives and hearts of large numbers of Israeli Jews who wish to strike roots in the Jewish religion without being transplanted into the arid wastes of isolationism, bigotry, and petrifaction.

Conservative Judaism in Israel will obviously not be a copy of the movement in America. It will, however, share the two great fundamental principles of Conservatism: *Growth is the law of life, and the law is the life of Judaism.* The half dozen Conservative congregations already in existence in Israel need to be increased. American Jews send tractors and medicines, technical knowledge, and scientific skills to Israel, along with vast financial assistance. If we believe in the vitality and value of the Jewish religion, we must be prepared to offer financial assistance to the struggling groups of Conservative Jews in Israel. We need to send some of our ablest rabbis to guide and direct them and give them the assurance that they are not alone in the battle to build a meaningful and vital Judaism in twentieth-century Israel.

The *Malkhuyot,* which proclaim the centrality of the Jewish religion, speak not only to our brothers in Israel, but also to us in America, with equal force. We must undertake to revitalize the Jewish religion for ourselves. The period of feverish building in America which produced the so-called "edifice complex" is apparently over. Dotting the country are resplendent structures, often with equally imposing mortgages, and frequently lacking both people and content within their walls. These structures are not to be despised. They are symbols of the basic pride that Jews take in their heritage, of which they know so little. They are evidence of the sense of at-homeness that Jews feel in America and of their desire to attract their children and children's children to their heritage.

Today we cannot content ourselves with contributions, however liberal, or with membership lists, however extensive. We need

a campaign of personal commitment to Jewish learning and Jewish living in concrete, visible, and contentful form on the part of
individual Jewish men, women, and young people. Notice that I
did not say "Jewish belief," because faith cannot be commanded;
it must grow in the human soul. But as Salvador de Madariaga
said, "Belief in God means to desire His existence and to act as
though He existed." Every one of us, even the Jew who believes
that he does not believe, can therefore share in the rebirth of the
Jewish religion.

Obviously, the revitalization of Judaism cannot happen overnight, but the longest journey starts with a single step. If one Jew
out of five in the United States were to undertake to add one
significant Jewish *mitzvah* to his regimen of life at the New Year
season, one observance, whether it be daily prayer, however
brief, or regular synagogue attendance on the Sabbath, the restoration of the Sabbath and Festival spirit in the home, how the
level of Jewish experience would be raised! If he were to set aside
two hours a week for Jewish reading and study, it would give
meaning and content to the Jewish existence of a million men
and women. How the quality of Jewish life in the entire American
Jewish community would be lifted! What a new sense of meaning
the Jewish tradition would take on! It would justify all the blood,
sweat, and tears, and the sacrifice of time, strength, and substance
now expended on Jewish life!

The Shofar will also sound the *Zikhronot,* the Memorials recalling the pageantry of history as traced in the Bible. Here is a
call to rediscover the richness of our culture, addressed both to
Israeli Jewry and to us. For our Israeli brethren it means that they
cannot blot out the nineteen centuries of Galut as though they
had not been, for nothing in life is meaningless. There can be no
blank page between the Bible and Chaim Weizmann, between the
destruction of the Temple by the Romans and the establishment
of the State of Israel. The nineteen hundred years of exile were
marked by tragedy and defeat, to be sure, but that was not their
dominant characteristic. There were ages of great heroism, both
passive and active, as a tiny, scattered, and defenseless people was
able to outlast its tormentors and retain its humanity in the face

of brutality. These were centuries marked by great creativity which immeasurably broadened the horizons of Torah. Poetry and philosophy, history and science, philology and law—all these entered the treasure house of Judaism during the period of the Exile.

Perhaps the greatest achievement of the long centuries of the Exile was the fashioning of Jewish character, the building of *Yiddishe menshlichkeit,* the Jewish personality, marked by *sekhel* and *rahmanut,* by understanding and compassion, by courage and patience, by insight and faith. The Jew at his best understood his fellow men, and yet loved them. He was aware of their human weakness, but never despaired of them and retained a sense of responsibility for them. He was clearly aware of the frustrations of life, and yet he loved and held fast to it.

These qualities are reflected not only in profound masterpieces or great men. They find expression also in simple tales drawn from the wells of Jewish humor. During the days of the First World War the Jews of Galicia, who were Austrian subjects, were impressed into the Austro-Hungarian army. In a small Galician village two friends, Shmuel and Hayyim, were drafted. While Hayyim remained a private, Shmuel became a corporal and was bedecked in a resplendent uniform with shining brass buttons, boots, and epaulets. One day, as Shmuel was walking down the main street of the village, Hayyim met him and greeted him as always. Shmuel was offended at his friend's casual manner, and said to him, "Hayyim, don't you see I am a corporal in the Austro-Hungarian army—Why don't you salute me?" Hayyim looked at his friend and said, *Zog mir, Shmuel, kein gressere dayges hostu nit?* "Tell me, Shmuel, you have no greater worries than this?" How this simple tale cuts through the swagger and pretense of military glory! How it understands men's weaknesses and loves them! How deep is its comprehension of life, infinitely precious for all its limitations!

The *Zikhronot* sound the call to our Israeli brothers to know and to cherish Jewish culture in all its fullness, the achievements of Jewish genius through the ages, and the qualities of Jewish personality which are our precious heritage from the past. If *they* need a deeper awareness of the content of Jewish culture, how much greater is the call *for us* in America to undertake in earnest the study of the Hebrew language, the Bible, Rabbinic literature, Jewish history, literature and thought?

A century and a half ago, the English critic Sydney Smith said, "Poverty is no disgrace, but it is damned inconvenient." Regarding ignorance, which the rabbis describe as *'aniyut hada'at,* "poverty of the mind," we may say that it is a disgrace, and dangerous to boot. Cheating our fellow man is a crime, but cheating ourselves is a cardinal sin. It is time that we stopped going through the motions of giving our children any kind of makeshift Jewish education, fragmentary, short-lived, lacking in content, approach, or dedication. If we worry why our children shake off so easily the remnants of Jewish loyalty, why they wander into the morass of alienation and defection, and often fall prey to intermarriage and total estrangement, the reason is not far to seek. We are content to keep them ignorant of Judaism in an adult sense, treating our rich heritage, which was created by men of profundity and genius, as though it were a pastime for youngsters. As a result, when our children outgrow childhood, they put away childish things.

Jewish ignorance has always been a threat to Jewish survival. Today it has taken on a new and more dangerous form. For in the past the *'Am Ha'aretz,* the Jewish ignoramus, was bereft of general culture as well. As a result, within the limits of his capacity, he deferred to those more knowledgeable than he. Today the Jewish *'Am Ha'aretz,* in increasing measure, possesses a substantial degree of general culture, since Jews are flocking to colleges in unprecedented numbers. American Jewry already possesses the highest percentage of college graduates of any group in America. In 1919 there were 15,000 Jewish college students. Today the figure is 300,000. By 1970, it will rise to 400,000. On the other hand, a survey showed that only 17% of the Jewish students of one college could identify the name of the holiday with which the Maccabees are associated, and only 16% could name three of the prophets.

This well-educated, self-assured generation of our youth con-

the light of general culture, about which it knows a good
or thinks it does—with the dark obscurity of Jewish culture,
which it knows little or nothing. Our youth then draw the
natural, though totally mistaken, conclusion that general culture
is contentful and Jewish culture is meaningless.

At the same time, a thousand subtle, and not so subtle, influences play upon our youth, urging them to surrender, or at
least to minimize, their Jewishness. Is it any wonder that alienation and desertion from the Jewish community are on the increase?
The emphasis must be placed where it rightfully belongs, upon
the education of our adolescents and young people. We need to
remind ourselves that adults are teachable. He who persists in
Jewish ignorance testifies to the truth of the comment of our
sages on a passage in *Deuteronomy: Ki lo dabhar reik hu' mikkem
—Ve'im reik hu' mikkem hu' reik,* "It is not an empty thing for
you—and if it be empty, it is because of you that it is empty"
(32:47).

A story is told of two American tourists who had heard of the
Mona Lisa in the Louvre as the most expensive painting in the
world. The tourists looked at the painting for a few moments and
then one said to his companion: "I don't know what people get
so excited about. I don't see much in it." A nearby guard overheard the remark and said, "Monsieur, that painting is no longer
on trial. The spectators are!"

Today there is no excuse for any Jew, however difficult the
conditions of his existence may have been earlier, to remain Jewishly uninformed. Schools, texts, and methods for the teaching
of the Hebrew language are available everywhere. A rich literature
in English now exists on every phase of Judaism, geared to every
level of understanding and written from every standpoint. The
opportunities for adult education under competent and even exciting auspices are to be found in hundreds of Jewish communities today throughout the land.

The *Malkhuyot* are a clarion call to revive our faith. The
Zikhronot summon us to remember our culture. The third call of
the Shofar, the *Shofarot*, challenges us and our brothers in Israel
to ethical action. We must measure up to our role as "the wit-

nesses of God," in the words of the ancient prophet; as "warriors on the battlefield of humanity," as a modern poet put it. The entire thrust of Jewish history declares that Israel cannot live for itself alone. For this is the destiny promised to our father Abraham, *Venibhrekhu bekha kol mishpehot ha'adamah.* "In thee shall all the families of the earth be blessed."

The *Shofarot* join the past and the future, linking Torah to the Messianic age. Israel may always remain a small nation, but it need not be a petty one. Our brothers in the homeland can be united through time with all the Jewish generations of the past, and through space with millions of their brothers throughout the world. American Jews and their brethren throughout the Diaspora need not live in fear of decay or in terror of extinction, if we remember that we are the bearers of great ideals and truths for mankind. Together with our brothers in Israel we can labor to help usher in justice, freedom, and peace for all men, races, and nations. We shall be not merely the descendants of the prophets, but the fulfillers of their word, the instruments of God's cause, the builders of human brotherhood.

The philosopher Friedrich Nietzsche once said: *Was mich nicht umbringt macht mich staerker,* "What does not destroy me makes me stronger." From the trials of this age we can emerge stronger than ever before, with meaning in our lives and purpose for our actions. Our goal is not merely our survival, but our service to mankind through the nobility and the wisdom of the Torah. For our work will not be done until the prophetic word is fulfilled, with which every Jewish worship service ends: *Vehayah Hashem lemelekh 'al kol ha'aretz,* "The day will surely come when the Lord shall be king over all the earth. On that day the Lord shall be one and His name one" (*Zechariah* 14:9).

MAN

XII

Why Do Men Suffer?

I

The long and solemn day of Yom Kippur begins in the evening with the unforgettable and haunting melody of the *Kol Nidre*. It will end with the majestic and awesome service of *Neilah*, as the sun begins to set in the western sky. Throughout the day there are many mountain peaks of experience, but towering above them all is the moving and poignant hour of *Yizkor*. Is it any wonder that when we recall the blessed image of those whom we have loved and lost, our eyes fill with tears and our hearts contract with pain?

In an hour such as this, we ask once again the immemorial question, "Why?" Why were we given these blessings only to be robbed of them later? Why were we permitted to taste joy only to have the cup dashed from our lips? Why the fleeting happiness—and why the long agony of suffering?

It is here that we come up, each of us in his own time and way, against the greatest stumbling block to religion. It matters not whether we be poet or peasant, philosopher or man in the street, scholar or simpleton. The mystery of man's suffering is the rock upon which the ship of faith has foundered and crashed for untold men and women. It is because men experience disease and pain, death and bereavement, that so many of our fellow men have lost their faith in God and with it their sense of commitment to any command spoken in His name.

II

It is true that no one can prove the existence of God by a cast-iron logical demonstration, especially since even mathematical proofs rest upon an assumption of faith. But if we cannot "prove" God, *Q.E.D.*, the recognition of a Supreme Power of the universe is by far the most reasonable explanation of reality. God's essence is hidden from man; in the words of the Torah, *Panay lo yera'u,* "My face cannot be seen" *(Exodus* 33:23). But the signs of God's activity are everywhere to be discerned by the sensitive spirit in the world of life and of man. In "A Faith for Moderns," I have sought to present the grounds upon which those who believe in God base their faith that man does not stand alone in the universe.

First and foremost is the hand of God in nature. Observe the harmony and the pattern of the natural world as revealed by the telescope and the microscope. See the symmetry of structure in an atom, in a flake of snow, in the veins of a leaf on a tree. Consider the miracle of the human body with its limbs and organs so wonderfully made, or the intangible wonders of the human mind, with laws that we are now just beginning to learn. Recall the atomic blocks out of which the universe is built. Think of the vast reaches of space in the planetary system and of the long sweep of the evolutionary process from the one-celled amoeba to man.

When one observes the beauty and order of nature, it is difficult to see how anyone can refuse to see the workings of a great Intelligence creating and directing all. What modern science reveals in increasing measure, the ancient Hebrew Psalmist saw with his poetic insight: *Hashamayim mesapperim kevod 'El,* "The heavens proclaim the glory of God and the work of His hands the firmament reveals" *(Ps.* 19:2).

This is not all. The hand of God is revealed perhaps a little less clearly, but nonetheless significantly, in the processes of history. He who studies the experience of the human race, the rise and fall of empires, the slow but unmistakable progress of man from savagery through barbarism, to the first glimmerings of civilization and upward, can discern a movement, a goal, a law which presupposes a direction in the history of mankind. For, as the Biblical teachers first proclaimed to the world, there is a law of retribution in the universe: evil leads to catastrophe and righteousness to well-being. In the words of the Biblical Sage: *Be'ein hazon yippara 'am, veshomer torah 'ashrehu.* "Where there is no vision, the people perish, but he who keeps the law will be blessed" (*Proverbs* 28:18).

Finally, God reveals Himself not only in the world of nature about us, and in the history of the human race, but also in the nature of man. "What is man?" the Psalmist asked centuries ago, and the question has echoed down the centuries. What is this strange creature, shaped like his cousins, the apes, yet aspiring to the stars? He is, in Hazlitt's words, the one creature who can laugh and cry. He weeps because things are not what they should be; he laughs because they are better than they might be.

He is the one creature gifted with conscience and consciousness of self. He, and he alone of all living things, has a sense of right and wrong, however mistaken or perverted it may be. He, and he alone, is aware of his own existence. He, and he alone, knows that he lives and some day will die. In the priceless words of the opening chapter of the Torah, he is fashioned *betselem 'Elohim,* "in the image of God." However blurred and distorted the image may become, he is a reflection of God, in whom God's attributes are enshrined in some degree. It is the Divine in man which expresses itself in the hunger for righteousness, the search for truth, the love of beauty, and, above all, in the power to create, to fashion embodiments of justice, truth, and beauty.

We have, of course, only sketched in broadest outlines the evidence for God in nature, in history, and in man. It is this imposing body of evidence which impels the religious believer to declare: *'Adonai 'Elohei Yisrael melekh umalekhuto bakol mashalah,* "The Lord God of Israel is King, and His sovereignty is over all."

III

Yet all this impressive testimony, and there is much, much more, is often powerless to persuade the heart and convince the mind of men, because of one stark, naked fact in human experience—the mass of misery, the burden of pain, that comes to man.

It is noteworthy that the Bible does not argue the existence of God or seek to demonstrate it with logical proofs. This it takes for granted. The great burning issue is the problem of human suffering. To it, the greatest book in the Bible, the book of *Job*, was addressed; with it, the Torah and the Prophets wrestled; over it, the Psalmists and the Sages agonized.

To be sure, it is not suffering in general that is the problem. That sin should be punished, that the guilty should suffer, is no stumbling block to faith. It is the suffering of the innocent, or at least of the not guilty, that remains the mystery and the challenge.

To claim that we have the answer to this great and fundamental crux at the heart of the universe, that we have solved the mystery of the problem of man's suffering, would be an act both of folly and of conceit. For our Sages have spoken the wisest word on the subject: *'Ein beyadeinu lo' mishalvat haresha'im ve'af lo' miyis-surei hatsaddikim* (*Abot* 4:19), "It is not in our power to explain either the prosperity of the wicked or the suffering of the righteous."

Yet even if the full truth is not within our power to grasp, we are not on that account free from the obligation to seek to understand as much of the truth as we are able. The mysterious universe in which we live is a dark cavern through which we walk with only a lantern in our hand, the lamp of reason. We do not imagine that its light can banish all the darkness. But neither do we cast the lantern aside because it does not dispel all the shadows. We cherish it for whatever light it can shed. A wise faith goes beyond reason but it does not scorn reason or ignore it. On the contrary, we should use this most precious of gifts as far as it can take us. And this is further than we sometimes imagine. From what we understand of the known world, we can surmise something of the unknown. For we live in a *uni-verse,* not a *pluri-verse*—one world, governed by one God, under one great law, the embodiment of His will.

Santayana was right when he said: "It is not wisdom to be merely wise." But the obverse of the coin is equally important:

Bekhol derakhekha da'ehu, "In all thy ways, know Him" (*Proverbs* 3:6). Seek to know God in all your ways, with all the means at your disposal.

IV

There is a precious instrument available to us for grappling with this mystery. It is the *Mahzor,* the traditional prayer book for Rosh Hashanah and Yom Kippur. Rich in insight, it can shed light on the great and agonizing mystery of human suffering. It can help us to attain some understanding of God's plan and thus make it easier for us to believe in Him and find life worth living.

An instrument needs, however, to be understood and used properly. The prayer book is poetry—it suggests more than it declares. Its implications are more eloquent than any explicit statements would be. The great Maimonides pointed out that God and His nature cannot be expressed in human language, however exalted, precise, and philosophical. For our vocabulary, like all our ideas, derives from human contacts and human experience and belongs to an altogether different order of being from that of God. All that we can conceive of God, all that we can say and affirm about Him, is our own poor, human approximation, a weak effort to touch the hem of the garment of the Divine. We may talk of Him, but only by analogy, by comparison. These figures of speech are never perfect because they are always partial, but nonetheless they can prove very helpful.

If we remember that prayer is poetry, that its phrases hint at truths, that its metaphors can give us glimpses of the divine reality, our worship on Yom Kippur will not merely warm our hearts, but will also enlighten our minds. It will sustain our flagging spirits with faith and courage and hope.

V

Scattered through the pages of the *Mahzor* are some simple yet profound phrases which shed light on the mystery of mysteries. From these familiar words there emerges one great truth—*God's love is not disproved by man's suffering, for man's suffering is at times part of the process of God's love.*

First and foremost, we must disabuse ourselves of the notion that love is the same as kindness. When we ask, "If God loves us, why does He let us suffer?", what we are asking is not for *'Avinu shebashamayim,* "our Father in heaven," but, as C. S. Lewis points out, for a "grandfather in heaven"—a senile benevolence who "likes to see young people enjoying themselves" and whose plan for the universe is simply that it may be truly said at the end of each day, "A good time was had by all."

Love is not sentimentality, which is inverted cruelty, as the psychoanalysts have taught us. Love is not lawlessness. When a youngster drives a hot-rod at eighty miles an hour and crashes into a wall, it is no sign that God does not love His children. We cannot ask God to stop the car in its tracks, and by that token, destroy the world which is governed by the laws of momentum, gravitation, and impenetrability, all the principles that apply to the relations of physical objects.

Basically, *love means concern.* God cares too much for His children to be indifferent to what they are. He is deeply concerned in what they do, what they can be, and should be, and are not. It is from people we care nothing about that we expect nothing. We make demands on our friends, our family, our children. We would rather see them suffer than be happy in contemptible and unworthy ways.

Love means concern, and the greater the love, the more profound the concern. This truth is reflected on every level of love that we know, all of which is referred to in our Yom Kippur Service.

Perhaps the lowest type of love is that of an artist for his handiwork. On Kol Nidre Eve, we recite a *Piyyut* which is based on a passage in the Prophet *Jeremiah* (18:1): *Hinneh kahomer beyad hayotzer,* "For behold, we are as clay in the hand of the potter." To be sure, the analogy is not perfect. The clay in the hand of the potter, or the stone in the hand of the sculptor, has no feelings, as the craftsman chisels away, scrapes, and pounds at the raw material on which he is working. Now we can imagine that if the stone could speak, it might very well say: "Let me be as I am. You are hurting me with all this pounding. I am willing to dispense with the glory. Spare me the agony of the chisel and the hammer." But even if the stone could speak, the artist would not listen, for he would be driven on by a vision of what the shapeless mass could become. In fact, the higher the artist's goal, the more pains he would take, and the more pain he would inflict on the raw material. Thus if a painter makes an idle sketch to amuse a child, he dashes it off in a few minutes and lets it go at that. But if he is working on his masterpiece, years of toil and agony are not too high a price to pay.

Then there is another, a higher love, that of a man for a beast, which lives, feels pain, and elicits affection. The Bible speaks of God as our shepherd, *'Adonay ro'i lo 'ehsar*, "The Lord is my shepherd, I shall not want" (*Psalm* 23:1). On this day we repeat again and again *ki 'anu tsonekha ve'attah ro'enu*, "For we are Thy flock and Thou, our shepherd."

The Bible tells us that when Moses fled from the Egyptian court, he became a shepherd for Jethro in the wilderness. This incident is amplified by a beautiful Rabbinic tale. One day, Moses noticed a little lamb straying from the flock, running over hill and dale. He followed after it, until he saw it come to a spring, where it thirstily lapped up the waters. Tenderly he bent down and said, "Poor little lamb, you were thirsty and I did not know it. Now you must be tired. Let me carry you back to the flock." Whereupon God's voice was heard, proclaiming, "Moses, you are a loving shepherd, and are therefore worthy to be the shepherd of my people, Israel."

Man's love for an animal, for his dog, is a higher rung in the ladder of love than that of an artist for the raw material which is his handiwork. When a man loves his dog, he cleans it, washes it, and house-breaks it. He teaches it, and because he loves it, he wants to perfect it. Perhaps the dog might wish to be left alone, unspoiled and untrained, but because he is loved he cannot avoid being an object of concern to his master.

Much higher and much more meaningful is the love of a parent for his child. *'Abhinu Malkenu*, "Our Father, our King," we cry

out again and again, *ki 'anu bhanekha ve'attah 'Abhinu,* "For we
are Thy children, and Thou art our Father." Here the relationship is much more intimate and the concern correspondingly
greater. The father who cares for his child seeks to rear and educate him, to improve and elevate him. In the words of the Prophet,
"Habhen yakkir li 'Ephraim, 'im yeled sha'ashuim," Is not
Ephraim my beloved son, the child in whom I delight? Whenever
I am about to speak against him, I earnestly remember him. My
heart is moved for him; I shall surely have mercy upon him,
says the Lord" (*Jeremiah* 31:19). Yes, a father pities his son when
he suffers, but if he really loves him, he does not say, "I love him,
I don't care what becomes of him, I want to spare him any pain
at all cost. All I want is for him to be happy." *'Et 'asher ye'ehabh
Hashem yokhiakh ukhe'ab et ben yirtzeh* (*Proverbs* 3:12), "Whom
the Lord loves, He chastises, and speaks as a father with his son."

Are there quarrels between father and son? It is because the
father cares, because their destiny is linked together. We do not
get upset about those who mean nothing to us. To be sure, the
father's reproof may fail in its object, if the son proves resentful
and hostile and lacking in understanding. It succeeds in achieving
its purpose and working an improvement only if the son recognizes that these are *yissurim shel 'ahabhah,* "chastisements of love."
At the same time, they become easier for the child to bear.

The story is told of a rich *Hasid* who came to his rabbi, and said,
"Rabbi, all through my life I have tried to observe fully all the
commandments of the Torah, yet there is one obligation which
I have never been able to discharge with true inwardness of spirit
—the Talmudic command, *Hayyabh 'adam lebharekh 'al hara'
keshem shemebharekh 'al hatobhah* (*Ber.* 54a), 'A man is obligated
to thank God for evil as sincerely as he blesses Him for good.'
Teach me, rabbi, how I may fulfill this commandment." "Very
well," said the rabbi, "go to the other end of town to Hayyim,
the water-carrier, and he will teach you." The rich *Hasid* proceeded to obey the rabbi's instructions. He traveled to the slum
where Hayyim lived, and found him sitting in a hovel with his
poor, barefoot children all about him. "The Rabbi has sent me
to you in order that you may teach me how to fulfill the com-

mandment, 'A man is obligated to thank God for evil as sincerely as he does for all his blessings,' " said the rich *Hasid* to the poor hovel-dweller. "The Rabbi sent you to me?" said Hayyim. "I can't possibly understand why. I have never received anything but good from the Almighty!"

Finally, there is a still higher level of love, the most intimate in human experience, which also serves as an analogy for God's love for man. It is the love of a man and a woman. Who can forget the poignant words of the prophet Jeremiah (2:2), *Zakharti lakh hesed ne'urayikh, 'ahabhat kelulotayikh, lekhtekh 'aharay bamidbar be'eretz lo zeru'ah,* "I remember for you the love of your youth, the devotion of your bridal state, when you went after me in the wilderness, in a land unsown." Again and again we chant during this Yom Kippur day, *Ki 'anu rayatekha ve'attah dodenu,* "We are Thy beloved, and Thou art our Lover."

Where there is love, there is yearning for perfection. When we fall in love with a woman, do we cease to care whether she is clean or dirty, fair or ugly? Love may forgive infirmities and love in spite of them, but it never ceases to hope and pray for their removal. The true lover will cherish his beloved even when beauty is lost, but not *because* it is lost. On the contrary, it is the memory of beauty that sustains love when physical beauty is gone.

In the words of the beloved poem by Thomas Moore:

> Believe me, if all those endearing young charms,
>   Which I gaze on so fondly today,
> Were to change by tomorrow, and fleet in my arms,
>   Like fairy-gifts fading away,
> Thou wouldst still be adored, as this moment thou art,
>   Let thy loveliness fade as it will,
> And around the dear ruin each wish of my heart
>   Would entwine itself verdantly still.

God's love for His children is unique, and all other levels of love are far below it. But each sheds some light on the love of God which concerns itself with us and therefore brings us suffering as well as joy. God loves us with the persistence of an artist who seeks to fashion a masterpiece. He loves us with the insistence of a man

who loves his dog and wants him to be his companion. He loves
us with the wisdom of a wise and good father who suffers himself
and causes his son to suffer, so that he may attain to true manhood.
He loves us with the ardor of a lover who seeks the vision of per-
fection in his beloved.

VI

The suffering which comes to us may not make us better, but it reveals our unknown potential. It strips away the layers of convention, etiquette, and pretense and reveals us as we really are. Justice Felix Frankfurter put it in homely, pungent words: "Old age and sickness bring out the essential characteristics of a man, just as they bring it out in dogs, or so I'm told, as they grow older. Their basic psyche dominates. A gentle dog grows gentler, and a dog that is not gentle, though he might cover up his ungentleness, in his old age becomes a bad, mad dog."

Once we recognize the truth that man's suffering may often be the mark of God's concern and love, we may understand why it is the righteous who so often undergo this grueling experience. The rabbis in the Midrash declare, "A potter does not test defective vessels, because he cannot give them a single blow without breaking them. Similarly, God does not test the wicked but only the righteous, thus. 'The Lord tries the righteous.' " R. Jose Bar Hanina said: "When a flax-worker knows that his flax is of good quality, the more he pounds it the more it improves and the more it glistens; but if it is of inferior quality he cannot beat it at all without its splitting. Similarly, the Lord does not test the wicked, but only the righteous, as it says, 'The Lord tries the righteous.' "

There is one more fundamental question which will continue to agitate us: "Why does God concern Himself at all with man, to love him and to chastise him? Why not leave him alone?" Here is the mystery within the enigma—Why is it that all the creatures that God has created blindly obey their instincts, while one only— or one at least—was chosen by God for His concern? Perhaps we can glimpse part of the answer in the love of a man and a woman.

Their love is not an end in itself—for out of their love they create new life.

God's plan for the world would be incomplete without man. The process of ongoing creation needs the cosmic partnership of God and man. This vast universe came into being with the formation of untold heavenly bodies, stars, and planets, all incapable of supporting life. Finally, one small planet emerged, which became, as far as we know, the only environment where life is possible. Aeons passed—then the first glimmerings of life appeared. Millions of years more elapsed and myriad forms of life were now spawned on this planet. Finally, one day, one creature came into being with the capacity to think, to feel, to create, to love. From the first fashioning of matter to the emergence of man—a cosmic process and a cosmic purpose. Man is the bearer of God's purpose in the vast universe. God needs man as man needs God.

This truth the Midrash expresses with classic directness and simplicity: " ' 'Attem 'edai, ne'um Hashem, va'ani 'el.' Keshe'attem 'edai, 'ani 'el ukheshe'ein 'attem 'edai, 'eini, kebhayakhol, 'el." " 'You are My witnesses, saith the Lord' (Isaiah 43:12). When you are My witnesses, I am God, and when you are not My witnesses, I am, as it were, not God" (Midrash Psalms, ed. Buber, p. 255; Sifre, ed. Friedman, 144a and parallels).

Because God loves us, He cares. Because He cares, He strives to perfect us. Because He labors over us, we undergo trial and tribulation.

This is not the whole truth about man's suffering, which takes on untold forms. But this insight is an essential element in that truth, and it can help to sustain us in our tribulations. Let us hold fast to the lamp as we walk and we shall not fall prey to the darkness of disbelief and despair.

As we recall the sweet memories of our loved ones, let us pray, "Almighty Father, bring home to our hearts the thought of Thy wisdom and justice and of that fatherly love with which Thou dealest with all Thy children. Teach us to feel that in the Divine order of Thy Providence, life and death, joy and sorrow, serve equally beneficent ends, and that in the fullness of time we shall

know why we are tried, and why our love brings us tears as well
as highest happiness."

Through the goodness of God, we may attain courage in the
face of suffering. Thus we shall rise from our experience to ever
higher levels of being, and make ourselves worthy partners of God
in building His world—and ours.

XIII

Who Desires Life?

I

If we consult the great dictionaries of the English language, such as the unabridged Oxford or the one-volume Webster, we discover that English is a very rich tongue. It contains over half a million words, all neatly catalogued and precisely defined. After all the definitions are given, only a handful of words remain unexplained, but they are the most important: "Love, honor, faith, man, God." Perhaps the greatest mystery of all inheres in the words "life" and "death." That death is a mystery is no wonder, since it is an experience which none of us has yet undergone, a land from which no traveler has yet returned. But life, which is an experience which all of us know at first-hand, is equally difficult to explain.

Nevertheless, life is inexpressibly precious. Therein lies the powerful appeal of the High Holy Days to the heart of the Jew, modern and ancient alike. On Rosh Hashanah and Yom Kippur we pray for life to the Author of life, *zokhrenu lahayyim melekh hafetz bahayyim,* "Remember us for life, O King, desirous of life." On these Days of Awe we become conscious of what we should never have forgotten—life is perilously uncertain and our destiny is in the hand of God: *Berosh hashanah yikkathebhun, uveyom tsom Kippur yehatemun . . . mi yihyeh umi yamut mi bekitzo umi lo' bekitzo,* "On Rosh Hashanah man's destiny is inscribed and on the Day of Atonement it is sealed—who is to live,

173

who is to die; who at his timely end, and who in an untimely hour."

Yet, paradoxical as it may seem, it is not God who really has the power to determine who shall live or die. Yes, if we define life purely in terms of biological processes, the breathing of our lungs, the beating of our hearts, the coursing of the blood in our veins—that aspect of life is not in our hands but in God's. But these biological processes are not life. They spell only mere existence, whether we call it animal being or vegetating.

For man, life must mean much more, or it is worthless. Not every man is a philosopher like Plato, who declared: "An unexamined life is intolerable for man." But every human being would agree that life must have some meaning, or at least a measure of satisfaction, if it is to be worth having. It is not enough to pray merely for more pages to tear off from the calendars of the passing years. Of our father Abraham, the Torah tells us that he died *zaken usebha' yamim,* "old and satisfied with days." Of this double blessing, part is within God's power to bestow and part within ours to achieve. It is God to whom we must pray for length of days—it is we who must fill them with abiding satisfaction.

II

Our Sages understood the great truth that there are many who walk the earth, who breathe and talk and eat and sleep, who are not really alive. And so they declared, *Arba'ah hashubhim kemethim, 'ani, summa, metzora' umi she'ein lo banim (Avodah Zarah* 5b), "Four are considered as though they were dead: the poor, the blind, the leper, and he who has no children."

When the ancient rabbis spoke of poverty, they meant, of course, the kind of grinding want which few of us experience today in our affluent western society. But we need not go back to ancient times for examples. There are the millions who scramble for a tiny piece of ground on which to sleep in India. There are untold hundreds of thousands who are born, live, and die on the sampans and junks, the rat-infested boats that fill the foul-smelling rivers and streams of China, which I saw in 1946. There are the billion and more human beings on this globe, one out of every three living creatures, who never go to bed free from the symptoms of chronic hunger. To our wise and compassionate Sages, these poor are to be reckoned as dead. Indeed, they are far worse, for they are the tinder-box out of which revolution and war and epidemic are ignited that threaten to destroy the human race. They are dead and they spread death and devastation.

Even in our own prosperous country, the slums that disfigure our great cities, the shanty-towns of the countryside, the filth and squalor of parts of the South, all testify that poverty is by no means gone even from the richest land on the face of the globe. And how much of true living is enjoyed by the Italian laborer who was put on the witness stand of a law court. He was asked his occupation and answered: "I digga da ditch to getta da mon' to buya da food to getta da strength to digga da ditch."

Are we not all, or most of us, afflicted with this death called poverty, even if we live in split-level homes and drive Cadillacs? Our most significant, active, our most meaningful hours, are spent in making money. Necessary—to be sure—but what else do we do? Our occupation absorbs all our abilities and energies. We have substituted making a living for learning to live. Comes the retirement age and we are left with no resources for life. The mortality tables and the obituary columns tell the story of retirement disease. Yes, the poor are reckoned as dead. But their ranks also include those who are frightened to death by the mere prospect or the possibility of poverty.

Falling within the same category is the blind person, the man or woman who has been beset by the affliction of the loss of sight, so that he cannot see the spectacle of existence. Two blind beggars sat in Central Park. The first carried a sign, "Help me, I am blind." Most passersby passed him by. Not so the other. He carried the shield: "It's May, and I am blind." A major physical disability like blindness or deafness gravely reduces the range of life's experiences of which we are capable, and makes us little better than dead.

The third category of living death is the leper. This dreadful scourge of the East, which is not unknown in the West, is today

susceptible to treatment. But in the ancient world the leper was
a hopeless outcast. Living on the dungheaps outside of the cities,
in deserts or waste places, these poor, hideously deformed creatures
would wander, hunting for scraps of food. When another human
being would approach, they would call out, *Tame' tame'*, "Unclean, unclean," to warn him against getting too close, lest he
contract the disease.

The fourth category of those who are reckoned as dead is the
man who has no children. As we grow older and come closer to the
end of our earthly careers, we discover how right our ancestors
were in their passionate concern for children, in their yearning
for offspring to survive them on earth. The Bible tells us that
when God wanted to bless Abraham, the Patriarch disconsolately
declared, *Mah titten li va'anokhi holekh 'ariri,* "What canst Thou
give me, seeing that I walk childless?" Rachel was deeply loved
by Jacob, who labored for her twice seven years. But all his love
could not fill the emptiness in her heart when she cried out:
Havah li bhanim, ve'im 'ayin metah 'anokhi, "Give me children,
for otherwise I perish." All the generations of Jewish men and
women have echoed this pathetic cry—"Give us children, or we
die." Yes, Judaism teaches us that death does not end all and that
the spirit of man is eternal. We may therefore hope for immortality in the life beyond. But we know that in this life we live on in
our children.

Now to a considerable degree these four classes of unfortunates,
the poor, the blind, the leper, and he who has no children, do
not have the power to alter their tragic destiny. It was a great
American religious thinker, Reinhold Niebuhr, who prayed: "O
Lord, give us the courage to change what we can and to bear what
we cannot and give us the wisdom to know which is which." What
cannot be cured must be endured; what cannot be transformed
must be transcended.

Yet we are not altogether helpless even in the face of trials such
as these. The *ro'a hagezerah,* the tragic effects of the decree, can be
overcome by the human spirit. Poverty can be conquered, not by
making money, but by developing standards of value, interests,
and ideals that are not tied to the dollar sign. Many of the best

things in life *are* free. Blindness did not shut out life for Helen Keller—it opened for her new horizons of nobility and service to humanity. There have been lepers who have served as missionaries among the stricken, as volunteers for scientific experiments, as moving symbols of human brotherhood. There are childless couples who have been among the best fathers and mothers in the world—either to an orphaned child whom they have adopted and brought into their own home, or to untold other children who received their help and their love through acts of benevolence.

These four types of sufferers listed by our Sages deserve our compassion and understanding. When they rise above their affliction, as they can, they deserve much more. They become worthy of all admiration and honor.

III

Our Sages taught us, *Hatorah nidreshet lemem tet panim,* "The Torah may be interpreted on many levels of meaning." We may therefore see in the utterance of the Rabbis another connotation that transcends the literal. If we interpret the physical categories in spiritual terms, we shall find a clue to perils which threaten our lives that are wholly within our control. If we succumb to these dangers, we have no one to blame but ourselves.

"Four are reckoned as dead: *'ani,* "the poor." This refers to *'ani beda'at,* "the poor in mind." Never have people been as conscious as today of the importance of good health. Thanks to medical science, cosmetics, and plastic surgery, we pamper our bodies, but how often do we neglect our minds and, through the poverty of our spirits, condemn ourselves to death?

For consider a human life in time and in space. We may live sixty, seventy, eighty, or ninety years, yet it is only a momentary flash of light between two eternities. Each of us can live in only one period of history out of countless centuries. And we can live in only one segment of space. We are now residing in New York, and by that token nowhere else, in none of the other great cities of the world, Chicago or San Francisco, London or Rome, Vienna or Athens, Tel Aviv or Jerusalem. Destiny has placed us by the

shores of the Atlantic. We are not in the Alps or the steppes of
Russia, or the islands of the Pacific. In other words, our bodies
keep us earth-bound, tied hand and foot to one place at a time,
to one short era in history. For every other place and every other
age, we are nonexistent, we are as dead. We are as though we had
not been for all times and places except our limited own.

We *can* come alive to other eras and civilizations, but only if
we overcome the poverty of the mind, if we undertake to grow
in our understanding and our experience of the world and our
appreciation of world culture. Horace Mann once said, "Be
ashamed to die until you have won one victory for humanity." In
more modest terms, but I believe with equal truth, I would say,
"Be ashamed to go to sleep until you have learned one new thing
during the day." One need not be a scholar to adopt the Latin
phrase as a guide: *Nulla dies sine linea,* "No day without a new
line written or learnt." The Jewish tradition has maintained to
our day the principle that one learns as long as one lives. Do you
desire life today? What have you learned this day?

What Jewish tradition has known for centuries, modern research has demonstrated. No longer can we hide behind the alibi
that we are too old to learn. Dr. Wilma Donahue, Chairman of
the Department of Gerontology of the University of Michigan,
tells of research conducted at the University of Michigan in the
mid-1930's which showed that there were no differences in the
ability of young and old to recall instances from the same passage
of a book. Although the younger persons reread the material less
often, older persons recalled it more accurately. She concludes
quite properly: "Each of us must be alert to the ease with which
habit can take over our thinking. To keep our minds healthy we
must continue to use and enjoy them."

Her observations are borne out by other objective tests. Tests
administered to a representative sample of the population thirty
years ago show that younger persons were more intelligent than
older. Now a recheck by Iowa State College of those who were
tested when young shows that *none of those taking the test a
second time did more poorly than they had done three decades
ago.* The initial tests were misleading because they failed to con-

sider the rise in the national educational level. The young had more formal education than did the older people with whom they were compared. Poverty of the mind is of our own making— we can overcome it.

Closely related is the *summa baruah*, the blind in spirit, he who is impervious to the glory and beauty of the world. You remember Stevenson's familiar lines:

> "The world is so full of a number of things,
> I am sure we should all be as happy as kings."

But what of those whose vision on the ophthalmologist's chart is fine, but who are blind to the world, who look, but do not see— sunrise and sunset, ocean, hill, and valley, spring and autumn? A rich man once proudly escorted an artist over his lavish estate. "You see," said the millionaire, with a lordly sweep of his arm, "I own all this land." "Yes," replied the artist, "but it is I who own the landscape."

We live in one of the most overcrowded and uncomfortable cities of the world, but also one of the most exciting and thrilling places on earth. The traffic jams, the noise, the dirt we cannot escape. But how many of us really see what New York has to offer in its colorful streets, its historical sites, its music, its art, its museums, its libraries, its theatres, off Broadway as well as on? How many of us are afflicted with T. V. eyes, the numbing paralysis of the mind, engendered by the little black box? How many of us have become blind to the real key to the world, which lies between the covers of books, because we have lost the capacity to read, to extract ideas from a page or gain pleasure from the process?

He, too, is dead who is a leper. This refers not merely to the man who is isolated by his fellows from society. It refers also to the man who in his selfishness and unconcern isolates himself and cuts himself off from his fellow men. He places himself *mihutz lamahaneh,* "outside of the pale." He may be described, bluntly but fairly, as a moral leper of his own making.

We all know so-called respectable citizens whose claim to respectability lies in the fact that they have not been caught committing robbery or murder. Let Tom, Dick, or Harry or Al, Ben, or Dave do it. Ours is an age of specialization. Those who are much too weak or exhausted to work do not lack the energy to criticize and to slander, to complain about cliques, to explain that their neighbors work for glory and prestige. They themselves are too modest, and so they content themselves merely with sniping from the sidelines.

The man who isolates himself from the community may explain that he asks for nothing from anyone and therefore need give nothing in return. But he is profoundly mistaken. He has come into a world, into a community, into a people and into a country, built by the labor and sacrifice of untold generations. Each of us who is not a savage has inherited a rich civilization from unknown ancestors. The greatest benefactor cannot give to society as much as society has given to him.

But the selfish isolationist, who, like the leper, is "outside of the camp" is an outcast of his own making. His penalty comes both during his own lifetime and afterwards. While he lives he knows none of the joy of achievement, the sense of identification with a cause beyond himself, which will live after he is gone, be it a synagogue, a school of learning, a hospital, or a park, an agency battling for justice or cultural progress, or an ancient people coming back to creative life. When the moral isolationist passes away, he is really dead. He leaves behind him no influence, no memory, only a stone monument in the cemetery, where even the letters will grow illegible with time.

Most tragic of all, and often linked to the third category, is the fourth, *mi she'ein lo banim,* which we may render as "He whose children are not his own." In the early formative years of a child's life, the parent gave these directions to his child, "Don't do as I do, do as I say," but our children are too bright, too honest for that. They hold the mirror up to us and say, "Look at yourselves," and all too often we do not like the image we see.

Tension between the generations is a natural phenomenon that has always existed. It is a necessary and beneficial, though painful, fact of life. For all growing up is in some measure growing away. But never has the sense of alienation and total estrangement, even downright hostility, between the generations been as widespread and as intense as in our time. Often the reason lies in the fact that there are no ideals, no convictions, no purposes that the parents really cherish, that they can share with their children, and transmit to them both as a heritage and a link.

For years on end we trample Judaism under foot, give our children the finest of general education, expose them to untold non-Jewish influences, and content ourselves with shadow-boxing as far as Jewish education is concerned. Then, at the eleventh hour, we discover that our children are not merely indifferent, but hostile to and contemptuous of our tradition and way of life, which they never knew and never understood. If, as happens all too often, they desert Judaism entirely—through total alienation or intermarriage or conversion—we are as dead, because our children are not our own.

Yet there is hope for our latter end. Precisely in the most basic and intimate area of human experience all need not be lost. Here where our own flesh and blood is concerned, we sometimes are able to enjoy a privilege which is rarely given us anywhere else— we get a second chance. Even if we have not succeeded as fully as we would like with our children, we can sometimes save our grandchildren. We can see to it that the third generation receives a genuine and contentful Jewish education. By example as well as by precept, in our homes and synagogues, we can show our grandsons and granddaughters Jewish life in all its beauty, nobility, and truth. We can strive to make sure that our grandchildren, and through them our children, will really remain our own.

"Four are considered as dead—the poor, the blind, the leper, and he who has no children." Sometimes these sufferers are victims of outer circumstances, but often they are the architects of their own misery. He who seeks life has but to reach out for life and it shall be given unto him.

Who desires life for himself, for his loved ones, for his people? On these Holy Days, sacred to life, let us pray to God that we may be spared poverty and blindness, leprosy and childlessness. But let us also give wings to our prayers and sinews to our hopes by doing battle against the poverty of the mind, the blindness of the soul, the isolationism of selfishness, the alienation of our children.

Let us resolve to build a vital Judaism for ourselves and our brethren that will be deeply rooted in the soil of Israel, with branches that will reach out to all the world and with fruit that will sustain the spirit of mankind. Then shall we indeed be worthy of the blessing pronounced by the prophet: *'Ani 'Adonay keratikha betsedek ve'ahzek beyadekha ve'etzorekha ve'ettenekha libherit 'am le'or goyim (Isaiah* 42:6), "I, the Lord, have called you in righteousness. I will sustain you and watch over you. And I will make you a covenant to the peoples, a light to the nations."

XIV

The Sins of Good People

In a few moments each of us will enter into his own private universe. We shall cross the threshold into our special Holy of Holies, shutting out the world, and we shall commune with those who are dearer to us than life itself. During the rest of the year we sometimes seem to have forgotten them. Comes Yizkor and we remember that we remember.

Many in our midst have lost a cherished brother or sister, a member of our own generation, whose passing brought home to us the end that awaits us all. Not a few among us have been deprived of a faithful life's companion, with whom we had planned to share many years of life, only to see our hopes dissolve in ashes. And in our midst, too, are some who have had to bear the heaviest of burdens, the darkest of all mysteries, the death of a beloved child in the springtime of life.

Not all of us, fortunately, have had these trials to face. There is, however, one tragedy which is universal. It is the law of nature that children generally survive their parents. Hence nearly all of us will recall with love and gratitude a hard-working and dedicated father, or a tender and self-sacrificing mother, who not only understood us, but loved us with all our faults and weaknesses.

Borne on the wings of memory, we are carried back to the days that have fled. Life a generation or two ago was far more difficult than it is today. Poverty was widespread. The immigrants who had escaped from the lands of oppression had come into a new and unfamiliar environment. They struggled desperately to establish a foothold in the *goldene medina,* where, they had been told, gold lay in the streets. Our parents and grandparents quickly discovered that at best America offered them an opportunity—and that was enough. There was no limit to their labors, their sacrifices, their ingenuity—all their energies they directed toward making life easier and better for their children.

It is a human tendency to idealize the past. Memory is not a camera photographing with fidelity every detail of the landscape. It is a painter's brush glossing over all that is painful or ugly, and spreading a soft glow of beauty over the remainder. As a contemporary playwright, Brian Friel, puts it, "Memory becomes divested of all its coarseness, and all that remains is pure gold." It is, therefore, entirely natural that when we recall our loved ones at Yizkor or at other occasions, we tend to magnify their virtues and overlook and even deny their weaknesses. Because we love our parents, we see them as paragons of all virtue, embodiments of perfection. In actuality, of course, saints among them were few and far between. To be sure, there were not many great sinners in their ranks either. By and large, they were good people, neither lily-white nor coal-black. They were men and women of varying shades of gray, with perhaps a streak of white or a dash of black here and there to vary and enliven the pattern.

Now there is a classic passage in our literature which declares, *Sheloshah sepharim niphtahim 'ehad shel resha'im gemurim, 'ehad shel tsaddikim gemurim, ve'ehad shel beinonim,* "There are three books open before God in the Heavenly Court. The first contains the names of the totally wicked, the second those of the totally righteous, and the third the names of those in between. The totally righteous are inscribed and sealed for life immediately (on Rosh Hashanah). The totally wicked are inscribed and sealed immediately for death. The fate of those 'in between' remains undecided until Yom Kippur. If they prove worthy, they are then inscribed for life; if not, they are consigned to death" (*B. Rosh Hashanah* 16b).

We can be reasonably sure that the volume containing the names of the totally wicked is not very thick, and that of the perfectly righteous, thinner still! Doubtless, the largest and thickest of the books open before the Heavenly Court is the one in which you and I, let us hope, are inscribed—the one for the people in the middle. In fact, the rabbis go further. In another passage in the Talmud they all but deny the existence of the first category. *Kol haneviim lo' nitnabe'u 'ela lebha'ale teshubhah 'abhal tsaddikim gemurim 'ayin lo' ra'athah,* "All the prophets prophesied only for those standing in need of repentance. As for the totally righteous, no eye has ever seen them!" (*Berakhot* 34b).

Today is, therefore, our last chance. It marks the climax of this process of self-examination, repentance, and rehabilitation, so that we become worthy of being inscribed in the Book of Life.

No one I know has ever complained that the Yom Kippur Service is too short. Perhaps the single most striking element in the long and complex ritual of Yom Kippur is the *'Al Het* prayer, the Great Confessional. Here, in alphabetical, form, forty-four transgressions are listed under the formula. *'Al het shehata'nu lephanekha,* "For the sin that we have committed before Thee—for all these forgive us, pardon us, grant us atonement."

This alphabetical catalogue of sins has often aroused the derision of the cynical and the irreverent: "Who can possibly commit this long list of transgressions? One would need to be a genius in sin to be guilty of them all!" But, as is so often the case, the cynic is more naive than wise. He fails to note that the *'Al Het* is couched in the plural: "For the sins which *we* have committed before Thee." Each Jew is called upon to confess not merely the sins which he has committed as an individual, but the collective sins of society in which he is involved. Beyond the sins of which we are guilty are the sins for which we are responsible—the manifold sins of commission, omission, and permission, which are rampant in our society.

The use of the plural in the *'Al Het* should remind us of a passage in the Holiness Code in *Leviticus* (chapter 19). This important Sedrah contains the Golden Rule, "Thou shalt love thy neighbor as thyself" (v. 18). It includes another great and neglected injunction: *Lo ta'amod 'al dam re'ekha,* "Thou shalt not stand idly by the blood of thy neighbor" (v. 16). This forgotten comnandment sheds a lurid light upon the major sin of the twentieth century. In our lifetime Hitler and his associates were guilty of mass murder, but the free nations, their statesmen, their religious leaders and the masses, were guilty of indifference, silence, and acquiescence in this monstrous sin. As Edmund Burke declared two centuries ago, "For evil to triumph, it is only necessary for good men to remain silent."

This moral weakness of "standing by idly" applies not only to nations but also to individuals who are concerned, not with major issues, but with so-called minor problems. In his *Reminiscences,* Justice Frankfurter asks why men who have position and, by speaking out publicly could turn on the currents of reason and decency, remain silent: "What is it that makes so many men timid creatures? I can give myself some answers. People want to avoid unpleasantness. Life is hard enough even if you've got a bank account. Life is hard enough as it is, why take on something extra? 'Why go out on a limb?' as the phrase runs. 'Why stick your neck out?' that other lovable invitation to do nothing! Even people who are economically independent are not socially independent. They may have money in the bank, but that isn't all they want. They want to be asked to dinner at certain houses. They want to run for office. They want to get a degree from some college or university. They don't want to make trouble for their wives. They have silly wives with social interests or ambitions. Or if they get into public controversies their boy in prep school will be a marked character. 'Oh, it's your Dad who says this.' " The plural in the *'Al Het* confessional is designed to make us conscious of our collective responsibility.

The cynic may ask another question: "What good does Yom Kippur really accomplish? One goes through the ritual of atonement. One fasts and prays to be forgiven, and goes out again into the world and commits the sins afresh!" This very question was once put to a rabbi by his disciple. His master replied, "Go, my son, to the creek at the outskirts of the town and stay there for a full week. Watch what takes place there, and you will then understand the value of repentance." The disciple carried out the instructions of the master. He finally returned, still troubled by his old question, and baffled even more by the strange procedure that his master had suggested to him. "All I saw were women doing their laundry by the creek," he reported. "They come with dirty garments, scrub them clean, and at the end of the week they return with more dirty garments and scrub them clean all over again."

"My son," said the master, "there lies the meaning and value of repentance. Our souls are like those garments scrubbed by the women. In our encounter with the world, our souls become soiled, and they must be scrubbed repeatedly. Repentance is a kind of scrubbing, to remove the filth which is on our souls. And cleansing must be continuous, because the accumulation of filth is perpetual."

A third question will occur to the inquiring mind: "Why is it that the 'Al Het is repeated so many times during Yom Kippur, twice in the Kol Nidre Service, and twice again at Shaharit, at Musaf, and at Minhah? Why must the worshipper be exposed to this catalogue of transgressions eight times in the course of one day?" The answer is suggested in the book of Job, which Thomas Carlyle called "the grandest book ever written with pen." In this book of God and man, a great poet and profound thinker presents a debate by Job and his friends on the agonizing mystery of the suffering of the righteous in a world governed by a just God. Suddenly a striking character in the book interrupts the discussion. He is a brash young fellow called Elihu. He suggests an idea which had not occurred either to Job or to the friends with whom he argues. Elihu declares that troubles sometimes come upon the righteous, not because of the sins they have committed in the past, but in order to serve as a warning against sins in the future. Suffering, he suggests, safeguards them against the sin of complacency, the danger of smugness, the feeling of self-satisfaction, which is the besetting weakness of good people. Let a rabbi deliver a hard-hitting sermon attacking some widespread evil, and how does the average congregant react? Oy, hut er zei gegeben, "Boy, did he let them have it!" Always "them," never "us," never, never "me."

To break through this hard shell of smugness is not easy. We are therefore made to run the gauntlet not once, or twice, but eight times during the day, in the hope that as we recite this list of transgressions, one or another will pierce through to our hearts, and arouse us to contrition and repentance. The American scientist J. Robert Oppenheimer expressed this truth somewhat differently: "When we are blind to the evil in ourselves, we dehumanize ourselves, and we deprive ourselves not only of our own destiny, but of any possibility of dealing with the evil in others." If we are sincerely concerned with our character and destiny, we desperately need to recite the *'Al Het,* for all of us are involved in individual guilt and collective responsibility. The repetition is designed to make us aware of this wholesome, if unpalatable, truth.

It is noteworthy that the great Confessional is not recited until Yom Kippur. It is therefore clear that it is intended not for the totally righteous, who conceivably have no sins to confess, nor for the incorrigibly wicked, who are beyond the pale of redemption. It is intended for the people "in the middle," for the vast majority whose fate is not determined until the Day of Atonement. This fact needs to be kept in mind if we wish truly to understand the meaning and intent of the Great Confessional. In a word, the *'Al Het* may be described as *the catalogue of the sins of good people.*

Let us note at the outset what the *'Al Het* does *not* contain. *It does not deal with major crimes.* Murder and robbery, blasphemy and idolatry, do not occur among the forty-four transgressions. Indeed, they are all lumped together and dismissed in one line, at the very end of the prayer: *'Al hata'im she'anu hayyabhim 'aleihem 'arba' mitot beth din,* "For the sins for which we would have been guilty of capital punishment by the Sanhedrin, we ask Thy forgiveness."

There is another striking category of offenses omitted in the *'Al Het. It does not contain any reference to the ritual sins,* which are so important in Judaism. There is no mention of the violation of Kashruth, the omission of daily prayers, the failure to observe the Sabbath and the Festivals. Here, too, the vast area of Jewish observance is disposed of briefly in the closing section of the *'Al Het: 'Al hata'im she'anu hayyabhim 'aleihem 'olah, hattat,* etc.,

union and the bribing of witnesses. After his conviction, the members increased his salary to $100,000 a year! The story can be repeated in every sector of the national life.

There is another aspect of our behavior that we tend to take rather lightly—*the area of speech.* After all, here we do nothing overt and physical; we simply say a word or two or three or ten. What is more delightful and titillating than gossip? What is more juicy than slander? What harm is there in it—just a breath? So widespread is the practice of gossip and slander that someone has said: "Any time that you discover that neither your friends nor your enemies are saying unkind things about you, you have reason to be alarmed. You may be dead and not know it!"

On the subject of the sins of speech, Jewish ethical teaching is thoroughly uncompromising. The Book of *Proverbs* declares: *Mavet vehayyim beyad lashon,* "Life and death are in the power of the tongue" (*Proverbs* 18:21). Time and again the *'Al Het* reminds us of this heinous sin to which good people are particularly prone. It warns us against *rekhilut,* "talebearing," and calls attention to *leshon hara',* "slander," as sins against which we must guard. The sins of *dibbur peh,* "the speech of the mouth," are not to be laughed away. They may be compounded of breath, but within them is the power of death.

Some years ago a glazier on West 42nd Street in Manhattan put out homely bits of advice in his dusty store window. One of them ran as follows: "Avoid heart attack—Don't run *up* stairs, don't run *down* people." I know of no better advice for physical or mental health.

One of the most remarkable items in the catalogue of *'Al Het* is *tipshuth peh,* "folly of the mouth." As Koheleth reminds us, the fool is a sinner and foolish speech is therefore criminal. There is the familiar story of the young rabbi who preached a sermon. After it was over and the congregation came up, one individual insisted on saying, "That was a terrible sermon you preached, Rabbi." The rabbi naturally felt very much downcast, but the president, who was a kindly soul, said, "Pay no attention to him, Rabbi. He has no mind of his own—he just repeats what everybody else says!"

Nor is this sin limited to the slandering of individuals. The twentieth century has demonstrated the horrible power of mass lying. The rabbis were right in calling slander *lishan telita'ah,* "the triple sword," because it slays the speaker, the hearer, and the victim of the slander with one blow. Millions of dead human beings in our time prove that propaganda is the prelude to genocide. Slandering a race or a people or a religion lays the groundwork for murdering the members of the race, the people, or the religion. The *'Al Het* therefore correctly stigmatizes as a crime *cahash vekhazabh,* "lying and deceit." Before we permit an attack upon an entire group to cross our lips, we would do well to recall the words of Edmund Burke: "You cannot indict a whole nation"—and remember, too, that we shall be among the victims.

Because the *'Al Het* is concerned with the sins of good people, whose acts are usually right and proper, it is particularly sensitive not merely to outer actions, but to *inner attitudes.* It warns us against *'immutz halebh,* "the hardening of the heart," in the face of human suffering. Callousness appears in no criminal code, but I know no more horrible evil than to be impervious to human need, to cherish a grudge—in a word, to persevere in evil. Closely connected with it is what many of us regard as a peccadillo, indeed, often as a virtue: it is *kashyuth 'oreph,* "stiff-neckedness and obstinacy." Of course, we all understand that *we* are persistent; it is our neighbor who is obstinate! But from the vantage-point of God there is no difference—persisting in a course which is mistaken is obstinacy. This is a lesson that our national leaders today could learn to their advantage—and to ours.

There is another inner attitude which is the basis for vast evil. Its importance is highlighted in the greatest moral code in the world—the Decalogue. The Ten Commandments deal almost entirely with deeds, with actions that are committed against God, like the violation of the Sabbath, or with crimes against man and God, like murder. Only one of the Ten Commandments deals not with an overt act, but with an inner sentiment, with a state of mind. It is the last of the Ten Commandments, from which all the others may be derived: *Lo tahmod,* "Thou shalt not covet."

It was through envy that crime entered into the world. The

Torah tells us that Cain was jealous of his brother Abel, whose sacrifice God favored more than his. Jealousy filled Cain's heart, and hatred nerved him for murder. The '*Al Het* does not let us overlook the gravest of sins when it insists that we confess to *tzarut 'ayin,* "the envious heart," and strive to overcome our inability to rejoice in the well-being of others.

Envy is not a crime on the statute books; it is a cardinal sin. All too often it leads to one of the besetting ills in Jewish character, the sin of *sin'at hinnam.* This is generally translated as "causeless hatred." Causeless hatred does not mean hatred without cause. On the contrary, those who are guilty of this vice are strongly convinced that they are thoroughly in the right, that there is "an issue of principle." Insulated by self-righteousness, the practitioners of hatred regard it as a virtue, *leshem shamayim,* "for the sake of Heaven." That is the principal reason why *sin'at hinnam* is so deep-seated and difficult to eradicate. Actually, "causeless" hatred is hatred without *due* cause.

The symptoms of this grave malady of the spirit are easily recognizable. First of all, the strength of the antagonism is out of proportion to the importance of the issue at stake. Second, the differences between the parties have been so exaggerated as to block out any comprehension of the elements of unity or similarity between them. Because the effect is not really the result of the cause, even the removal of the alleged cause has little impact upon the effect. The entire record of Jewish history validates the moral judgment of the tradition that *sin'at hinnam* is a cardinal sin that has brought our people to the verge of disaster time and again.

The great catalogue of sins reaches what is perhaps its climax in *Hillul Hashem,* "the profanation of God's name." These are acts which bring disgrace upon the name of God, whose witnesses we are, and which desecrate the honor of Israel, which is entrusted to the keeping of every Jew. Vulgarity and deception, cruelty and indifference, selfishness and blindness—these prevent us from living up to our highest aspirations. When we fall prey to these evils, we bring the name of God and Israel into disrepute. For this major sin we must ask forgiveness on Yom Kippur. In the words of one of the great rabbinic authorities of our century, Rabbi

Baruch Halevi Epstein: *Mi sheyesh bo 'azzut panim 'o 'akhzariyut veson'e 'et haberiyot ve'eino gomel lahem hesed, hosheshim bo beyother she'eino mimmishpahath yisra'el,* "He who is characterized by impudence or cruelty, who hates his fellow men and practices no lovingkindness toward them, may be suspected of not being truly of the household of Israel."

The *'Al Het* seeks to make us conscious of our sins. But even when we become aware of our shortcomings a pitfall awaits us—the human tendency to offer alibis. The Torah tells that in the Garden of Eden, when Adam disobeyed and ate of the forbidden fruit, Adam, being human, blamed it on Eve: "The woman Thou gavest me, she fed me the fruit." Eve, equally human, accused the serpent: "The snake seduced me and I ate." Only the serpent, not being human, said nothing and took his punishment "like a man."

When we cannot blame our misdeed on some one else, we have another escape—we offer the alibi that we really didn't mean it—we meant no harm. The *'Al Het* does not let us off so easily. It catalogues these offenses, and warns us against the sins that we commit, not only *beyode'im* but also *belo' yode'im,* "knowingly or unknowingly." We need to repent the sins that we commit *be'ones uveratzon,* "under compulsion or of our own free will," *bezadon uvishegagah,* "willfully or unconsciously." Since man is created in the image of God with the power of reason, Talmudic law declares, *'Adam mu'ad le'olam, bein beshogeg bein bemeizid; bein 'er ubhein yashen,* "Man is always responsible for his actions, whether he acts willfully or unconsciously, whether awake or asleep" (*Mishnah Baba Kamma* 2:6).

When an accused is brought before a human court, the judge should deal with the degree of his culpability and inquire about extenuating circumstances. But when we stand in judgment upon ourselves, these alibis should fall away. We should hold ourselves guilty even of the sins which we have committed *bibheli da'at,* "without knowledge." Ignorance before the Law of God is no excuse.

The message of the *'Al Het* is clear. It is concerned not with the major crimes of master criminals, but with the sins and transgressions of good people, which are by no means minor. The Great

Confessional seeks to break through the shell of our complacency and satisfaction, to send us trembling for mercy in sincere contrition to the throne of God.

It is particularly at the turning of the year that we become conscious of the flight of time and aware of the uncertainty of life. None of us knows whether we shall be alive to welcome Rosh Hashanah and Yom Kippur next year. Before it is too late, let us resolve to try to order our lives in the spirit of Abraham Lincoln, who prayed, "When I come to lay down the reins of power and may have lost every other friend on earth, I pray that I shall at least have one left, and that friend shall be deep down inside me." We may then hope to attain to the blessed serenity of spirit embodied in the Sanskrit utterance, "A child when it is born weeps, while everyone around it smiles. So live, that when you die all around you may weep and you may smile."

If we let the words of the 'Al Het penetrate our hearts, Yom Kippur will indeed have been a success for us. We shall not only have the satisfaction of having observed the day, maintained the fast, and read the prayers. We shall also enjoy the feeling of at-oneness with God, with our ancestors, and with our brothers on this Day of Atonement. We may then hope that the heartfelt prayer of these sacred days will be fulfilled for us: Zokherenu lahayyim melekh hafetz bahayyim vekhotebhenu besefer hahayyim lema'anekha 'Elohim hayyim, "Remember us for life, O King desirous of life, and inscribe (and seal) us in the Book of Life, for Thy sake, O God of life."

XV

Forgiveness—The Divine Art of Being Human

I

Ours is the age of the child—and we are proud of it. Earlier generations gave primacy to age on the theory that the elders possessed the wisdom which comes with maturity and experience, while children were expected to be seen and not heard. Today the tables have been turned. The younger people are in command, and the older folks are not expected to be either seen or heard. To be sure, they still have a few practical uses, but essentially they are expected to be as quiet and unobtrusive as possible.

We live in an age whose slogan might very well be: "What Junior wants, Junior gets, and even before he knows he wants it!" Visit a toy shop today, and you marvel at the extraordinary ingenuity which is expended upon every conceivable game and mechanism, all intended to trap the parents and grandparents into buying them for the youngsters. Little girls, just out of swaddling clothes, are dressed like junior debutantes, and, when little more than infants, are taken to the hairdresser. Our children are so bright nowadays that they seem to leap right out of the baby carriage into the motor car. Whether it will be a hot-rod or a sports car, depends primarily on the economic level of the parents.

Many of our schools are now child-centered, which is a great improvement over the situation two generations or more ago. Unfortunately, it is often assumed that a progressive school is one which caters to what the pupil wants to do rather than to what the teacher thinks he ought to learn. Some time ago a cartoon appeared in "The New Yorker" which is undoubtedly an exaggeration, but it possesses too much of the truth to be altogether comfortable. In this particular cartoon we see a modern "progressive" classroom, and a child frantically waving his hand to his teacher, and saying, "Teacher, I'm tired doing what I want to do; tell me what to do!" That children should be taught any given subject only when they show "readiness" for it is now taken pretty much for granted. If it does not interest them, or if it requires some hard work, such as memory drill or concentration on details, we go to any length to "spare" them such unpleasantness.

By and large, we modern parents give our children everything within our capacity, or virtually everything. Especially if we ourselves knew deprivation and poverty in our youth, we assume that if our children lack for nothing, they will avoid any unhappiness, such as we once knew. Few of us have ever heard Oscar Wilde's saying—and fewer still believe it—that "wealth is somehow the negation of childhood."

Yet there comes a dark moment in the life of every parent today when he begins to wonder just how well he has succeeded. Has he really been able to win the love of his children? Are we much more than a convenient necessity while they are young, and an inconvenient nuisance when they get older?

There is, of course, a great deal of physical affection between parents and children, especially when they are young. But what about the old-fashioned, outmoded concept to which the Fifth Commandment points, "Honor thy father and thy mother!" Not amused tolerance or patient forbearance, but "respect," which is an intellectual quality, and includes a sense of concern for the values and the ideals that the parents cherish. To what extent have our principles played their part in molding the lives of our children, and to what extent will they command the attention, both moral and intellectual, of the generation that comes after? To put it in the simplest terms, how many of us can be certain that in the years that lie ahead our children will be in the synagogue at Yizkor time to recall our memory, exactly as we have assembled here to honor our fathers and mothers in this solemn hour?

We shall be raising up their living presence in affection and in gratitude. For what? For if it is true that we give our children everything, or nearly everything, it may be argued that our parents gave us nothing, or practically nothing, primarily because they had nothing to give. Consider, for example, the clothes we wore, cheap and good, and made to last, even if they were a little too large for us, and very often a "hand-me-down" from some one else in the family. The toys we used were the toys we made ourselves, or we did without. Perhaps we built a wagon from a wooden grocery box mounted on wheels. Or we played "pussycat" with two pieces of wood, using the rim of a sewer in the middle of a street as the home base. Or we played marbles in the channels of the gutters of our overcrowded streets. As for the long summer vacation days, we did as well as we could with them. Camps were unheard of in most of our circles. Who would ever have dreamt of coming to his mother, and complaining that we were "bored." We might very well have gotten the classic answer, *"Geh shlug zikh kup un vant,"* a pungent Yiddish phrase that pales into a caricature when it is translated, "Go bang your head against the wall!" Boredom was a disease of the well-to-do, which we could not afford.

What did our parents really give us? They gave us none of those comforts and luxuries which we regard as necessities today, and without which our children could not conceive of life. Many of us went to work before our teens and were contributing to the family coffers throughout our youth.

What debt of gratitude do we really owe them? What our parents gave us was nothing material or tangible. They gave us something far more significant and enduring. They gave us a sense of values, setting before us standards of conduct by which they lived. By and large our parents were not formally educated, and they were certainly not articulate in presenting their ideals to us in the language we understood. But every moment of their lives was a vivid illustration of the truths to which they held fast, an unspoken yet eloquent summons to behold the vision of life to which they gave their wholehearted allegiance. This light which governed their actions, they tried to transmit to us.

II

If we consider our parents' careers, we shall see that their entire philosophy of life, in all its essentials, is embodied in the message of these High Holy Days. Rosh Hashanah and Yom Kippur are not distinct and separate festivals. They are parts of a single whole, representing the two fundamental and interdependent laws of life. For each of these two *Yamim Noraim,* or Days of Awe, represents one aspect of a great truth about God and man.

Rosh Hashanah is known in Jewish tradition as *Yom Hadin,* "The Day of Judgment." It underscores the principle of God's justice and of man's responsibility. It reminds us that the consequences that flow from men's actions are inescapable and unavoidable. The other great day is *Yom Kippur,* "the Day of Atonement," stressing the possibility of a new chance in life, a fresh beginning. It is both these elements, and not one, that constituted the view of life by which our loved ones governed themselves. Rosh Hashanah emphasizes the truth that we live in a world which is not haphazard, which is not based upon chaos or chance or luck. It highlights our faith that the world does not operate according to the standards of Las Vegas, but that, on the contrary, this is a world of law. All our scientific discoveries, as well as our ethical principles, are based upon this insight.

This faith the Rabbis graphically expressed in their utterance: "No man strikes his finger here below, unless it is proclaimed from above" (*Hullin* 7b). Their words recall the saying of Judge Learned Hand, "Not a sparrow falls to earth unheeded." In the words of the Prophet Isaiah, *Vayigbah hashem tsebha'ot bamishpat veha'el hakkadosh nikdash bitsedakah,* "The Lord of hosts is exalted in judgment, and God, the Holy One, is sanctified by righteousness" (*Isaiah* 5:16). The teaching by which our parents lived was summarized by the same Prophet when he said *'Imeru tsaddik ki tobh,* "Tell the righteous that it will be well with him, for he will eat the fruit of his deeds," *'Oy larasha' ra',* "Woe to the wicked, for it will be ill with him, for the recompense of his deeds will be done to him" (*Isaiah* 3:10-11).

To be sure, the Prophets and Sages saw that there are many exceptions, or seeming exceptions, to this law of consequence, that all too often we see the wicked prosper and the righteous suffer. They proposed many answers to this most agonizing of human questions, notably in the greatest book in the Bible, which is the Book of *Job.* But they never faltered in their conviction that we live in a world governed by the law of righteousness, a universe in which ultimately well-doing creates well-being, and evil necessarily leads to catastrophe.

But all men are weak and imperfect, prone to error and sin. The Bible teaches that "there is no man altogether righteous on the earth, who does the right and never sins" (*Ecclesiastes* 7:20). If this be true, all men must carry a burden of punishment.

It is natural for a human being to try to avoid the consequences of his actions. Indeed, the oldest human trait known is giving an alibi, "passing the buck," or trying to find a substitute to carry the penalty for our actions. If we cannot find someone else to blame for our sin, we try to find someone else to bear the punishment. This is the origin of the deeply rooted human desire for a "scapegoat," a word which is derived from the English translation of the Torah reading of this Yom Kippur morning. For the Bible tells us that in ancient Israel, on Yom Kippur, a goat would be selected to be sent away into the wilderness by a messenger, thus symbolizing the desire of the entire community to be separated from its sins. In the consciousness of the masses, however, the "scapegoat" tended to become not only a symbol, but a substitute.

The great appeal of Christianity, which helped it to conquer the world, was precisely this human desire to escape the consequences of one's actions. Christianity preached the doctrine of vicarious atonement—that the Savior had died for men, and thus absolved them of their punishment. This doctrine Judaism never accepted. It recognized another idea, with which it is often confused—vicarious suffering.

That we suffer for one another is the law of life, for no man is an island, entire of itself, cut off from the main. A gangster commits murder, his heartbroken mother suffers with him and for him. An alcoholic undermines the health of his innocent children. The Nazis inflicted disaster and death upon millions of peaceful and inoffensive men and women. All these are examples of vicarious suffering, for the lives of all men are interwined and interdependent, but vicarious atonement—that our sin is borne by others—that normative Judaism never could believe, because this is a world in which *'ith din ve'ith dayyan,* "There is both judgment and a judge," and each man must shoulder the consequences of his actions for good and for ill.

This is the truth proclaimed by Rosh Hashanah, but it is not the whole truth concerning life. According to Jewish tradition, God has two thrones, the *Kissei' hadin* and the *Kissei' harahamim,* "the seat of judgment" and the "the seat of mercy." Our religion teaches that man is not imprisoned by an iron law of necessity. The circle of cause and effect, of deed and consequence, of sin and punishment, can be broken through the divine attributes of mercy and forgiveness.

III

This long twenty-four-hour vigil of prayer and supplication, of meditation and fasting, underscores the truth that *forgiveness is possible.* This does not mean that we can escape the consequences of our actions, or that sin goes unpunished. Forgiveness means that we can avoid the inner penalties of sin, for when we sin we become conscious of our estrangement from God and our own unworthiness. Modern psychology lays great stress upon the evil effect of guilt feelings. It would do better to emphasize rather the evil effect of guilt, which brings in its wake a sense of alienation from God, a feeling of worthlessness, the collapse of self-confidence, the loss of faith and joy in life. Moreover, sin leads inevitably to the progressive deterioration of character. Not only is it true that *'abherah goreret 'abherah,* "one transgression leads to another," but *sekhar 'abherah, 'abherah,* "the consequence of one misdeed," as the Rambam explains, "is that it paves the way for the next misstep and makes it easier."

What forgiveness can do is, therefore, to free us from the intolerable burden of estrangement from God and the ensuing decay of character. As a modern Jewish teacher acutely pointed out, this is the deeper meaning of the great affirmation in the *Unetanneh tokeph* prayer: *Uteshubhah utephilah utsedakah ma'abhirin 'eth ro'a hagezerah.* Correctly rendered, this declaration means that repentance, prayer, and righteousness avert not the evil decree, the outer consequences of our sin, but *ro'a hagezerah,* "The *evil* of the decree," the inner effects of our wrongdoing. When we cease to do evil and make restitution for our offense, we free ourselves from the incubus of guilt through the act of forgiveness, whether it be God or our fellow man against whom we have sinned. Forgiveness is possible.

Moreover, Yom Kippur teaches us that *forgiveness is real,* that it is not a figment of our imagination, or an illusion fostered by our desires. In our rich and expressive Hebrew tongue there are many terms for forgiveness, and we repeat them time and again in the *'Al Het: Ve'al kullam, 'eloah selihot, selah lanu, mehal lanu, kapper lanu,* "For all these sins, O God of forgiveness, forgive us, pardon us, grant us remission." While the three verbs used in this moving prayer are synonyms, they each suggest a different conception of the nature of forgiveness.

The minimum view is expressed by the Hebrew term *selah.* The root has an Akkadian cognate, *salahu,* which means "to besprinkle, to water." There are those who conceive of forgiveness as a kind of deodorizer. The sin remains intact, but we add a little perfume, so that the odor is not quite so pronounced, or clean it up a little by besprinkling it with water, so that it is easier to bear.

At the other end of the spectrum is the term *mehal,* which is derived from the Hebrew root *mahah,* "to wipe out." According to this maximum view, forgiveness means blotting the sin out completely, erasing it as though it had never taken place. Unfortunately, however, once the face of innocence is corrupted, it can never be restored in its pristine purity. Deception, theft, cruelty, unfaithfulness, let alone a major crime like murder, cannot be blotted out, because they cannot be undone.

Basically, forgiveness is more than besprinkling the sin, but it is less than blotting it out. It is noteworthy that neither of these two terms gives its name to our Sabbath of Sabbaths. Yom Kippur derived its name from a root *Kafara,* which in Arabic means "to cover over." Forgiveness does not mean pretending that the offense was never committed, but neither does it mean constantly recalling the wrong and reviving the resentments and hurts of the past. "Kippur" means "covering over," and beginning afresh.

To be sure, forgiveness is desperately hard to practice. The reason for the difficulty is highlighted by the French proverb, *"Tout comprendre, c'est tout pardonner,"* "To understand everything is to forgive everything." But human beings, unlike God, never understand all, either about themselves or about their fellow men, and therefore they find it difficult to practice the divine art of forgiveness. An injury we find it hard to forgive, but even worse is an insult, a blow to our pride, to our self-esteem, to the trust we find misplaced, and so we say, "revenge is sweet," and we call it justice. "An eye for an eye," we say, quoting Scripture and misinterpreting it.

But the sweetness of revenge is transitory; it quickly turns to gall and wormwood, to bitterness in our hearts. Hard as forgiveness is to practice, it is harder still to live without it. The Count of Monte Cristo had been grievously wronged in his youth, and he decided to devote his life to avenging himself upon his enemies. When it was all over, he discovered that he had sacrificed his life and destroyed himself in the process.

The divine art of forgiveness will become easier to practice if we remember that not only is this virtue possible, but it is real; that it is not only real, but absolutely necessary. Life cannot go on without it, not only for the sinner, but also for the victim, as well as for the society of which both are a part.

The Eichmann trial was in many respects an infuriating spectacle. The cool aplomb of the mass butcher, his unshakable insistence that he was living by a moral code of obedience to his superiors, his total lack of any compunction, pity, or grief at the greatest blood bath in history—all these were maddening to behold. To speak of forgiveness where there was no contrition and no regret was a contradiction in terms. At the time I opposed his

execution, because, as I said, "His crime is cosmic, and only a
cosmic punishment, which is beyond a human power to inflict,
can do justice to his monstrous acts. Any governmental execution
would be anti-climactic." Perhaps in view of the agonizing problem that his life-long imprisonment would have posed, the Israeli
government had no real alternative.

Eichmann was not asking for forgiveness, and deserved none,
but Eichmann is not Germany. There are Nazis in Germany today,
to be sure, far too many for comfort, but there are also many
Germans who are deeply ashamed of Nazi bestiality, and who
seek to make restitution as far as is humanly possible. There is
an order of German nuns who were members of the Hitler Youth
in the heyday of Nazism and who have now dedicated their lives,
both in Germany and in the State of Israel, to helping Jewish
people, and thus making atonement for the sin of which they
were a part. Let us remember that the West German Republic
paid out millions of dollars in reparations both to individuals and
to the Jewish people, and that much of the recovery and progress
of the State of Israel is due to these funds and goods coming from
Germany.

Before we dismiss these reparations too cavalierly, let us note
that the East German Communist Republic and Austria have not
made any payments at all to their Jewish victims. Let it not be
forgotten that even our own free country has acquiesced in the
Arab anti-Jewish boycott, and contented itself with a few weak
protests. It has even degraded American citizens of the Jewish
faith to the level of second-class citizenship, and barred them from
U.S. military or civilian posts in the Arab countries, whom we
are helping with millions upon millions of dollars. On the other
hand, the West German Republic has steadfastly refused to surrender to the threats of the Arab League. It has continued to do
business with Israel, and never supplied the names of Jewish firms,
or of German firms doing business with Israel, to the would-be
boycotters.

Two hundred years ago the great English statesman Edmund
Burke declared, "You cannot indict a whole nation." Certainly
no people in the world has ever paid a heavier price than Jews

for the failure of men to remember this truth. We Jews cannot afford to forget that this principle is true always and everywhere— even of the German people today.

"To err is human, to forgive divine." What we cannot forgive, we must try to forget; what we cannot forget, we must forgive. We must cover over the offense committed against us and start a new chapter. The business world is traditionally hardheaded rather than sentimental, but we can learn a lesson from the world of practical affairs. When a firm or an individual cannot meet its obligations, the law provides for a bankruptcy proceeding. The business community salvages what it can from the remaining assets, and then begins anew to do business with the same principals.

IV

Forgiveness is necessary if society is not to fall apart and life is to go on. We can train ourselves to practice the art if we recall some basic truths taught by life and by religion:

No man is without some value. The worst criminal, and we rarely meet him, has a spark of God in his soul, perhaps deeply overlaid, almost extinguished, but never quite dead. The Torah tells us that each human being descended from Adam is created *betzelem 'elohim,* "in the image of God." Perhaps all that remains in a criminal is the ideal, "Honor among thieves," loyalty to his own gang, but it is honor and loyalty still. If we possess the requisite skill and patience, sympathy, and endurance, it is possible to work a miracle, to rehabilitate the criminal and reveal a man. One of the greatest utterances of the Talmud declares: *Hamekayyem nefesh 'ahat, ke'illu kiyyem 'olam male',* "He who preserves a single human soul is as though he saved an entire universe." But the Hebrew can also be rendered, "He who sets straight a single human spirit has saved a whole world."

That is not all. *No man is perfect, and the least perfect of all is he who believes he is.* As a wise Hasidic teacher put it, "Better a thousand times a sinner who knows he is a sinner, than a saint who knows he is a saint." Albert Schweitzer sought to express the same truth when he said, "A good conscience is the invention of

the Devil." Each of us might well repeat whenever he encounters
or hears of some criminal, "There, but for the grace of God, go I."

The Rabbis were profound students of human nature when
they declared: *Kol hagadol mehabhero, yitzro gadol mimmenu,*
"The greater a man is, the more powerful is his impulse, his
temptation to sin" (*Sukkah* 52a). Long before Freud, they understood that great creative energies may also be manifested in
stronger desires, in more powerful drives toward love, toward enthusiasm, toward life, but also as stimuli to the sins of lust and
pride, envy and greed.

The saintly founder of the Hasidic movement, Israel *Bal Shem
Tov,* describes his own nature in a profound parallel. A king once
entrusted a treasure to four lords of his court who absconded with
it. Shortly thereafter, the first reconsidered his act and returned.
The second consulted a sage and was persuaded to go back. The
third came to a place where punishment was being meted out for
such crimes, and was overcome with fear of the consequences and
returned to the court. The fourth did not come back at all. The
first courtier was rewarded by the king with a position of greater
dignity than he had ever had. Not so the second. As for the third,
the *Bal Shem Tov* went on to relate, the king appointed him as
governor of the province in which the convicted criminals were
expiating their offense through suffering. The *Bal Shem Tov*
identified his role with the third and saw it as his destiny to share
the evil of the world, including the sin and the punishment that
befell his fellow men. Then he wisely added, *'ephshar 'adam
metakken 'eth ha'olam vehu' 'atzmo nidbak bo min hara'.* "A man
may be able to improve and elevate the whole world, but something of the world's evil will cleave to him."

You may remember the old anonymous jingle:

> "There's so much good in the worst of us,
>   And so much bad in the best of us,
>   It ill behooves any of us,
>   To find fault with the rest of us."

If we recall the truth of the first two lines, and keep in mind
that great gifts are often marked and compensated for by equally

great weaknesses, we shall find it easier to practice the divine art of being human. We shall not be too grievously hurt to discover, as the phrase has it, that the idol which we worshipped has feet of clay. We shall treat our fellow men as we implore God to treat us—with mercy as well as with justice, with forgiveness as well as with fairness.

V

As we recall the living presence of our parents, let us remember how they reacted to us, their children. We disappointed them time and again, and broke their hearts, trampling their dearest wishes under foot, but they never ceased to love us because they understood us, and forgave us. The noblest tribute which we can pay them is to try to emulate them by practicing the art of forgiveness, first toward those near to us, then to neighbors and associates, and ultimately to all God's children. Forgiveness is the key to life, both for the sinner and for his victim, and for the society of which both are a part.

If we truly seek life, we must strive to cultivate the divine art of being human.

XVI

The Dangerous Age

I

It is only when we confront the mystery of death that we are led to contemplate the miracle of life. It is in an hour such as this that we ask ourselves the question which is eternal because it is unanswerable: Is life worth living? Or we may repeat the jocular answer given by the well-known after-dinner speaker Chauncey M. Depew, who lived to a ripe old age. When reporters once asked him whether life was worth living, he answered, "It depends on the liver."

Less epigrammatic, but far more profound, is the teaching of Jewish tradition on the subject. The Talmud tells us that this very question was discussed in the Academy between the schools of Shammai and Hillel. The Hillelites, always optimistic, declared that it is better for a man to have been born than not to have been born. The Shammaites, of a more somber disposition, held the opposite opinion.

The final decision reached by our Sages reflects the practical wisdom and idealistic aspiration characteristic of our great tradition: *Noah lo le'adam shelo' nivra' yother mishenivra', ve'akshav shenivra' yephashpesh bema'asav*, "It would have been better for a man not to be born than to be born. But now that he has come into the world, let him scrutinize his actions" (*Erubin* 13b). There is a charming comment on this Talmudic passage in Jewish folklore: "Of course it is better not to have been born than to be

208

born, but what person in ten thousand has that much good luck?"

The wisest of men have recognized the basically tragic character of existence. In the words of the poet: "Tragedy is life's true guise; Comedy lies."

The greatest poet of the English language, and perhaps of all the world, expresses this sense of the tragic character of man's march from infancy to death in his description of the Seven Ages of Man:

> All the world's a stage,
> And all the men and women merely players:
> They have their exits and their entrances;
> And one man in his time plays many parts,
> His acts being seven ages. At first the infant,
> Mewling and puking in the nurse's arms.
> And then the whining school-boy, with his satchel
> And shining morning face, creeping like a snail
> Unwilling to school. And then the lover,
> Sighing like a furnace, with a woeful ballad
> Made to his mistress' eyebrow. Then a soldier,
> Full of strange oaths and bearded like the pard,
> Jealous in honour, sudden and quick in quarrel,
> Seeking the bubble reputation
> Even in the cannon's mouth. And then the justice
> In fair round belly with good capon lined,
> With eyes severe and beard of formal cut,
> Full of wise saws and modern instances;
> And so he plays his part. The sixth age shifts
> Into the lean and slipper'd pantaloon,
> With spectacles on nose and pouch on side,
> His youthful hose, well saved, a world too wide
> For his shrunk shank; and his big manly voice,
> Turning again toward childish treble, pipes
> And whistles in his sound. Last scene of all,
> That ends this strange eventful history,
> Is second childishness and mere oblivion,
> Sans teeth, sans eyes, sans taste, sans everything.

As a matter of fact, Shakespeare had been anticipated by many centuries in the Midrash. The majestic opening verse of the Book of *Ecclesiastes* reads, "Vanity of vanities, saith Koheleth, vanity of vanities, all is vanity." In the Hebrew text the Rabbis find seven "vanities," which they refer to the seven ages of man (*Midrash Koheleth Rabbah* 1:1):

> Seven worlds does a man behold:
> When he is a year old, he is like a king,
> Placed in a litter with a canopy
> And all kiss him and embrace him.
> When he is two or three, he is like a little pig,
> Who reaches out to play in every form of filth.
> When he is ten years of age, he jumps like a young kid.
> When he is twenty, he is like a neighing horse,
> Preening himself and seeking a wife.
> When he marries, he becomes like a donkey
> Carrying a heavy burden.
> When he gives birth to his children,
> He becomes strong-willed like a dog in order to support them.
> When he becomes old, he is like a monkey,
> A caricature of a man.

Here is a priceless blending of realism and idealism, of honesty and hope. Both Shakespeare and the Midrash were deeply conscious of the limitations of life, but they held fast to the joy of life. They felt that life was an experience for man not to be missed, the greatest blessing of the Living God.

II

Why argue whether life is worth living or not? "Now that we are alive, let us scrutinize our actions," our Sages urge us. When should we begin? Which is the dangerous age?

Until very recently, the first period of life was exposed to great physical danger. Infant mortality was extremely high, even in civilized countries, as it is in the underdeveloped nations of the world. Because the first thirty days of a child's life are fraught with hazard, the ceremony of the *Pidyon Haben,* "the redemption of the first-born," takes place on the thirty-first day of the baby's life, when we may feel secure that he is *bar kayyama,* permanently alive, well and here to stay.

Then come the early childhood years, which we were wont to call "the years of innocence." If Freud is to be believed—and experience seems to bear him out—the basic traits of character, both negative and positive, go back to these first years. It is the love given or withheld, the disciplines taught or denied, which create the basic patterns of security or insecurity in which the youngster and the man will live ever after.

Then come the later years of childhood, which have all but disappeared in our modern-day society. Today parents do all in their power, abetted by television, the movies, and advertising, to rob children of their childhood and make little boys and girls into lovers and sweethearts, competing for popularity, for prestige, for position. Perhaps you saw the full page ad in the newspapers, "For your daughter, aged 13 going on 17. Macy and Revlon agree with her!" One wonders why.

As for the carefree years of youth that follow, they are no more. However much our youth today may pretend to be carefree and careless, self-assured and self-sufficient, they deserve our deepest understanding and sympathy, for theirs is a difficult lot. They live in an age of cosmic fears and dangers. They are torn by tensions and conflicts without end. More than a little of the revolt, the estrangement, and the apparent lack of responsibility among our present-day youth is an expression of their basic insecurity in the present and their dread of the future: "Let us eat and drink, for tomorrow we may die."

Then come the twenties, the years of marriage and adjustment. The young people must first find each other and discover their real character, which is often hidden behind the patina that we call "glamor" and "personality." The young people enter into marriage and embark upon the slow, serious, and difficult process of adjustment to one another, to which far too little attention is paid in our age, when marriage is expected to be a perpetual courtship à la Hollywood. The young man, and very often his wife, too, are now in the thick of the economic struggle, striving to find a foothold on the ladder of success.

Then come the thirties and the early forties. These are perhaps the happiest years of life. At this time the children are young and still close to their parents, and the parents are in their prime, able to share the interests of their children without being patronized or dismissed as the "old man" and the "old lady." These are the years when our children become Bar and Bat Mitzvah and the cup of our joy runneth over.

Then, suddenly, like a thief in the night, the late forties are upon us. We discover that we are suffering from a disease—the feeling of failure. In the words of a contemporary observer (John C. Cort, in *Commonweal*, September 8, 1961):

"There are many symptoms to the ailment, of which the physical are only the most obvious. The change in the texture of the skin on the back of the hands is more important than it might seem, because a man is likely to be noticing the back of his hands more often than his face. When he does look at his face in a mirror it strikes him that the countenance that had always looked too young has suddenly begun to look too old. He finds himself doing things he never believed he could do, such as letting the hair grow long on the sides so that he can comb it over the bald spot in the middle.

"He drinks more often than he used to, and sometimes more deeply than is wise. If a young woman goes out of her way to talk to him at a party he is likely to fall in love with her out of sheer gratitude, and more likely if he has had a few.

"And almost every male in the forties is disappointed by the lack of success in his career. Men whom I have envied for their bright achievements confess that their hopes have far outstripped reality. I suppose that John F. Kennedy is one man in the forties who would have to be listed as an exception to this rule. And there are others. But give them time. From their eminence they will look up to higher peaks of glory and fulfillment. If there are no higher peaks, they will invent them, creating visions of magnificence out of thin air.

"In the thirties a man can still tell himself that he has been unlucky. Give him another ten years and sheer ability is bound to triumph over circumstance. Ten years later, in the forties, the realization begins to dawn that maybe he hasn't got it, or that circumstance is so relentlessly unkind that he isn't going to make it, or a little of both. He begins to resign himself to mediocrity."

Then comes the next decade, which Dr. John F. Briggs, addressing the American Medical Association, called "the frenzied fifties":

"The age is upon a man when he has squandered his reserves of emotional, intellectual and physical strength and realizes he no longer has what it takes to do everything he wants and needs to do.

"The symptoms are clear-cut as the rash that goes with scarlet fever. The underlying cause is a failure to learn one's limitations early and to frame one's life within them.

"The state, which strikes most men sometimes in the mid-forties or mid-fifties, can mimic the diseases prevalent in this age group, can aggravate existing disease and makes rehabilitation difficult, because the victim tends to retreat into his real or imagined disease as a psychological shelter from the frustrating facts of life.

"The essential fact is that the man has gone as far as he ever will up the ladder of success and perceives at last that the only direction remaining is down.

"He is living the artificial life of a successful man. He is continuing to exhaust his intellectual, emotional and physical reserves. He is no longer on the ladder of success. He is on a merry-go-round that goes faster and faster and then suddenly he wakes up and realizes that he has reached his 'frenzied fifties.'

"The first reaction is insecurity, the second is depression and the next is anxiety and tension. The man becomes chronically tired and irritable and eventually even his favorite hound dog crawls under the sofa when he comes home."

Then come the years which few people in earlier generations ever reached. Thanks to modern medicine, more and more of us may look forward to the sixties, the seventies, and the eighties. Here the problems, while still psychological, are aggravated by the natural decline of physical powers, the onset of ailments and disabilities, which are designed to prepare us for the inevitable end. How poignant is the old prayer which we repeat time and again on Yom Kippur: *'Al tashlikhenu le'et ziknah Kikhelot kokhenu 'al ta'azebhenu.* "Cast us not off in old age. When our strength fails, do not forsake us."

Which is the dangerous age? The answer is clear—every age

has its problems and its perils. In every age we need to pray: *'Al
tashlikhenu milephanekha veruah kodshekha 'al tikkah mimmenu,*
"Do not cast us off from Thy presence. Thy holy spirit do not remove from us."

III

How can we prepare to meet the problems and conquer the
perils? How can we continue to find life worth living? The great
leisure-time pursuit of modern men and women is the search for
the elusive bluebird of happiness. The effort to supply answers to
this quest has become a major enterprise in twentieth-century
civilization. Columnists, radio and T.V. programs, religious re-
vivalists, psychological counsellors and psychiatrists, the populous
tribe of the writers of "How to be Happy" books,·all offer their
answers, running the gamut from the conventional to the most
radical.

Judaism has always been deeply concerned with the well-being
of men and women. But when we pray for *refu'at hanefesh urefu'at
haguph,* we place "the healing of the spirit" before "the healing
of the body." The goal of religion is not to make men *feel* better,
but to help them *be* better. Judaism grapples not with our symptoms, but with our sins. It is not satisfied to have men rid themselves of their guilt feelings; it strives to have them get rid of their
guilt.

Describe the ages of man as you will. It is not the age which is
dangerous, but man who is prone to sin. In a striking Talmudic
passage (*Derekh Eretz* 5:1, p. 120, ed. Higger), our Sages describe
not the seven ages of man, but the seven stages of sin:

> *Tehillat 'abherah hirhur halebh, sheniyah lah letzanut, she-
> lishit lah gassut haruah, rebhi'it lah 'akhzariyut, hamishit lah
> habattalah, shishit lah sin'at hinnam, shebhi'it lah 'ein hara'.
> Hu she'amar Shelomo Ki yehannen kolo al ta'amen bo, ki shebha'
> to'abhot libbo.*
>
> "The beginning of transgression lies in giving rein to the im-
> pure imagination of the heart. Then come scoffing and mockery.
> This is followed by arrogance of the spirit. The fourth stage is

cruelty; the fifth, idleness; the sixth is hatred without cause; and the seventh, the ungenerous and envious eye.

"It was of these perils emanating from the *yetzer hara'*, the evil inclination, that King Solomon spoke when he said: 'Even when the enemy speaks sweetly to you, do not believe him, for seven are the abominations in his heart' " (*Proverbs* 26:25).

"Even when the enemy speaks sweetly"—our ancient sages understood that the path of perdition is paved with flowers. The sins which tempt us always look attractive and often seem of trifling importance. Yet step by step we are led down the road to total destruction.

What remedy is there against these dread diseases of the spirit? Our one great weapon of defense is familiar to us all by name, but, unfortunately, it has been debauched and vulgarized in our day. If it is to save us, we need to restore its pristine purity and vigor. It is the greatest Commandment of the Torah, *Ve'ahabhta*, which is directed both toward God and man: "Thou shalt love the Lord thy God with all thy heart, with all thy soul, and with all thy might" (*Deuteronomy* 6:5); and "Thou shalt love thy neighbor as thyself" (*Leviticus* 19:18).

What does the Torah mean when it commands us to love God with all our heart? It means to serve God without asking for any reward beyond the joy of doing right. As Rabbi Levi Yitzchak prayed, "God, I do not want Thy heaven, I do not fear Thy hell. I want only Thee." H. Wheeler Robinson spelled out the meaning of "love of God" in modern terms: "It means to conceive of God in moral terms, so that He is attractive in Himself, loved for His own sake, served gladly, and it may be without hope of any visible reward at all."

What is asked of us in the Golden Rule? We are commanded, "Thou shalt love thy neighbor *as thyself*," not "more than thyself." It does not mean the denial of our own rights and impulses. It means, however, that our arithmetic must progress beyond Number One, and that our geography must extend beyond the tiny bit of earth which we personally occupy. It must include our fellow men, whose rights and wishes have an equal claim with ours for fulfillment. For, being God's children, they are our brothers and our partners in God's world. If this is our obligation to strangers, how much greater is our duty to those near to us, to our parents, our husbands, our wives, our children, our neighbors, our friends, our fellow countrymen?

If we go out to face life armed with such love for God and man, we shall prove invincible.

IV

Seven are the paths of perdition. Perhaps the first is that of idleness. We all remember the old-fashioned proverb, "The devil finds work for idle hands to do." Today all of us enjoy far more leisure than was even dreamed of by earlier ages. It was Judaism that originated the revolutionary concept of the Sabbath, of man's right to a day of freedom from toil and responsibility, a day to be devoted to rest and the recreation both of body and of spirit. Today this great Jewish contribution to civilization has been extended to such features of modern life as the shorter work-week, summer and winter vacations, and long week-ends. That is not all. Men today find it possible to retire at a relatively early age, with their faculties and powers virtually unimpaired.

But leisure, which could have been a blessing, has become a problem, a threat, even a curse, for modern man. Far too many of us have emptied our lives of every interest except making a living. When the day comes and making a living is no longer necessary, there is nothing left in our lives. It sometimes happens that husbands and wives "get on each other's nerves" when retirement comes. They have never lived together, except in the most limited sense. There is no genuine bond of interests, activities, and ideals that they share.

Every man and every woman should have more than one string to his bow. While we are active, we should be preparing another career for ourselves for the years of retirement—a career which need not, indeed, should not, be attached to a salary tag. During our middle years, most of us are so busy doing the things we must, that we have no time to do the things we wish. The later years can be the Golden Age if we free ourselves from the obsession of gold. Retirement from money-making should make it possible for us to devote ourselves to the pursuit of interests and cultural activities that we have pushed into the background. Now we can devote ourselves to the love of God and the service of man without the need of material reward. As we lose ourselves in causes greater than ourselves, we shall find ourselves anew.

The second great path of perdition threatens us at nearly every stage in our lives. It is what the Rabbis, with their unflinching realism, called *hirhur 'abherah,* "the obscene imagination," the sinful meditating of the heart. Our entire civilization today seeks to stimulate sexuality, and then piously stigmatizes it as sinful. Our books and plays, our popular music and art, all our advertising media, are concerned with stimulating this basic element of human nature and exaggerating it out of all proportion. All too often the word "love" has become a four-letter word for physical gratification.

Now Judaism has always regarded sexual attraction as natural and potentially holy, but it has never made it the be-all and end-all of love. To treat "love" and "desire" as synonyms means to degrade love and to distort desire. Nowadays, when a young man declares, "I love her," that is assumed to be the unanswerable argument against all considerations of religious loyalty, family responsibility, and career. In the name of "love," young people rush into marriage in haste and repent almost as quickly, leaving the wreck of their happiness behind and often learning little from the tragic experience.

Judaism has never underestimated the power of the sexual impulse, nor stigmatized it as unworthy. It has always recognized its tremendous power for good and for evil. How can its evil be checked and its good be manifest? How can we learn the true art of love?

The great Hasidic sage, Rabbi Levi Yitzchak of Berditchev, once declared that he had learned the real meaning of love from a drunken peasant, whom he had overheard one day in a country inn. The peasant and his friend were seated at a table, both already far gone in their cups. They were at the sentimental stage, throwing their arms around one another and declaring how much hey loved each other. Then Ivan turned to Peter and said, "Peter, tell me what hurts me." "How do I know what hurts you?" Peter answered. Whereupon Ivan said, "If you do not know what hurts me, how can you say you love me?" "That," said Rabbi Levi Yitzchak, "is the true meaning of love."

We may go further. True love can save us from self-destruction. If we keep before us the vision of what hurts those we love, we shall not fall easily into sin.

Another sin that seems petty and pleasant in the beginning, but turns out to be pernicious in the end, is *letzanut,* the "spirit of mockery and scoffing." When Goethe in his *Faust* sought to picture Satan, the spirit of evil in the world, he described him as "the spirit that always says 'No.'" There is so much that is false and hypocritical in the world that it seems not only easy but honest to become a cynic, to strip away men's pretensions and laugh all their exertions to scorn.

But there is a great difference between unmasking falsehood and insisting that there is no truth, between laughing at sanctimoniousness and mocking at the sacred, between recognizing men's weaknesses and denying men's strength. He who insists that "man is only an animal" may quite likely attempt to demonstrate it by his own beastly actions. There is nothing in the world that cannot be mocked, be it God, love, patriotism, truth. But when we do so, we are tearing down the very fabric of civilization, painfully erected over the centuries, which alone stands between man and savagery.

It is a sign of our times that we have a talent for accentuating the negative, but little gift for articulating the positive. Our satirists can mock at what is wrong with the world. Our political analysts can skillfully describe the symptoms of illness in our society. Our psychological analysts can lay bare the complexes and maladjustments of men. But ask about their positive program and they become tongue-tied. Against the temptation to cynicism, we must mobilize all our resources for love by insisting that man counts in the eyes of God and man.

Two more perils threaten the life of man that seem, at first blush, to be so natural as to be quite forgivable. What is more

natural than to be aware of our gifts and talents and to be just
a little conceited? And what is more normal than to envy those
better situated than we? Conceit and envy—how unimportant they
are! Indeed, they seem to be opposites, cancelling each other out.
For conceit tends to be the supreme vice of the successful; and
envy, of the unsuccessful. Yet in spite of all logic, human beings
are so gifted that they can often manage to combine them both!

Of such characters the Psalmist declares, *Gebhah 'einayim ure-
habh lebhabh, 'otho lo 'ukhal,* "The man who is haughty-eyed
and envious of spirit, him I cannot abide" (*Psalms* 101:5). A modern Jewish moralist offers this striking insight into the verse. If
a man is conceited, what is the remedy? Tell him to look above
him and let him see those who are better than he! On the other
hand, if a man is envious, what is the cure? Tell him to look
below him and see those whose lot is worse than his! But what
happens if a man is both conceited and envious? If we try to cure
his conceit by telling him to look above him, we make him all
the more envious. If we try to cure his envy by telling him to
look below him, we make him even more conceited. That is why
the Psalmist declares, "The man who is haughty-eyed and envious
of spirit, him I cannot abide." For him there is no help.

The monstrous character of these two evils of arrogance and
envy cannot be exaggerated. It is noteworthy that nine of the
Commandments in the Decalogue deal with actions and only one
with a state of mind or feeling. That is the Tenth—"Thou shalt
not covet." Envy is the root of all evil. When it is coupled with
arrogance, it begets limitless cruelty.

The most horrible manifestation of brutality in the world,
Nazism, combined both these sins. On the one hand, the puny,
unsuccessful house-painter, Adolf Hitler, became the mouthpiece
of the Germans, the symbol of their rankling sense of inferiority,
for they had attempted world conquest and had been beaten at
their own game. And with this envy of others came the arrogance
which expressed itself in the doctrine of the master race, so that
the German was trained to believe that he had no obligations to
his fellow men, because he was a race above and apart from the
generality of men.

The penalty of these sins is tragically clear on a far smaller scale. How often are we guilty of cruelty to friends and neighbors, even to our own flesh and blood, because of envy or conceit? Envy destroys our sense of fair play. Conceit creates an artificial abyss between us and them, so that we lose the common touch, the feeling for our brother.

What remedy is there for these two dangerous and deep-seated maladies of the human spirit? Here, too, the secret lies in cultivating our capacity for love, in a world where every man is now literally our neighbor. We shall then recognize that we are part of a larger whole. When we behold the suffering of our brothers, their inadequacies and failures, our hearts will be filled not with conceit, but with pity, not with *Schadenfreude,* but with compassion. On the other hand, the achievements of our brothers, their successes and triumphs, will be not a source of envy, but of joy in our hearts, for we shall be participating in their good fortune.

To counter arrogance and envy, we need the contrasting qualities of humility and self-respect. As a modern Jewish teacher said: "A man should always carry two stones in his pocket. One should bear the inscription, 'I am but dust and ashes.' The other, 'For my sake was the world created.' And he should use each stone as needed." If we love God, we shall know that our place in the scheme of things is as secure as that of our brothers. We shall conquer the twin perils of arrogance and envy that corrode man's spirit.

The last of the seven cardinal sins is causeless hatred. One may recall the lines written by Tom Brown while still a student at Oxford:

> "I do not love thee, Dr. Fell,
> The reason why I cannot tell,
> But this I know, and know full well,
> I do not love thee, Dr. Fell."

We today tend to regard dislike without a reason as a minor peccadillo. Our high "society," our country clubs, our "exclusive" sets, all are nourished by our "constitutional" right to dislike our neighbor.

Our Sages were far more realistic. They did not hesitate to declare that the Temple in Jerusalem was destroyed because of *sin'at hinnam,* "causeless hatred." Causeless hatred is nothing but another name for prejudice, the great cancer devouring the life of the twentieth century. For it is causeless hatred which sets man against man, invoking the differences of color, or race, or creed, or class to justify itself. Hatred is always evil. But when it has a tangible basis, remove the cause and you can recreate the sense of fellowship. But when hatred is causeless, how can it be conquered?

When, therefore, we find ourselves indulging in the pleasant little vice of hating or disliking someone "just so," without a reason, let us sternly take measures against this sin within ourselves. Let us recognize our duty before God to strive to love our neighbor. If we seek honestly to understand the person to whom we think we have an aversion, we may discover the truth expressed by the English essayist Charles Lamb. He was once heard attacking a contemporary. "How well do you know the man you hate so much?", Lamb was asked. "Know him? I do not know him at all. If I knew him, I could not hate him!"

Seven are the ages of man, and seven are the perils that threaten man at each stage. Idleness and lust, conceit and envy, cynicism, cruelty and hatred, are our constant companions. As we journey along life's highway, they are perpetually lying in ambush, ready to ensnare us. Eternal vigilance is the price of liberty. Only as we cultivate the love of God, to whom we owe everything, and the love of man, without which we would not be human, can we hope to overcome the enemy.

For the dead, the pain, the fever, and the struggle are over. But for us, who still walk the earth, life still holds rich promise, if we strive to overcome its perils and set our sights on perfection.

XVII

Time for Life

I

Of all the days of the Jewish year, the Sabbath and the Festivals are the most sacred. Of all the festivals of the year, Rosh Hashanah and Yom Kippur are the most solemn. Of all the hours of Yom Kippur, Yizkor is the most poignant, the most deeply personal— for now we shut out the hue and the cry of the world, the clamor of nations and the clang of the Machine Age, and look inward to the very sources of our being. These sweet, sad moments are dedicated to those who gave us life, who fashioned our goals and shaped our ideals. Since loneliness is the greatest of all calamities, these moments of intimacy and fellowship with those we love most become increasingly precious as the years go by. For we each have more and more dear ones in *beth 'almin,* "in the house of eternity."

Even if we have been singularly spared, and there are no empty places around our family table, none of us is a stranger to death. We think not only of our kinsfolk who have gone before us, in accordance with the law of nature, but of those who were the warriors in the war against man's inhumanity to man, the heroes and the martyrs of the House of Israel and of mankind. That long roster gives no sign of coming to an end. We pause in silent tribute to those whose names have been added during these long, bitter years. We think of two young men of our people, among many others, who left home to fight for civil rights and died for other men whose skin was of another hue, whose religion was not their own, but who were linked to them and to us by the kinship of our common humanity.

The Yizkor hour is not only sacred to the dead. It can be of the greatest value to us, the living. For such is the tenor of our days that it is only when we stand in the presence of death that we take time out to ask ourselves the meaning of life. A long time ago Koheleth said: *Tobh lalekhet 'el bet 'ebhel millekhet 'el bet mishteh, ba'asher hu' soph kol ha'adam vehahay yitten 'el libbo* (*Ecclesiastes* 7:2): "It is better to go to the house of mourning than to the house of feasting. For this is the end of every man, and the living can take the lesson to heart."

II

What is life? How can we judge it? In setting the title for this sermon as "Time for Life," the goal was not to give free advertising to two very popular magazines. The truth is that most of us regard "time" as a synonym for "life." When a man dies, we ask, "How old was he?"—as though that told us anything really significant about the life that ended. We forget that the longest life is merely a breath.

In the old days, monuments carried long inscriptions extolling the virtues of the deceased and undoubtedly exaggerating his merits. Now, tombstones have practically no text except the name and the age. If epitaphs were true as well as kind, many a monument would read, in Voltaire's words, "He died without having lived." Or the inscription would say, "Died at thirty, buried at sixty."

How wise is the Prayer Book which we hold in our hands on these High Holy Days! Again and again we pray, *'Abhinu Malkenu kothebhenu besefer hayyim tovim,* "Our Father, our King, inscribe us in the Book of *Hayyim Tobhim.*" Not *Hayyim Arukim,* "a long life," but *Hayyim Tobhim,* "a good life."

What makes a good life? The wisest and the best of men, the Hebrew prophets, the Greek philosophers, have wrestled with this question of questions. There is a striking answer suggested by our ancient literature. The Rabbis tell us that when a man dies

and comes before God's judgment seat, some questions are put
before him, of which three are basic:

> *Natata venasa'ta be'emunah?* "Have you conducted your affairs
> honorably? Have you been honest in business?"
> *'Asakta batorah?* "Have you occupied yourself with the Torah?"
> *Tsippitha liyeshu'ah?* "Have you hoped for the redemption of
> your people, and the establishment of God's Kingdom of justice,
> freedom and peace for mankind?" (*Shabbat* 31a).

This utterance of our ancient teachers is eloquent not only in
what it says, but also in what it leaves unsaid.

Natata venasa'ta be'emunah? "Have you conducted your affairs
honorably? Have you been honest in business?" There are so
many other questions, some important, others not, that are *not*
asked: "Have you been successful in business? Have you made a
lot of money? Do you give your children everything they need
and much that they do not? Are you popular in a crowd? Do your
name and your picture appear in the papers?"

The intent of our Sages is clear. The first test of a good life
is whether it has been an ethical one. Whether we have lived
honorably and responsibly toward our fellow man. Whether we
have avoided not merely such crimes as murder or robbery, but
whether we have cheated him of his substance, of his good name,
or his faith in human nature. Whether we have used our personal
needs and desires to provide for our family as an excuse to ride
roughshod over our brother's rights and possessions. Have we
clambered to success on the ladder of life across the prostrate
bodies of our fellow men? God's first question to us is, "Have you
conducted your affairs rightfully?"

'Asakta batorah? "Have you occupied yourself with the Torah?"
Not, "Are you a great scholar? Do you know much Torah?" but
"Did you occupy yourself with the Torah—whatever your level of
knowledge or your power to comprehend?" What we *know* from
the past may be dead and useless; only what we *learn* in the
present is alive and meaningful. Notice that the question is addressed not to the scholar in his study, but to the worker, the

businessman, the bread-winner, "Have you occupied yourself with the Torah?"

The third and final question ranges even farther afield. "Have you looked forward to salvation for your people and the world?" "Have you demonstrated your faith in God and in His purposes for His people and all humanity?" Again some very important questions are not asked: "Did you observe the Sabbath? Were you devoted to prayer? Did you attend the synagogue?" Only the fundamental question is asked: "Did you limit your gaze to the here and now, to your own petty self, your own little circle, your home, your family? Or did you use your God-given gifts to contemplate ideals and to serve goals beyond your own circumscribed life? What have you done for the cause of your people, its homeland, its growth, its safety, its creative spirit? What have you done to help bring all men a greater measure of equality and justice, a sense of hope for a better day?"

'Abhinu Malkenu kothebhenu besefer hayyim tobhim, "Our Father, our King, inscribe us in the book of a good life." The test of a good life lies in dealing honorably with our fellow men, in occupying ourselves with the Torah, and in making our faith in God manifest by advancing the cause of His kingdom.

III

In our expressive Hebrew language, the phrase *Sefer hayyim tobhim* has another meaning as well. In fact, if you consult English translations of the Prayer Book, you will find that they invariably translate it as "The book of a happy life." Human nature being what it is, what most of us crave is happiness above all else! For every one who strives to be good, there are a thousand who desperately want to be happy.

When our Sages tell us of the questions that will be put to us before the judgment seat of God, they are disclosing the secret not only of a good life, but of a happy life as well. For they are indicating the three indispensable ingredients of happiness for man—not pleasures and passions that intoxicate and devastate, that pass like a hurricane, leaving ruined lives in its wake, but happiness, genuine, deep, enduring, joy that never palls, but grows deeper with time.

When we are asked the three questions, "Have you been honorable in business?" "Have you occupied yourself with the Torah?" "Have you looked forward to salvation?", we are being reminded of the three pillars of happiness for all men—labor, leisure, and loyalty to goals in life that go beyond one's personal existence.

How can we speak of labor as a basic element in a happy life? Are not all our energies bent toward labor-saving devices? In fact, it is often argued, the Bible itself regards labor as a curse. When Adam and Eve sinned and were driven out of the Garden of Eden, they and their descendants after them were told: *"Beze'ath 'appekha tokhal lehem,"* "With the sweat of thy brow shalt thou eat bread" (*Genesis* 3:19).

As is so often the case, a little knowledge is a dangerous thing. It was not labor in the Garden that was a curse, but unremitting toil beyond one's strength, without limit, without hope, without purpose. The Torah tells us that at the very outset Adam was placed in the Garden *le'obhedah uleshomerah,* "to till the garden and to guard it" (*Genesis* 2:15). Labor within his capacity, for a purpose that he could see, was part of Adam's happy life in the Garden of Eden before he was driven into exile from Paradise.

Our Sages point out that the Fourth Commandment has two injunctions, not one. The first of these, *Sheshet yamim ta'abhod ve'asita kol melakhtekha,* "Six days shalt thou labor, and do all thy work" (*Exodus* 20:8) is an integral part of the injunction of Sabbath rest. The Wisdom teachers in the Bible constantly exhort men to industry: "Go to the ant, thou sluggard, consider her ways, and be wise" (*Proverbs* 6:6). Ben Sira summarizes the authentic teaching of Judaism when he tells his reader, "Hate not laborious work nor husbandry, which the Most High has ordained" (7:15). The first and the greatest worker in the world was God Himself, the Creator of heaven and earth. It was He who set the pattern for man, in the six days of creation, as well as in the Sabbath which followed.

It is a tragedy that modern man has a fatal talent for converting his blessings into curses. A century ago, the English philosopher John Stuart Mill said that he doubted whether all the machines that were ever invented had really decreased man's enslavement to work. Since Mill's time, the average work-week has been cut in half, the physical strain of labor has been radically reduced, and wages have increased tremendously. Nonetheless, in a large and painstaking work entitled "Of Time, Work and Leisure," Professor Sebastian de Grazia argues that the thirty hours or more which have been subtracted from the standard work-week of 1860 have all been dissipated in "work-related" drudgery.

What is even worse is that modern technology has made so much of labor monotonous and meaningless. In days gone by, a shoemaker working at his last fashioned an entire shoe, from the leather to the finished product. He was able to express what Thorsten Veblen has called "the instinct of workmanship." He could develop a sense of pride, a joy in his skill. Today the employee in a shoe factory does not manufacture a shoe; he may hammer one nail or, more likely, stand watching the machine to make sure that it does not get out of order and upset the assembly line. As C. Wright Mills points out: "The detailed division of labor means, of course, that the individual does not carry through the whole process of work to its final product; but it also means that under many modern conditions the process itself is invisible to him. The product as the goal of his work is legally and psychologically detached from him, and this detachment cuts the nerve of meaning which work might otherwise gain from its technical processes" (*The Meaning of Work in Our Time*).

How can work be redeemed from its meaninglessness today? Reducing the hours of labor is an economic necessity, if we are to avoid overproduction and the threat of depression. In the second instance, we must continually strive to remove, or at least radically reduce, the element of drudgery in the day's program for the factory hand, the farmer, the housewife. Better physical surroundings, music where possible, interludes of relaxation help substantially.

But these devices are not enough. What is needed is not only a change in the work, but a new spirit in the worker. He who labors will have new zest if he is constantly aware of the goals of his labor, of the goods he is helping to produce, to whom his product will go, and what benefit it will confer upon men. There are some glorious old words whose full meaning needs to be recaptured.

When we describe an occupation as a "calling" or use its Latin equivalent, "vocation," we are being reminded that each of us in his labor is answering a call from God, to share with Him in building the world. The Hebrew word *mela'khah,* "work," comes from the same root as the word *mal'akh,* "angel, messenger of God." *'Abhodah* means both "labor" and "worship." To modify the great injunction written across the Ark, *Da' liphenei mi 'attah 'obhed,* "Know before whom you labor." There is no menial work; there are only menial workers.

With the growth of labor-saving devices, running a household has become easier—though not much, when we recall the automatic laundry worked at home and the task of shopping and carting groceries from the supermarket. Nevertheless, an intelligent woman can find time for other interests, cultural and communal, beyond the four walls of her home, when her children are no longer small. But keeping house will not make her unhappy, if she remembers that she is not a houseworker, but a home-maker. She needs to remind herself that her labor is truly a calling, that she is building a sanctuary for her husband and her children, a shelter for their bodies and their souls, an anchor of unity and safety in the world.

A passerby saw some men working on a construction job. "What are you doing?", he asked the first laborer. "I am laying bricks," was the gruff answer which he received. "What are you doing?" he said to another. "Can't you see?", was the tired response, "I am earning a living for my family." The third replied, "I am building a cathedral." At the end of the day, the three workers would all be fatigued and be paid in dollars and cents. But only one would be receiving a bonus, not specified in his union contract. His and his alone would be the reward of inner satisfaction, a sense of meaning and value in his exertions.

That even the most difficult and least interesting of jobs gives a man a sense of worth can be demonstrated through a negative proof. Consider the state of mind of the unemployed, even of unskilled laborers, whose labor is the most back-breaking and the least rewarding, who do not earn much more from work than they receive from relief and social security. Nevertheless, the demoralization that sets in among the unemployed is unmistakable. The indolence and the lack of responsibility of which we often complain in these unfortunates are the end-result of a process which began with the breakdown of self-esteem, the loss of the feeling that one is a respected member of society, however humble.

The tragic violence of the Negro riots during the past few years is in largest measure an expression of the frustration of the unemployed and the unemployable. Their antisocial behavior was a destructive expression of their need to work. "When work goes," says H. A. Overstreet, "we know that the tragedy is more than economic. It is psychological. It strikes at the center of our personality. It takes from us something that rightly belongs to every self-respecting human being." Hear also the melancholy refrain of the unemployed in T. S. Eliot's "Choruses from 'The Rock' ":

> Only the wind moves
> Over empty fields, untilled
> Where the plough rests, at an angle
> To the furrow . . .
> . . . In this land
> No man has hired us.
> Our life is unwelcomed, our death
> Unmentioned in "The Times."

Most Americans, fortunately, are not at the bottom of the social and economic ladder. As we ascend the scale, our occupations become more and more interesting. Talk to a hard-working businessman and he may tell you, and honestly believe it, that he toils as strenuously as he does in order to provide for his family. Actually, they have more than they possibly can spend. The truth is that he is working for the sheer joy of working, for the satisfaction which he derives from facing problems, meeting new situations, solving difficulties, overcoming obstacles, opening up new vistas.

Here we come upon one of the neglected truths of our time—for millions of men and women today the line of demarcation between labor and leisure becomes less and less sharp. At work, we have such practices as the morning and afternoon coffee-break and the piping of soft background music into factories and offices. There is the lunch hour among professional and business people, where, it has been said, wheels make deals over meals. Consider the new consumer industries created by the "do-it-yourself" movement, when a man undertakes the most strenuous jobs voluntarily after his day's occupation.

The lesson is clear—if we truly wish to be happy, we must include work in our regimen of life. Work, which is the hallmark of God Himself, is a blessing. It is we who must recapture its inner meaning, its sense of direction, the conviction that it has a Divine purpose, that it is '*Abhodah,* the service of God, *Mela'khah,* our mission as His messengers.

IV

The second element of a happy life, leisure, will seem more obvious in our play-oriented society. Yet here too, the fatal capacity of modern man to convert a potential blessing into a curse poses a major problem.

For ages men had a vision of leisure, but the dream has become a nightmare in our day. If our ancestors could have been told that we would have a five-day week, a thirty- or thirty-five-hour schedule, longer vacations, and sabbatical periods, they would have thought that we were describing Paradise or a reasonable facsimile thereof. Today more than one authority believes that the steady increase of crime and violence, the growth of juvenile delinquency and adult misbehavior, are due to the increased leisure available to all.

In the ancient world of the Greeks, leisure was the prerogative of a handful of aristocrats, while their slaves, who were the majority of the population, labored from sunrise to sundown, from childhood to old age. Now the blessing of retirement beckons not only to a fortunate few, but also to the vast majority of men and women in our affluent society. But all too often retirement has brought a mass of problems in its wake, physical, intellectual, and moral. Experts in geriatrics speak of "retirement disease," of the boredom which leads to the breakdown of mental and physical vitality. At times there is even an increase in family dissension when the husband no longer leaves for work. A husband and a wife, who have for years lived side by side, suddenly discover that they do not know how to live together.

The truth is that we do not know how to live with ourselves, and that is why leisure is a major problem.

What is leisure? It has been defined as the time we are free from the duties which a paid job imposes upon us. Obvious as this definition seems, it is too superficial to be true. Free time is not the same as leisure, as any unemployed worker or a prisoner in a cell, or a patient in a hospital, can tell you. Far too many of us have too much time and too little leisure. That is why we exhaust ourselves in the process of "saving time" and then hunt for ways of killing it.

Leisure, like labor, becomes a blessing only if we approach it from within. A physician who is worthy of his sacred calling, a lawyer who sees the law as the product of men's drive toward a just society, a teacher who knows that he is creating human beings, a religious leader who seeks to help his fellow men and lead them to God's wisdom and truth—these men have no time off. Every moment of their leisure is dedicated to enlarging their capacity for service.

It is no wonder that the happiest people of our time are its creative figures, its scientists, artists, musicians, and scholars, for they are paid to do what they enjoy for its own sake. In the medieval Jewish classic, *Sefer Hasidim,* the pious author declares that the most perfect prayer was pronounced by an illiterate shepherd who, standing before the Holy Ark, said, "O Lord, my God, if You had sheep, I would guard them for You for nothing."

Those who do the kind of work that they would do for nothing find that their lives are meaningful. They are enjoying *leisure in work*.

Equally fortunate are those who enjoy *work in leisure*. In our society there is a growing number of men and women whose economic position makes it possible for them to choose an area of public activity without regard to financial return. They work very hard at their self-assumed tasks, but they would not have it otherwise. During the past few years we have seen men of great wealth in America, who could spend their days as playboys and indulge every whim and desire, undertaking the most arduous and gruelling of tasks in the field of politics, philanthropy, and public service. The Roosevelts, the Kennedys, the Harrimans, the Rockefellers, are the heirs of great fortunes. They voluntarily subject themselves to great physical strain. They expose themselves to public misunderstanding, even vilification, but they find their self-fulfillment through work in leisure.

Nor is this blessing open only to multimillionaires. We have only to look around us and we observe some of our friends and neighbors. They carry the same burdens and have the same obligations as we, yet they undertake the obligations and responsibilities, yea, the heartaches and the tensions of community service. Our temples, our schools, our community organizations, our philanthropic agencies, all are headed not by angels—far from it— but by men and women of flesh and blood. Confronted by problems, beset by fears, prone to error, sensitive to misunderstanding, they give up days and nights to causes beyond themselves. Often they complain, as did Moses himself under the inhuman strain of leadership, but they carry on. They have added to their lives the dimension of significance, the sense of achievement, which is the inner meaning of leisure. For a man to be well, he must dedicate his leisure to the well-being of others.

But not *all* his leisure. Judaism teaches us that there are *mitzvot* we must fulfill not only for our fellow men, but also for ourselves. Leisure offers us the opportunity of fulfilling these obligations. There is a clue to this truth in the Greek word for leisure, *schole,* which entered into Latin as *schola*. From this word *schola* comes

our word "school" and the beautiful Yiddish word for a synagogue, "shul." There is a close and intimate relationship between
leisure and education. The Greek philosopher Aristotle, who addressed himself to the fortunate minority of Athenian free men,
said, "The goal of education is the wise use of leisure." The Rabbis
of the Talmud, who were dedicated to the ideal of the equality
of all men, expressed the converse of this truth—the goal of leisure
is the achieving of an education. They remind us, *'Al to'mar
likheshe'eppaneh 'eshneh shema' lo tippaneh* (*Abot* 6:2). "Do not
say, 'When I shall have time, I shall study,' lest you never have
the time."

To wait until the years of retirement to develop interests and
activities is dangerous and sometimes fatal. These interests need
to be cultivated during our active careers, when our mental
muscles are flexible and vigorous. And we can do so, because today
all of us have free time at our disposal, every day, every week of
our lives. The world of human thought and achievement beckons
to us all. We who live in New York have no fewer than fifty
museums at our disposal, dealing with all the arts and sciences,
all the occupations and interests of men, each of them a world of
interest and stimulation to us.

Vacation trips are necessary not merely because they take us
away from our usual responsibilities and burdens. The new sights
we cover on our travels are not as important as the new insights
we discover. When we undergo new experiences in an unfamiliar
environment, we live more intensely, we see more vividly, we feel
more sharply.

We Jews are singularly fortunate, for our people's culture offers us a double blessing. The study of the Bible, the Hebrew
language, Jewish history, the Talmud, have fascinated men of
every background for centuries. But for us, the study of Torah is
not merely a voyage of discovery, but an adventure in self-dis-
covery. As we reveal to ourselves the innermost sources of our
being, we become more truly ourselves.

Finally, there is one other blessing in leisure which is all the
more necessary because it is not easy to learn. It is a secret that I
must confess I have yet to master myself. Our activistic society

places great stress upon doing things and being busy. But the Latin orator Cicero said, "He does not seem to me to be a free man who does not sometimes do nothing." To learn how to loaf and invite the soul is a rare and difficult art. The Hasidic teachers underscored this virtue which they called *Hitboddedut,* "learning to be with one's self." It will be easier to learn the art, if we remember that when we are with ourselves, we are not alone, because God is with us.

V

Labor and leisure, properly understood, intelligently cultivated, and wisely used, are both indispensable for happiness. But they are not enough. George Bernard Shaw once said, "The surest way to be miserable is to have the leisure to ask ourselves constantly whether we are happy." The Russian writer Maxim Gorki said that the wisest words he had ever seen were the utterance of the great Hebrew sage, Hillel: *"Im 'ein 'ani li mi li, ukheshe'ani le'atzmi mah 'ani, ve'im lo 'akhshav 'eimatai"* (*Abot* 1:14). "If I am not for myself, who will be for me? But if I am only for myself, of what good am I? And if not now, when?"

As we have already seen, the full use of leisure must include striving for a goal beyond ourselves. This truth is embodied in the third question which we must answer before the heavenly seat of God: "Have you hoped for and striven for redemption?"

We flatter ourselves today that we live in our affluent society, but we are surrounded by misery and want, not only abroad, but at home. We dare not shut out the cry of the oppressed. We dare not blind ourselves to the poverty, the ignorance, and the disease which even now constitute the lot of the vast majority of the human race. The Peace Corps has been a revelation of deep fountains of idealism in the American people. But it has been more—it has been a reservoir of happiness, of true inner satisfaction, for thousands of Peace Corpsmen and Corpswomen.

If we want to be truly happy, we must not be too happy. The function of religion is not only to comfort the afflicted, but to afflict the comfortable. As a wise Arabic proverb puts it, "Contentment is of the nature of domestic animals." To be content with our personal lot and discontented with the lot of mankind—that is the secret of genuine happiness for men. To enjoy the blessings that are ours and to labor to augment the blessings of our brothers—that is the true goal of life.

As we stand before God and our consciences, let us resolve to utilize the blessings of labor, of leisure, and of goals beyond ourselves, because we shall be fulfilling His will. Thus we shall be worthy of having our prayer answered:

Kothebhenu besefer hahayyim lema'anekha 'elohim hayyim.

"Inscribe us in the book of life, for Thy sake, O God of life."

XVIII

The Golden Years

I

Ordinarily we spend our days beset by petty problems and unimportant goals. Rarely do we have the time or the inclination to contemplate the fundamental issues of existence. It is only when Yom Kippur comes and we set aside our usual worries and occupations, disregarding even such elemental needs as food for the body, that we are led to consider the miracle of life that we generally take for granted as our due. And it is the approach of the Yizkor hour that impels us to face the mystery of death, the eternal sleep which rounds out our brief existence upon earth.

As we think of our dear ones whom we loved and lost, we begin groping after the meaning of life and death. Once they lived among us, but now we do not see their faces or hear their voices. Yet every fiber of our being proclaims that they live on. We refuse to believe that they are totally and completely gone. As the English thinker James Martineau said, "We do not believe in immortality, because we have proved it. We forever try to prove it, because we believe it."

The nature of the life that comes after death we cannot grasp. It belongs to an altogether different order of existence that we have never experienced. It is like asking a man blind from birth to visualize the colors of a sunset. The senses we possess are too gross to feel this unknown and subtler level of experience. But that God is *mehayyeh hametim,* that He gives life to the dead, that in some way life is mightier than death—that faith we affirm because life is too wonderful and too powerful to be totally obliterated.

There are religions, like those of the ancient Egyptians, in which the consciousness of death became an obsession and all of life on earth was regarded as of no account, useful only as a preparation for death. And in every society, creed, and age there are those who dismiss life here as unimportant and even as worthless.

Normative Judaism has always been too clearsighted and courageous to downgrade the life we know because of its faith in a life unknown. It refuses to belittle the here-and-now because of the hereafter. We believe in life eternal, but we respect life as we know it, limited, incomplete, and fragmentary though it be.

II

For centuries the liturgy on Rosh Hashanah and Yom Kippur has been replete with the prayers for this life. Traditionally, long life has always been regarded as the crowning blessing of God. Of Abraham the Torah says, *Ve'abhraham zaken ba' bayamim ve-Hashem berakh et 'abhraham bakol (Genesis* 24:1). "Abraham was old, advanced in years, and God had blessed Abraham with everything."

Our prayers have remained virtually unchanged, but a total revolution has taken place in the world with regard to the attitude toward old age. For the greater portion of recorded history, the aged possessed all authority and were accorded the greatest honor. Our language still reflects this familiar pattern. The word "senator" comes from the Latin *senex,* meaning "old man." "Alderman" means "elder man," and the Rabbis explain that the Hebrew word for "old," *zaken,* means *zeh shekanah hokmah,* "He who has acquired wisdom." The position of the aged in the ancient world is succinctly summarized in a verse in *Job: Bishishim hokhmah ve'orekh yamim tebhunah,* "With the aged is wisdom, and with the length of days, understanding" (*Job* 12:12).

The Midrash tells us that the external signs of old age came into the world only because Abraham had asked for it. "Without

of a white beard, how will people know to honor a father
the son?" (Midrash Bereshit Rabbah, sec. 65; see also
a Metzia 87a).

It cannot be denied that the total authority of the aged had its
share of evils. As Lord Acton said in an epigram which is justly
famous, "Power corrupts, and absolute power corrupts absolutely."
The authority of the old often degenerated into tyranny, and led
to the suppression and the exploitation of the young.

There developed the natural tendency to regard the old and
familiar as holy, not to be subjected to change, and the new and
untried as subversive. We find in our literature such statements
as Kol millei 'attikei ma'alye (B. Batra 91a), "All old things are
good." One of the Sages declared, Setirat zekenim binyan, binyan
ne'arim setirah (B. Megillah 31b). "When the old destroy, they are
building. When the young build, they are destroying."

The absolute power of the old, like every form of tyranny,
needed to be overthrown. Came the revolution and age toppled
from its throne. But, as is all too characteristic of human nature,
the pendulum swung to the opposite extreme. Age was cast to the
depths and youth was now set up on the pedestal, and this was
worse. For God has placed some safeguards in the older generation, which tend to check and prevent extreme abuses of power.
There is the natural love and tenderness that a parent feels for
the young, which is all but universal. There is the passage of time
that teaches us as we grow older to be satisfied with less than
everything. These built-in safety valves against tyranny the young
do not possess.

It used to be said, "Children should be seen, but not heard."
Now the old should not even be seen. We want them out of sight
and out of mind. In our day the triumph of science in extending
the life-span has proved a tragedy or, at best, a major trial. The
increased life expectancy of men and women, far from being the
blessing for which the generations prayed, has turned out to be—
if not a curse—at least a problem and an embarrassment.

A truly civilized society is one which is conscious of the past,
of the long, difficult struggles and boundless sacrifices by which
each step of human progress was achieved. But today we are con-

temptuous of the past, and, what is worse, totally ignorant of it. The Talmud tells us that Rabbi Johanan used to rise up before aged Gentiles and he would say, *Kammah harpatekei 'ado 'alaiho* (*Kiddushin* 33a), "How many difficult experiences have they gone through!" They used to tell of the old man who walked into the drugstore and asked, "What have you got for gray hair?" "Nothing but sympathy, sir," was the polite answer. Even the sympathy grows rarer by the hour!

A generation or two ago grandparents lived with their families as honored members of the household. They were able to exert beneficent influence upon the lives not only of their own children, but also of their grandchildren, serving as a symbol of the continuity of time and tradition. How many of us have been profoundly influenced by having known our grandparents? This privilege grows increasingly uncommon. The proliferation of homes for the aged, of hotels for senior citizens, of retirement villages, meets a need, but it is a sad symbol of our civilization. The aged are not wanted. Being bereft of any vital role in the lives of their family, they themselves prefer not to be close to their children, in spite of the dread of loneliness. Thus there has emerged the tragic paradox that we pray for long life, and if our prayers are answered, we are miserable.

III

How do we seek to escape from this *cul-de-sac?* We fight against old age and pretend it does not exist. We hide our age, deny our years, color our hair, or replace it altogether with wigs. We wear bright clothes and on the dance floor we vie with the youngsters in doing the most violent of dances that leave us limp and exhausted. Let me not be misunderstood. I am not criticizing these tactics as wrong. Quite the contrary, they are praiseworthy when they are in proportion. A medical authority recently pointed out that the unending efforts of people in middle age and beyond to remain young have a beneficial effect upon their physical health, and reduce the incidence of certain diseases of old age.

There is no reason why we should surrender to old age without a struggle. The Biblical sage, Koheleth, brings his great book to a climax with an unforgettable picture of old age. He calls to man to seek his happiness before old age sets in with its burdens of debility and failing powers: *Umatok ha'or vetobh la'einayin lir'ot 'et hashemesh (Ecclesiastes* 11:7ff.)

> Sweet is the light
> And it is good for the eyes
> To see the sun!
> For if a man lives many years,
> Let him rejoice in them all,
> And remember that the days of darkness will be many,
> And that everything thereafter is nothingness.
> Remember your Creator in the days of your youth,
> Before the evil days come and the years draw near,
> Of which you will say, "I have no pleasure in them."

Fighting against illness and declining powers, holding fast to our interest and joy in life—this is not merely forgivable, but worthy of all praise. As Koheleth reminded us, the enjoyment of life is perhaps the greatest *mitzvah* of all, because in cherishing life we are expressing our gratitude to God, the giver of life.

The inherent drawback in our efforts today to hold off the advent of old age is not that we are doing too much, but too little. We are going about it in the wrong way and in the wrong place. It is true that modern science has bestowed upon each of us the great gift of many more years of life expectancy, and that we have a right to hope for substantial good health during these added years. Not so long ago a man or woman in the forties had reached middle age and at sixty was old. Today the sixties represent middle age, and many men and women, in high places and in low, remain active and energetic into their eighth and ninth decade. Nevertheless, the miracles of science cannot totally negate the aging process. Our energies become more limited with time and need replenishment. We may do as much as before, but we must do it more slowly. Newspapers and telephone directories continue to be printed each year in smaller type!

If we wish to overcome the drawbacks of advancing years and make them significant and worthwhile, it is not to the physical realm alone that we must look, for there time must take its toll. It is in the area of the spirit that we can truly triumph. This great and fundamental truth, that we often overlook, is expressed in one of the most moving prayers of our liturgy: *Shema' Kolenu.* In this short but fervent petition, we ask not once, but twice: *'Al tashlik-henu,* "Do not cast us off." Each time, however, we append a different plea. In one case we pray for physical well-being, *Kikheloth kohenu 'al ta'azevenu,* "When our strength fails, do not desert us." In the other we ask for a spiritual boon, *Veruah kodshekha 'al tikkah mimmenu,* "Thy holy spirit do not remove from us."

What do we mean by God's holy spirit? The prophet Isaiah indicated the meaning of "the spirit of God" in his great Messianic vision: *Ruah hokhmah ubhinah ruah 'etzah ugebhurah ruah da'at veyir'at Hashem,* "The spirit of wisdom and understanding, the spirit of counsel and might, the spirit of knowledge and the fear of God" (*Isaiah* 11:2).

When we ask for God's holy spirit in old age, we ask for wisdom, for courage, and for faith. We need insight to recognize the true capacities of old age, so that we may understand the proper sphere for its activities. We need courage to bear the ills which come with advancing years. And, above all, we need the knowledge and the fear of God, which alone can endow our lives with glory.

IV

It is true that there are liabilities and drawbacks with age, but there are also great and abiding compensations. The first and foremost is *the blessing of ease.* We can avoid the stress and strain of the "rat race" that we call an active career. We need no longer drive ourselves to the breaking point in order to get there first, only to find someone else there already. The gospel of "drive," of "go-go," and "up-and-at-'em" is peculiarly American, but the entire world is rapidly being Americanized today.

In a perspicacious piece Russell Baker points out: "Some puritan perversity in the American character makes us hate the nothing-doers of the world. A man quietly doing nothing is a challenge to the American system. He must be cajoled, badgered and, if necessary, blackguarded into purposeful living" (*New York Times*, June 30, 1965). Baker insists, "Every once in a while it is important to do nothing." But he has the feeling that he is a voice crying in the wilderness. During our active careers it is not easy to follow this counsel "to loaf and invite the soul." It is only when the later years come that we can put into practice the wisdom of Dr. Samuel Johnson. He was once asked why he spent so much of his time in conversation with his friends, taking his ease in the coffee houses of London. "Sir, I am not obliged to do any more. No man is obliged to do as much as he can do. A man is to have part of his life to himself."

It is in our later years that we can afford the luxury of true *recreation,* which is re-creation. Because of the habit of unremitting labor we have lost the art of recreation during our so-called active years. Out of a sense of guilt we work harder at our pleasures. As Russell Baker points out, "People lying in the grass doing nothing put the whole community on edge. All that idleness—it is like having an infection in the neighborhood." Yet true recreation is not an activity, but a process. It needs a slow, silent, serene period of growth.

That is the precious secret of the Jewish Sabbath, which is not negative, but positive. Sabbath is rest, not merely absence from our job, but *menuhah shelemah,* total rest of body and soul, a turning away from all bustle and movement, including the pressure and stress of our so-called "good times."

But this blessing is fully possible only in later years. Who is there among us who has not cherished some goal for which we have had no time during our active career? We are so busy doing the things we need to do that we never have time to do the things we want to do. We are so occupied with people we must see that we rarely have the energy to cultivate the people we want to know. Be it friendship, or travel, or a hobby, it is the golden years that offer us the opportunity for ease and true recreation.

Perhaps the greatest blessing which the later years of life can confer upon us is *the opportunity for growth in knowledge.* We can resume the process of education which for most of us ended much too soon. By "education" I mean not training for a career, learning new techniques for added proficiency in our calling, but *educatio,* the drawing out of our capacities, the enlarging of our dimensions of knowledge. Judaism expresses it in an untranslatable phrase, *Torah lishemah,* "Torah for its own sake," study for its own abiding rewards.

Today, retirement disease is recognized as a major peril by medical authorities. The root of the malady was diagnosed centuries ago in the Talmud, *Zikenei 'amei ha'aretz kol zeman shemazkinin da'atan mittarepheth 'aleihem, zikenei talmidei hakhamim 'einan ken. Kol zeman shemazkinin da'atan mityashebhet 'aleihem (Kinnim 3:6),* "Those who are ignorant and untutored, as they grow older, find their minds becoming confused and increasingly bewildered. Not so students and scholars. For as they grow older their minds attain to new serenity and peace." The reason is not far to seek. He who during his earlier years has not developed any interest in the life of the mind, any cultural goals or concerns, nevertheless finds life tolerable in youth and maturity. During his active years he is immersed in the world of competition and strife, and is confronted by a succession of problems. He has no time to be bored. But when these fall away, and he no longer has his nose to the grindstone and his children move away, his life has been emptied of all content and interest. Not so the man who, in spite of all other preoccupations, never permitted his interest in the life of the spirit to atrophy, be it literature or music, science or art, the Torah or general culture.

It is not easy to begin to find and cultivate these interests in the retirement years. There is a verse in the Book of *Proverbs* (20:4): "When winter sets in, the lazy man does not plow; when he seeks at harvest time there is nothing." On this verse the Midrash (*Debharim Rabbah,* chap. 6) comments: "This refers to the man who does not study Torah in his youth and then seeks to learn in his old age, and cannot." To be sure, it is not easy to begin late, but it can be done.

I remember a striking instance very well. This man had come to the United States as a youngster and had become a salesman. For nearly fifty years he traveled the length and breadth of America selling his goods to support his family. Though he had virtually no Jewish education to start with, he had somehow developed a great respect for Jewish learning and a desire to achieve it himself. After his retirement he decided to begin to study. It meant starting practically from scratch. He was not particularly acute, and the studies were not easy for him. But with dogged perseverance he began to study the Humash and the Prophets. He studied Rashi and the other commentators. He went through the entire Bible and proceeded to the Mishnah. He even began the study of Talmud. When he died at an advanced age, he was at the floodgate of his powers—never bored, always alert, and interested in the fascinating world he had made his own.

Most of us are far more fortunately situated. We need not begin from the beginning. We have some background to serve as a foundation for the creation of habits of study. Bertrand Russell once defined the study of mathematics as "thinking God's thoughts after Him." Mathematics is a pursuit granted to only a few. But for us who are the children of the Jewish tradition, "thinking God's thoughts after Him" is not only a possibility, but a privilege and a duty. For every Jew is commanded to engage in the study of Torah and, by learning God's will, to make himself God's partner in the universe.

A rabbi in a tiny Polish village found, late one night, that his shoes were badly in need of repair. He went down to the cobbler and found him hunched on his stool, working by the light of a flickering candle. "It's very late, my friend," said the rabbi, doubtfully, "and your candle is pretty low. I suppose you can't do anything more tonight." But the cobbler answered, *"Nein, rebbe, kol zman dos lichtel brent ken men noch varrichten."* "So long as the candle glows we can still put things right."

V

These are the three blessings which we can enjoy in our later years—ease, recreation, and learning. Cultivating them makes it possible for us to achieve the greatest good in the world—*the true wisdom of life.* Perhaps the most valuable—and the most difficult—human attribute is contentment. It is never easy to achieve, but it is easier in this period. As Sidney J. Harris has written: "Then we learn, slowly but undeniably, that nothing belongs to us, completely, finally. The job is ended, the children grow up and move away, even the money (where there is money) buys little that we want. For what we want cannot be bought. And it is then, if ever, that we learn to make our peace with destiny. To accept the fact that our dreams have been half-realized, or unrealized; that we did not do what we set out to do; that our goals have receded as we approached them. There may be a sadness in this prospect, but also a serenity. Illusions lose their power to disturb us; we value life by what it has given us, not by the promise of tomorrow. For only by accepting Time can we, in a measure, learn to conquer it."

Now that we are free from the stress of competition we can view our fellow men not as enemies, but as brothers. We now can look upon them with pity for their trials, with forgiveness for their weaknesses. All our lives we have heard preachments to love our neighbor. Now we find it easier to practice this highest of all ethical commandments. It is in these years that we can fully cultivate the love of the world and the love of man, and take delight in nature and in society.

Some ten years ago, a Jewish leader in Mexico, Dr. A. King, reached his seventieth birthday. At a banquet in his honor he expressed his thoughts on the meaning of man's aging: "Ten years ago, when I noticed the approach of old age, I was not frightened by it; I was neither angry nor downhearted. I never knew the meaning of tiredness, until one day I felt weak. The doctor then told me it was a heart ailment, . . . Since then I have known that I have no time to waste . . . .

"Ambitions decline as you grow older. In my young years I used to find fault in everything. Now, however, everything around me seems so beautiful. The mountains, the fields and flowers, the streets, the people—far, far more beautiful than ever before. Every day I wonder where my eyes had been yesterday, why I had been blind to all this beauty. Every morning, every day and every evening I see how everything blooms around me. I feel warm and friendly toward my surroundings.

"To all those who reach the older years I say: take pleasure in your life and help others to have that same kind of happiness."

Freed from the cares and responsibilities that have weighed down upon us through the years, only now can we dedicate ourselves wholeheartedly to goals beyond ourselves, and make some contribution to an ideal in which we believe. We live in a world replete with problems. Instead of sitting and wringing our hands, lamenting the good old days and castigating the new, we can resolve to choose one tiny corner of the world and help to set it aright. As the old Quaker saying has it, "Let us not curse the darkness. Let us light a candle."

How desperate are the ills that confront our country! How many human beings are there weighted down by misery and illness, by poverty and ignorance! How much needs to be done to save our own people from decay and death! How difficult is the struggle to keep our institutions of religion, culture, and human welfare alive in an age where too many are always ready to owe too much to too few! Perhaps we were too busy before. It is in these later years that we can afford to dispense with the cynical question, "What is there in it for me?" and ask, instead, "What is there in me for it?"

The Midrash (*Vayikra Rabbah,* chap. 25) tells that the Roman emperor Hadrian was once riding through the countryside in the land of Israel. He found an old man planting a fruit tree. "Old man, what sense is there in your doing this? It will take years until fruit appears!" Whereupon the old man answered: "If I am found worthy, I shall eat of it. If not, just as my ancestors toiled for me, so I am laboring for my son." A few years later, when Hadrian passed that way again, he found the old man sitting under the tree and enjoying its fruit.

Our sages point out that the phrase *sebhah tobhah,* "a good old age," is applied in Scriptures only to three men: Abraham, Gideon, and David (*Bereshith Rabbah,* sec. 44). They traversed the same path as every other human being; each of them was once young, grew mature and old, and finally knew infirmity and death. But each lived for a goal greater than himself. Abraham first discovered the true living God. Gideon was the courageous battler for his people's security and peace. David was the sweet singer of Israel who gave immortal expression to man's love of God and righteousness. Their old age could be described as good because they had each dedicated themselves to something eternal—to truth, to righteousness, and to beauty.

What the Midrash teaches, the wise men of all nations have urged. George Bernard Shaw said, "This is the true joy in life, the being used for a purpose recognized by yourself as a mighty one; the being thoroughly worn out before you are thrown on the scrap heap; the being a force of Nature instead of a feverish, selfish little clod of ailments and grievances complaining that the world will not devote itself to making you happy."

If we use these golden years for ease and recreation, if we dedicate ourselves to growth in knowledge and understanding and devote some of our energies to an ideal, we shall attain to wisdom that is greater than learning, to a contentment richer than wealth. "Age means the acquiring of wisdom." Just as sunset is the most beautiful time of the day, the golden years will send a glow over our entire pilgrimage on earth. "Life," said Julia Ward Howe, who lived to ninety-one, "is like a cup of tea; the sugar is all at the bottom."

None of us is so young that he can postpone the preparation for these golden years, and none so old that he cannot capture its joy. Before it becomes too later forever, let us respond to the invitation which Robert Browning placed in the mouth of Rabbi ben Ezra:

> Grow old along with me!
> The best is yet to be,
> The last of life, for which the first was made;
> Our times are in His hand
> Who saith "A whole I planned,
> Youth shows but half; trust God:
>   See all, nor be afraid!"

XIX

The Ultimate Goal

From the time when man emerged upon this planet as a thinking creature conscious of his own being, he has sought an answer to the fundamental question: What is the purpose of his existence? Closely related is another: What are the criteria of the good life? This deep desire to discover the meaning of life has nurtured man's religious faith, whenever he has been persuaded to accept its view of God's purpose and man's duty. It has also been the fountainhead of his skepticism and unbelief, whenever he could not be convinced of the validity of its interpretation of life. Moreover, man's vision of the good life, whether clearly articulated or not, impels him to perpetual restlessness, an unceasing discontent with the imperfect face of reality, a constant reaching out for more than he can attain and hold fast.

Man has learned much about the world in the centuries of recorded history, but the ultimate remains a mystery which gives little evidence of dissipating. Today nonbeliever and believer alike are convinced that with regard to the purpose of existence we have made little progress; again, not merely *ignoramus,* "we do not know," but *ignorabimus,* "we shall not know." Here, all ages and temperaments are as one.

The fourth-century Greek poet Palladas of Alexandria seeks refuge from this melancholy thought in the joys of wine:

> How was I born? What place my home?
> So soon to go, why did I come?

248

How can I learn from books or men,
When all things are beyond my ken?
I came from naught this world to see,
To-morrow I shall nothing be.

O race of men, from nothing brought,
And nothing worth in deed or thought,
One thing alone contentment gives,
A drug 'gainst trouble while man lives,
The gift of Bacchus, fount divine—
So pour me out a cup of wine.

(Greek Anthology)

The same mystery of existence intrigued the Hebrew thinker
Koheleth, who sought to grasp the truth with the pincers of
reason, but his efforts, too, proved unavailing. Order and beauty
were everywhere in evidence, but the purpose of the cosmos was
forever veiled from man:

> I know the concern which God has given men to be afflicted
> with. Everything He has made proper in its due time, and He
> has also placed the love of the world in men's hearts, except that
> they may not discover the work God has done from beginning to
> end. . . .
> Who knows what is good for man in life, during the brief days
> of his vain existence, which he spends like a shadow? Who can
> tell man what will happen under the sun after he is gone? . . .
> . . . I saw that though a man sleep neither by day nor by night
> he cannot discover the meaning of God's work which is done
> under the sun, for the sake of which a man may search hard, but
> he will not find it, and though a wise man may think he is about
> to learn it, he will be unable to find it. . . .
>
> *(Ecclesiastes* 3:11; 6:12; 8:16-17)

It was this bafflement which led the Biblical sage to his insistence
that the enjoyment of life is the only reasonable goal for man.
Like Samuel Johnson, Koheleth was a pessimist with an enormous
zest for living. This sense of mystery induced in Koheleth a
brooding melancholy, which is not far apart from that of a believing saint, nearly a millennium and a half later, who lived in a

radically different milieu. The Hasidic Rabbi Bunam of Pshysha found his beloved disciple Enoch in tears. The Rabbi asked him, "Why are you weeping?", and Enoch answered, "Am I not a creature of this world, and am I not made with eyes and heart and all limbs, and yet I do not know for what purpose I was created and what good I am in the world." "Fool!" said Rabbi Bunam, "I also go around thus."

Nonetheless, religion, unlike secular thought, does not remain content with an agnostic position with regard to the goal of creation and the demands of the good life. The rationalist Moses Maimonides declared that though we cannot know God's purpose for the universe, we can and must believe that it has its meaning. His view recalls the utterance of Justice Oliver Wendell Holmes that each man is a soldier in a cosmic campaign, the plan of which he does not know. The mystics, on the other hand, believe that God, seeking an object upon which to bestow His love, called the world into being. God's spirit, unable to brook the unbroken calm of nothingness, called out: "Let there be a universe!" The religious spirit praises the Lord in the hymn, "Blessed be our God who has created us for His glory." Since man is the beloved creature and the child of God, the purpose of his existence is to fulfill the will of his Father in heaven, and thus enhance the glory of God.

What is the will of God and how can man minister to God's glory? Perhaps the finest definition is that to be found in the familiar words of the prophet Micah:

"Wherewith shall I come before the Lord,
And bow myself before God on high?
It hath been told thee, O man, what is good,
And what the Lord doth require of thee:
Only to do justice, to love mercy, and to walk humbly with thy God."

(*Micah* 6:6-8)

This threefold imperative, be it noted, is addressed not to the prophet's countrymen or coreligionists, but to all men everywhere and always. Both the content and the order of the injunction are highly significant.

It may be observed that for the prophet the ethical imperatives of justice and mercy precede the strictly religious ideal of "walking humbly with God." The emphasis upon ethical living as the primary demand of God is fundamental to the Biblical world view.

The relative order of the two ethical demands is also noteworthy; "doing justice" comes before "loving mercy." Justice is the only firm foundation of group living; without it no stable society, no assurance of peace, is possible. Moreover, justice, not being dependent upon our subjective emotional attitude, is binding upon men in all their relationships, to strangers as well as to kinsmen, toward enemies as well as toward friends. It is a debt which we owe to all human beings, who stand in the same relation to God as we do, as creatures and as children.

Basic as justice is, however, it represents the lower limit of the arc of the ethical life, while it is mercy or love that represents its uppermost point. The Hebrew noun *hesed,* which is generally rendered as "mercy," is more accurately to be translated as "lovingkindness" or "steadfast love." To enforce justice alone means to condemn the world to stagnation, for the ceaseless round of cause and effect, of act and consequence, offers no chance for growth and improvement. To practice love means requiting one's fellow beyond his deserts, thus freeing him from the burden of past errors and affording him the opportunity of rising to a higher level of existence. Hence love is the light of the world, the gateway of hope to the future.

Justice and love are mutually indispensable. Justice without love is cruelty; mercy without justice, sentimental caprice. As we have seen, the tension between these two attributes of God reflects both the order and the freedom that characterize His world, the element of stability and the aspect of hope in the universe. In our attitude toward our fellow men, each of us must manifest both these qualities of justice and mercy. Since each man is the center of a complex web of relationships, his duties and opportunities fall into many areas: his obligations to himself, to his family as parent, spouse, and child, to his community, to his country, to the world.

In each area, man is perpetually subject to countless temptations, compounded by the weaknesses of his own nature. Moreover, the ethical life is often confronted by the conflicting claims of two ideals, each valid and worthy of allegiance, or by the demands emanating from two areas of relationship, each legitimate and deserving of consideration. Accordingly, specifying the implications of justice and mercy in human affairs is complex and difficult.

It is to this task that the ethical philosopher seeks to address himself. The abiding glory of the Halachah, the structure of rabbinic law, is that it strove, and in largest measure succeeded, in translating the exalted ideals of the prophet into concrete enactment within the context of every-day life.

It is, however, a self-evident truth, all too often overlooked, that man's moral conduct remains the touchstone of his sincerity in obeying the call of God. Hence Micah properly places these ethical imperatives first in his call to man.

Because ethics are basic to the good life, it is often stated, in the name of religion, that righteous living is the goal of human existence. Reflection makes it clear, however, that ethical living cannot be the ultimate purpose of human existence, but only a means to an end beyond itself. That purpose is expressed in the climax of the prophetic call, "to walk humbly with thy God," every word of which is freighted with meaning.

"To walk with God" means to be conscious of His presence in every human activity and in every aspect of the world which He has called into being. It therefore follows that the failure to rejoice in the blessings of God's world means to be an ungracious guest in the home where God is host. The enjoyment of life, coupled with the recognition of its divine Source, is not merely every man's right, but every man's duty. However paradoxical it may seem at first blush, the conclusion is inescapable that the enjoyment of life ranks higher in the scale of values than the ethical life, for the ethical life is the means for assuring to all men the enjoyment of life, which is their due.

Why are murder and robbery, deceit and fraud, cruelty and exploitation accounted cardinal sins? Because they deprive the victims of their God-given right to share in such blessings of the world as food and shelter, liberty or leisure. If it were not true that these are inalienable rights, there would be nothing wrong in depriving men of them. As a matter of fact, it was argued with warmth and sincerity in more than one period in history that the suffering of the poor is a blessing, since it prepares them more perfectly for the beatific state in the world to come. For the prophet, no such casuistry is conceivable. For his passionate spirit, justice and mercy are God's imperatives to man, because they are indispensable instrumentalities for man's fulfilling his divinely ordained privilege: walking with God, and seeing His presence everywhere in a world aflame with beauty and aglow with truth.

This hierarchy of values, which gives primacy to the enjoyment of life's blessings even above ethical living, was obscurely sensed by the ancients. This insight helps to explain the position of a skeptical work like the book of *Ecclesiastes* in the Biblical canon. Undoubtedly, many factors, some even accidental, played their part in the inclusion of this masterpiece in Scripture. Unlike the Biblical legislators, prophets, and psalmists, the skeptical Hebrew sage is not concerned with buttressing faith in God or with urging righteous living upon his readers. But he is stressing the truth that joy in life is a Divine imperative. Even the most pietistic of the rabbis seem to have sensed that, however unconventional the route by which Koheleth arrived at this insight, he was focussing attention upon the highest level of human values, loftier even than the preachment of morality—the enjoyment of life's blessings as the fulfillment of God's will for man:

> Therefore I praise joy, for there is no other good for man under the sun but to eat, drink, and be joyful and have this accompany him in his toil, during the days of his life, which God has given him beneath the sun.
>
> (8:15)

> Go, then, eat your bread with joy,
> And drink your wine with a glad heart,
> For God has already approved your actions.
> At all times let your clothes be white,
> And oil on your head not be lacking.
>
> (9:7-8)

Rejoice, young man, in your youth,
And let your heart cheer you in your youthful days.
Follow the impulses of your heart
And the desires of your eyes,
And know that for all this,
God will call you to account.

Banish sadness from your heart,
And remove sorrow from your flesh,
For childhood and youth are a fleeting breath.

Remember your Creator in the days of your youth,
Before the evil days come and the years draw near,
Of which you will say, "I have no pleasure in them."

(11:9-10; 12:1)

"To walk with God" as the prophet enjoined means to fulfill His will. It embraces the practice of justice and love, but it goes beyond to include the living sense of His presence everywhere in His world.

But the phrase has not yet yielded up all its meaning. "To walk with God" means that man is to recognize himself as God's co-partner, sharing vitally in the task of building and governing the world. This recognition of man's innate dignity as God's co-worker is basic to a proper understanding of his nature, as manifested in his creative activity, his moral responsibility, and his untapped potentialities.

"To walk with God"—but humbly! Is the prophet here warning against the besetting vice of the virtuous—the tendency to self-satisfaction of those who know that they walk with God? "The wicked praises himself, while he blasphemes against the Lord," the Psalmist complains, but the boasting of the sinner is not nearly so common as the self-adulation of the pious. Now, the smugness of those who walk with God is no mere peccadillo, unpleasant but unimportant. To walk with God without humility means to build a wall of arrogance about us, estranging ourselves from our fellow men, who may make no claims to intimacy with Him or who may see Him differently from ourselves. It means to add fuel to fanaticism and to enlarge man's already substantial capacity for

hatred and intolerance by imbuing him with the proud conviction
that cruelty and persecution minister to the greater glory of God.
No wonder that a Hasidic teacher declared, "Far, far better a sinner who know that he is a sinner, than a saint who knows that he
is a saint." Only if a man walks humbly with God will he remember that he has brothers, whose dignity is equal to his own.

"To walk humbly with thy God." If this quality is needed in
our attitude toward our fellow men, it is the bedrock of man's
relationship with His God. To learn the art of humility does not
come easy in our age, which is so conscious of man's vast and
expanding powers and which has spawned the crass and brutal
idolatry of man's self-worship. To walk humbly with God is to
recognize that man is not the measure of all things, being neither
the center of the universe, nor its creator, but a creature, elevated
through God's love to the dignity of partnership with his Maker,
so that he may help achieve the Divine purposes, which he can at
best only dimly perceive.

Man's humility before God is a shield and buckler against
countless evils. It is a protection against the arrogance of the dic-
tator, who justifies his actions both against his own people and
against others on the ground that he is answerable to no one and
recognizes no law higher than his own will. Few men are likely
to attain the dizzy heights of unlimited power, but all men are
tempted, at one time or another, to regard their own desires and
capacities as the ultimate arbiter and justification of their actions.
So, too, we are all destined to descend into the valley of suffering
through the loss of our loved ones and, finally, through our own
death. To walk humbly with God means to recognize the limitations of man's understanding and thus attain to the wisdom and
the courage for resignation:

> For My thoughts are not your thoughts,
> Neither are your ways My ways, saith the Lord.
> For as the heavens are higher than the earth,
> So are My ways higher than your ways,
> And My thoughts than your thoughts.
>
> (*Isaiah* 55:8-9)

One final implication flows from the last phrase, "thy God." For all man's weaknesses, his brief hour on the stage of life, his foolish antics, his sorry misdeeds, he alone stands in conscious comradeship with his Maker and can call Him "My God."

We need to explore the full implications contained in Micah's call to men, "Walk humbly with thy God." The Chinese sage Mencius said: "I love life and I love righteousness; if I cannot have both, I choose righteousness." Vital Judaism believes passionately that man can have both and have them abundantly. This is the ultimate goal of human striving and its abiding glory.

Index of Sources

257

II. *Talmudic Sources*

III. *Post-Talmudic Sources*